Books: A Manifesto

Also by Ian Patterson

Guernica and Total War
War and Literature (co-edited)
Nemo's Almanac
Collected Poems

Translations

Marcel Proust, *Finding Time Again*
(In Search of Lost Time, Vol. 6)
Charles Fourier, *The Theory of the Four Movements* (1809)

Books: A Manifesto
or, How to Build a Library

Ian Patterson

W&N
WEIDENFELD & NICOLSON

First published in Great Britain in 2025 by Weidenfeld & Nicolson,
an imprint of The Orion Publishing Group Ltd
Carmelite House, 50 Victoria Embankment
London EC4Y 0DZ

An Hachette UK Company

The authorised representative in the EEA is Hachette Ireland,
8 Castlecourt Centre, Dublin 15, D15 XTP3,
Ireland (email: info@hbgi.ie)

1 3 5 7 9 10 8 6 4 2

A CIP catalogue record for this book is
available from the British Library.

ISBN (Hardback) 978 1 4746 1898 4
ISBN (Ebook) 978 1 4746 1900 4
ISBN (Audio) 978 1 4746 2527 2

Typeset by Input Data Services Ltd, Bridgwater, Somerset

Printed in Great Britain by Clays Ltd, Elcograf, S.p.A.

MIX
Paper | Supporting responsible forestry
FSC® C104740

www.weidenfeldandnicolson.co.uk
www.orionbooks.co.uk

for Olivia Laing

But what strange art, what magic can dispose
The troubled mind to change its native woes?
Or lead us willing from ourselves, to see
Others more wretched, more undone than we?
This, Books can do; — nor this alone; they give
New views to life, and teach us how to live;
They soothe the grieved, the stubborn they chastise,
Fools they admonish, and confirm the wise:
Their aid they yield to all: they never shun
The man of sorrow, nor the wretch undone:
Unlike the hard, the selfish, and the proud,
They fly not sullen from the suppliant crowd;
Nor tell to various people various things,
But show to subjects, what they show to kings.

George Crabbe, *The Library*

Contents

Introduction

> I love to lose myself in other men's minds. When I am not walking, I am reading; I cannot sit and think. Books think for me.
>
> I have no repugnances . . . I can read any thing which I call a *book*.
>
> Charles Lamb, 'Detached Thoughts on Books and Reading'

We're living in a time of cultural and political crisis. Wars and climate change, racism and the resurgence of far-right ideology, the huge gulf between the mega-rich and the poorest, years of attack on tax-funded services – education, social care, the legal system, libraries, the health service – have all contributed to it, as has the internet, especially social media. Climate change has exacerbated the exploitative relationship between the developed and developing worlds, which in turn has intensified both economic migration and war-driven asylum-seeking. With all that, the last decade or more in the UK has also seen an extraordinary and unprecedented attack on every aspect of serious culture: systematic and destructive underfunding of libraries, schools, universities, theatres, museums, art galleries, film, orchestras – in fact all the arts and all the humanities, with concomitant effects on publishing, arts broadcasting, newspaper reviewing and so on. The result has been a society that has become morally and culturally impoverished.

A crisis like this demands more than books, but without the breadth of imagination, sense of history, awareness of alternatives and hope for the future that can come from reading books, things will not get better. Nor will AI solve our problems. Very few discoveries are straightforwardly progressive: the undoubted benefits of laptops and tablets for teaching must be seen against the decline in attention span and reading ability, and in social media the instant responses, magnifying unfounded rumour or piling on to some momentarily fashionable target of hatred or admiration. The novelist Julia Bell has written cogently about the way the demands of the internet and social media distract our attention: 'Our capacity to make memories is most affected by this kind of divided attention. We can – just about – attend to several things at once but we do them badly. In the midst of all the overstimulation we are unable to lay down new memories . . . A new kind of human behaviour then emerges under this influence, a semi-automated for-profit personality which is being constantly nudged and notified and prompted.'[1] Warnings have long been sounded, notably in Nicholas Carr's 2010 book *The Shallows: How the Internet is Changing the Way We Think, Read and Remember*, but not enough has been done to counter the situation. And we've been made forcibly aware of new vulnerabilities where our overconfident reliance on computer systems can lead to disastrous consequences, as when in 2023 the British Library system was hacked into, depriving readers of access not just to electronic materials from the catalogue itself but also to large numbers of books – because the library, understandably but short-sightedly, had discontinued its policy of receiving a physical copy of each book published in favour of electronic copies. In the wake of the cyberattack, the weakness of that policy is very clear, and the advantage of the material object ought to be obvious, despite the space each book needs to occupy. (There are other reasons, too, for having physical copies of books, as we'll see later.)

Even for ordinary readers, there are advantages to having actual books. I know ebooks are convenient for travel and storage, but you can't so easily lend one to a friend or remember the particular feel of it in your hand. When I've read a book (if it isn't a library book), I like to have it around, on a shelf, fully present, separate but available, ready to be consulted again, shown to other people or borrowed (and returned). I've accumulated books all my life. In a sense, books have *been* my life, or at least they've usually been somewhere near the heart of it. I've been a teacher, an academic, a translator, a political activist, a second-hand bookseller, an editor, a writer and a poet. The constant theme linking them all is books.

I am a reader and an accumulator and collector of books. Since I was very young, I've wanted to read books and have them around me. I believe books and reading are important – all kinds of books and all kinds of reading. It seems natural to me to want to create a library of my books wherever I'm living, even if I'm only to be there for a short time. I used to feel guilty about it sometimes, prey to the accusation that absorption in books is an avoidance of the outside world, a feeble substitute for 'real life'. But that notion of 'real life' is dubious at best. At worst it's just bogus ideology, used by right-wing politicians and demagogues to belittle the whole array of creative thinking by accusing artists, writers, academics and intellectuals of retreating into ivory towers, when the rarefied world of parliamentary politics is itself much more of an ivory tower than universities, publishing or the media. Reality is complex. It's not just social reality, the things that actually happen in the world, practical matters, action; there's also the life of the mind, the imagination, the arts, history and memory, everything we think, remember, hope for, forget, everything that isn't the 'reality' that politicians are concerned with, but which belongs in another kind of reality, psychic reality, no less real for being imaginative, subjective or invisible, or confined in books.

Reading is a necessary part of reality, and an unavoidable part of everyday life. We live within language, and using it is as natural to us, and as unconscious, as breathing. When we think, it's what we think with. Exercising our use of language, both our receptivity to it and our control over it, is how we develop individual personhood, self-knowledge, knowledge of others and of the world. And although we live in language, the language we live in from day to day is like the sea, constantly shifting in permanent restlessness. It is only still when it's written down.

But how, and why, and in what medium it's written down also matter. So many crucial elements of our society are distorted by oversimplification. As the American novelist, activist and polemicist Sarah Schulman says, 'We have developed these reductive modes like email and texts to accompany reductive ideas that are supposed to serve large social functions but are not based in human complexity.

They seem to be time-savers, but avoiding real communication produces long-lasting problems that can endure forever. Shortcuts and speed-ups define our moment, and yet they simply do not address human reality.' Human reality is infinitely complicated, and our understanding of it changes all the time. One way to understand it better is to read, not just informative books but literature – novels, plays, poems, contemporary and from the past, including literature translated from other languages, different realities.

One of the great pleasures of reading is encountering the different ways language is used: different styles, different attitudes, different aims, language used for different purposes. The current focus in schools, and even in university courses, on exams and exam results tends to encourage uniformity and stifle independent thinking. It has probably always been like that: a hundred years ago, Gilbert Cannan wrote in his novel *Sembal*, though admittedly in the persona of his central character, that 'The atmosphere of education suffocated him. He wanted to learn and he had only been taught. His years at the University had been one long frustration of his desire to learn, and when they were over he had less capacity for learning than when he started, was left indeed with only a desperate and almost hysterical longing to recover the ardour with which he had begun.'

But as William Davies points out in a 2022 essay in the *London Review of Books*, it isn't as easy as that. Things have changed, whether we like it or not. Talking about the difficulty students can have navigating the expectations governing essay-writing, he explains that 'the discerning scholarly self on which the humanities depend was conceived as the product of transitions between spaces – library, lecture hall, seminar room, study – linked together by work with pen and paper. When all this is replaced by the interface with screen and keyboard, and everything dissolves into a unitary flow of "content", the identity of the author – as distinct from the texts [students] have read – becomes harder to delineate.' With the result that students muddle up the passages they've copied and pasted from the 'relevant' bits of online books or essays with their own thinking, in another illustration of the changing experience of reading texts.

Universities and schools need to find ways of accommodating their requirements to respond to this, while ensuring students know how to read and how to use books, whether the books are online or on shelves in a library. Nothing is more important than learning how to think for yourself.

The importance of books and the importance of recognising the connections between the books we read, the lives we live and the things we think and believe and hope for or struggle against was brought home to me quite powerfully a few years ago when I had to dispose of part of my own library when I retired, and again a year or two later when I had to dismantle what was left of it, put the books into store, move house and wait two more years until there was somewhere in the new house for them to go. The pages that follow trace those reflections of mine about what books are and what they're for and why we need them, why we should all be passionate about them, as I watch the reconstruction of a space for my own library and ponder what books mean to me, and what they have meant to me over a lifetime. Along the way, I'll be writing about all kinds of books and authors and thinking about what's worth reading and why it's worth building one's own collection or accumulation of books. As I talk about personal histories and global politics, expanded horizons and quiet pleasures, difficult poems, romantic novels, well-known writers, new writers, forgotten writers, other languages, other cultures, the uses of reading and the pleasures of the imagination, I hope things may spark the reader's interest and suggest books worth discovering, as well as encouraging the use of public and institutional libraries and the habit of acquiring and keeping books. Libraries of all sorts are storehouses of culture and knowledge and pleasure, a really necessary part of being human and understanding our common humanity.

I

The Library *or* 'I could not live without them'

When I'm grown up I'm going to have a library. With all the books there are, in every language.

Elias Canetti, *Auto da Fé*

It was a cold, bright day in January when I saw the library for the first time, though at that point it wasn't a library. It was a solidly built Victorian coach house, down at the far end of the garden. One half had been converted years ago into a garage and now it was showing its age, slightly damp, rather makeshift, gloomy and grimy, with the up-and-over door needing to be propped open. The other half of the building – the old stable and loose box – was just a store place for ancient discarded things and a home for spiders and their webs, probably undisturbed for a decade or more. The garage part contained a car (shrouded in a protective sheet), and there were shelves housing tins of paint, sundry tools, various pieces of wood, coils of cable and suchlike, and against the back wall, among other mementos of the debris of daily life, the large cut-out figures belonging to the local church's Christmas crib, complete with a camel or two. Nothing about the place looked in the least like a library. But the more I thought about it, the more I realised that it had the potential to be one, though I had no idea at that point whether we would be able to buy the house we were viewing, nor, if we did, how and when the transformation from garage to library would come about.

That January day was shortly before the onset of the pandemic. My life, not for the first time, was in flux. My wife had died some years earlier, and I'd retired from my job teaching English at Queens' College, Cambridge. I was now married again, and trying to find a new structure for my days, a project made more difficult by the unfamiliar rhythms of time the pandemic brought with it. Nonetheless a change was needed, and eight months after I'd first seen the house and imagined creating the library, we finally took possession of it and moved in, leaving Cambridge, the city I'd lived in for forty years, for a Suffolk village seventy miles away. The house and the garden were lovely, but there wasn't yet enough room for my books (a situation I was all too familiar with). A hundred and fifty boxes of them had to go into store. This meant that all the books that had been shelved or piled up in the studio shed in my Cambridge garden, including all the books of poetry, my main interest, were now expensively in store and out of reach for the foreseeable future. The contents of yet another seventy or eighty boxes had already been accommodated in my study and wherever else we could fit them around the house: I really needed somewhere to put the rest of my library. Which is why the coach house was already starting to metamorphose into a library in my imagination.

Why did I want a library? Why did I have so many books in the first place? Books and reading have always been an integral part of the fabric of my life, but sometimes I would look at the sheer quantity that I'd accumulated and wonder about them. How did they all get there? Surely they weren't all necessary, and surely I hadn't read them all? Indeed, I might ask myself these days how many books I could possibly read in the years left to me before death intervened. And in the twenty-first century, with so much material available online, wasn't a library of actual physical books an outdated idea? Wasn't there something pathological about wanting to own so many books? Why would anyone want a library of their own? Who has enough space for one? These were questions that, if I didn't ask them myself, other people asked for me. There are no easy answers, or not short ones at any rate; I'd been thinking about it for years, and as my retirement loomed, the questions took on a new urgency. At about the same time, my wife had developed terminal cancer, which gave me another reason to interrogate myself about my past, my purpose, my books, my future, and other difficult questions.

Books and my desire to collect them seem always to have been linked in my mind with loss, sometimes in contradictory ways. In childhood they sometimes played the part of transitional objects, giving me a sense of connection to the world, providing a feeling of permanence and protection I couldn't quite experience elsewhere. I often felt more at home in those fictional worlds than I did in the one I was required to inhabit, which seemed lacklustre and ordinary by comparison, and my rows of books became a defence against normality as well as a way to escape from it, functioning as a sort of carapace, almost as character-armour in the Reichian sense. But at the same time, I knew that the protection they offered was illusory, that they couldn't be truly permanent. The fictional worlds that engaged my imagination were all too obviously absent from the world I lived in. As the spell of those worlds faded, some time after the last page of the book had been reached, their sheer absence could leave me feeling bereft and that I belonged nowhere, out of place at home and unable to join in with the Treasure Seekers, or the Famous Five or the Swallows and Amazons. At least the books themselves were more permanent – but only if I owned them. Most of the books I was reading in those days came from the public library in Hoylake, the small town on the edge of the Wirral peninsula where we lived, and as I write this, the feel of those library books comes back to me, especially the mottled blue-grey and the shiny brown bindings, along with indistinct but powerful memories of the emotions the stories aroused. Some of them, the ones I was fondest of, I took out time and again, although sometimes to my dismay they vanished from the library shelves, discarded, and were never seen again.

Before I could read for myself, and for two or three years after I was able to, my father would read to my sister and me every night before we went to sleep. Not from library books, but from books of our own or books that he'd owned and enjoyed when he himself had been a child in the 1920s, which meant that they were there to be looked at whenever I wanted. Books like *Winnie-the-Pooh*, Beatrix Potter's stories, *Alice in Wonderland* and *The Wind in the Willows*. When I started to read for myself, I loved picture books like *Old Dame Trot and her Pig*, with the brilliant illustrations of Frank Adams; *Orlando the Marmalade Cat*, written and wonderfully illustrated by Kathleen Hale; my sister's Little Golden Books (*Pantaloon* by Kathryn Jackson, *The Saggy Baggy Elephant* by Kathryn and Byron Jackson and *The Train to Timbuctoo* by Margaret Wise Brown);* Rupert Bear annuals, all that sort of thing. But of all the books I read then, and especially as I grew older and read voraciously, the ones I enjoyed most, the ones I read and reread, were those where there was some kind of access to another world; first just to places that looked far more interesting and exciting than the ones I knew, but soon I was deep in books that led me to a quite separate or mythical or otherwise fantastical place, like finding a way into Narnia through the back of a wardrobe in *The Lion, the Witch and the Wardrobe*, or like *Tom's Midnight Garden* by Philippa Pearce, in which a boy slips back in time after midnight, when the clock strikes thirteen, and enters a Victorian garden that shouldn't be there, tantalising me with the puzzle of where or how the two worlds might coincide. More than anything, I wanted to find a way into them: the more intense my experience of the book, the more I felt a part of its world, and at the same time shut out from it. No matter how many times I reread them, the books refused to show me how to cross that borderline. That fruitless quest may be one key to my pathology, my wanting to keep my

* The Little Golden Books is a very popular American series of illustrated young children's books, which began publication with Simon & Schuster in 1942 and still continues, now owned by Penguin Random House.

own copies of the books I read: I wanted a library of my own so I could read the books whenever I desired, building a defence against them not being in the public library when I needed them.

Years later, when I was in my early teens, one event more than any other came to symbolise for me this precarious availability of books – a promise and what felt like a betrayal. The promise came when I must have been about eight years old. My sister and I were staying with my grandmother, who with two of her sisters had apartments in the large old house in Sussex that belonged to their brother, my great-uncle Ken, who bred racehorses. One day my great-aunt Ginny took me into her drawing room and showed me a tall breakfront bookcase full of similar-looking books. Opening a glass door, she took out a small blue volume, *Household Tales* by the Brothers Grimm. 'This is for you,' she said, putting it into my hands. Then, gesturing towards the bookcase, she went on, 'This is called Everyman's Library. The man who published it was a great friend of your great-grandfather's. I know you like reading, so one day these books will all be yours.'*

* Everyman's Library was founded in 1906 by Joseph Dent, a publisher influenced by William Morris's ideas about the need for objects to be both beautiful and useful, inspired by a mission to bring affordable editions of the best books to a wide public. The editor, and original instigator of the project, Ernest Rhys, was another socialist man of letters. The books were uniformly produced, the name derived from the medieval morality play *Everyman*, and most volumes contained the words of Knowledge to Everyman in the play, 'Everyman, I will go with thee, and be thy guide, In thy most need to go by thy side.' Dent's aim was 'to build up the most complete library for the common

Nothing before had equalled the excitement of that moment. It held out the promise of something that was almost grown-up, something that contained a guarantee of my sense of my inner self. As the inveterate reader I was, I felt a powerful need to have my books around me, and I dreamt of the day that bookcase full of books would be mine to explore.

By the time I was nine or ten, the eldest child of very literate but not bibliophile parents, living in a big enough house in the Wirral between the Royal Liverpool Golf Course and the sea, most of my pocket money went on books – Billy Bunter, Jennings (which made boarding school appear very attractive), Just William (freedom and destruction wrapped up in a past that looked odd and funny), War Picture Library, Biggles (men-but-really-boys having adventures with aeroplanes), Arthur Ransome (independence, adventure, hierarchy and a realistic but distant topography), bird books, wild-flower books. And every week I read comics, too, variously *Topper*, *Eagle*, *Rover*, *Adventure*, *Hotspur*, *Wizard*, preferring the ones that were printed text rather than comic strip. In the late 1950s, when I was ten or eleven, I used to send away for the Puffin Books catalogue and order books from it by post, the pleasure of opening the parcel rivalling the discovery of a new book in a Christmas stocking. For my ninth birthday, I had asked for and been given a glass-fronted bookcase (a step,

man the world had seen'. The books were priced at a shilling each, so that (as Dent put it), 'for five pounds (which will procure him a hundred volumes) a man may be intellectually rich for life'. I think it was Ernest Rhys who was my great-grandfather's friend.

as I saw it, towards that great glass-fronted bookcase full of Everyman's Library), and loved to organise the rows of uniform jacketed hardbacks and bright Puffin Books. I can still see the Puffins in my mind's eye: *The Phoenix and the Carpet*, *The Wouldbegoods*, *The Story of the Treasure Seekers*, *The Borrowers*, *Robin Hood*, *King Arthur*, *Tales of the Greek Heroes*, *The Saga of Asgard*, *Redcap Runs Away*, *Norman and Henry Bones: The Boy Detectives*, *The Magic Pudding*, *Kidnapped*, *Treasure Island* . . . They weren't just lined up behind glass and left there, either; they were frequently taken out and reread. It was one of the great pleasures of childhood (long periods of which I spent ill in bed), reading familiar stories over and over again. So the shiny rows of books in my bookcase continued slowly to expand.

Writing now, I find all this rather odd. I didn't know anybody else, child or adult, who acquired books, or collected anything seriously, except for my grandfather, who collected stamps. As I did, too, in fact. When I was seven, I'd tried to set up a stamp club with two boys in my class, both called Paul. It was to be known as the Victory Stamp Club (it was 1955 and the war was still a very live memory). It only had one meeting – even though tea was included – because it turned out that neither Paul was really interested in stamps at all. My collecting, like my reading, remained a solitary pursuit. I got through quantities of library books each week, but it wasn't the same as owning them myself. I suppose I felt that possession gave me a different kind of relationship with the stories the books contained; it certainly seemed to bring me closer to the kind of life I enjoyed imagining for myself: I could be living in a rambling old house in the country with priest-holes and secret passages, or alternatively, in a tall terrace in London with high dark rooms full of untidy piles of books and wildly interesting – more interesting than my parents – grown-ups. (I think that latter idea must have come partly from Noel Streatfeild's *Ballet Shoes*.) The sight of the books, the feel of them, their colour and their smell were a reliable source of pleasure and comfort, separate from but always associated with the narratives and locations to which they provided access.

I anticipated receiving the library of Everyman's books with mixed feelings: as I got older, I began to be anxious about the sheer size of the bookcase. Would I be allowed to have it in my bedroom? Would it even fit in there? I kept these worries to myself, in fact forgot about them and the bookcase until the day they were dispelled, which happened in a sudden and unpredicted way. My great-aunt, it transpired, was suffering now from dementia. When one day two strangers came knocking at her door and offered to take away unwanted furniture for cash, she invited them in. They took all the furniture they could find, including that bookcase and its contents, and left her with a five-pound note and almost empty rooms.

I still feel a pang of loss as I write about that, even though some sixty years have passed since my mother told me the news. It was a blow, but in a way the promise of that library had already served its purpose by validating my desire for books and giving me a sense that it was permissible to own lots of them. So when I was twelve or thirteen, I took my first opportunity. By chance, I spotted a large quantity of books at the local auction house. I went to the sale the following day and bid for them, successfully. There were more than a thousand altogether, Victorian novels and histories for the most part, along with some religious tracts and a few bound volumes of piano music. The whole lot cost me a pound. I went back to the saleroom the next day with an old pram and started the business of transferring the books to my room at home. It took several journeys there and back to remove them all. But at the end (discounting the religious tracts and suchlike), I had a very substantial addition to my embryonic library: a quantity of uniform quarter-leather hardbacks (I think probably from a set of the 'Hundred Best Books'),* and a variety of other books ranging from novels like *The Count of Monte Cristo* and Alain-René Lesage's *Gil Blas* to Napier's *History of the War in the Peninsula*, an almost complete set of Dickens (the last three volumes had been placed on top of a cupboard, and the dealer who'd bought it wouldn't let me have them as he claimed they were part of his lot), a set of Scott's novels, a great deal of Thackeray and Macaulay, some Jerome K. Jerome (first editions, I discovered later), Pardoe and Bartlett's *Beauties of the Bosphorus* (seven out of eight quarto volumes of steel engravings), the works of Homer, Milton, Bunyan, and so on and on and on. Not quite a treasure trove or the complete Everyman's Library, but getting so many books at once, with so few titles I would have chosen for myself, moved me suddenly much closer to possessing a real library, and catapulted me into reading books I would never have read otherwise. Some of them were very hard going – I could never get through anything by Hall

* One of a number of similar publishing ventures in the late Victorian and Edwardian period, aimed at the newly literate reading public.

Caine or Jeffery Farnol, sentimental novelists of the late nineteenth and early twentieth centuries – but there was enough enjoyable reading there to keep me productively occupied for quite a while. As Will Self puts it, 'By reading indiscriminately, I learned to discriminate – and learned also to comprehend: for it's only with the acquisition of large data sets that we also develop schemas supple enough to interpret new material.'

A couple of years later, a generous Welsh bibliophile my parents knew gave me a calf-bound set of the first forty volumes of *The Edinburgh Review*,* along with an early-seventeenth-century edition of *Foxe's Book of Martyrs*,† a 1615 history of England and a few eighteenth-century odds and ends, all of which extended my interests as well as extending my bookshelves. Add to this all the books I bought for myself, and it's clear that by the time I left school I already had a biggish, if miscellaneous, collection. The latest addition to it had been a complete set of bound volumes of *Punch* (which cost me five pounds), from its beginnings in 1841 to the 1950s, which I read avidly. As Max Beerbohm wrote many years ago, 'It is from the bound volumes of *Punch* that small boys derive their knowledge of life.' I didn't learn a great deal relevant to my own life from

* An important and influential nineteenth-century literary and political magazine started in 1802.

† John Foxe's *Book of Martyrs* (or *Actes and Monuments of these Latter and Perillous Days, Touching Matters of the Church*, to give it its full, original title) was a much reprinted and revised Protestant history of Christianity, first published in 1563 and illustrated with many very gruesome woodcuts of martyrdoms.

those pages, many of the cartoons relying on a familiarity with fox-hunting or the inadequacies of servants (nor was I any longer small), but, along with Richmal Crompton's Just William books, it was certainly where I learnt at least half of what I knew about social history.

I continued to buy books when I was a student. That's when I started to spend time in second-hand bookshops, which quickly became a consuming interest. Wherever I went, I would search out the bookshops and spend disconcerting amounts of time in them, after which of course I usually had to carry at least one bag of books with me for the rest of the day. (Some years later, leaving young children in the car with their mother, after spotting a bookshop and saying I'd just be a minute, six-year-old Jacob would ask, 'Is that a minute, or a bookshop minute?') My main criterion for choosing books was that I might want to read them some day, but not necessarily immediately.

As I got older, and my interests became more specialised, the books I wanted became commensurately harder to find, and sometimes, as with Wyndham Lewis, whose works I devoured in my twenties, more expensive. What I loved about Wyndham Lewis's writing was its polemical intelligence, its idiosyncrasy, its energy (such a change from most of the literary critics I'd read) and its unpredictable and bellicose style. Partly as a result of my interest in Lewis, in my late twenties I developed a consuming fascination with out-of-print or forgotten fiction from the first part of the twentieth century – books by writers like Ford Madox Ford, Mary Butts, Gilbert Cannan, Douglas Goldring, Carmel Haden Guest and Yvonne Cloud, as well as more overtly left-wing writers like John Sommerfield, Jack Lindsay and Ralph

Bates. By my mid thirties, I was spending so much time in second-hand bookshops that I decided I might as well capitalise on it by giving up my (part-time) job as a teacher in a further-education college and becoming a second-hand bookseller myself. A subsidiary motive for this, or so I told people who disapproved of my book-buying habit, was the hope that it would make me less acquisitive if I was buying books in order to sell them rather than keep them. Selling them would also be a sort of controlled loss. I spent much of the next ten years in that world, accumulating a large and somewhat specialised stock in the basement of my house in Cambridge (I specialised in modernism, left-wingery, the Spanish Civil War, ephemeral political pamphlets and the like), until my undiminished capacity for buying books outstripped my aptitude for selling them by a large overdraft, and I stopped, sold the stock and the shelves, started a PhD and fell into the equally bookish business of academia, teaching English at Cambridge University. After thirty years of that, my Queens' College rooms were a parody of dons' rooms in novels, most of the shelves double-stacked and the tables, chairs, window seats and much of the floor covered in piles of books and xeroxed articles and papers.

Those rooms were a comfortable place to work and to teach in. The large windows looked out over the green, and from the table where I worked, I could survey the rest of the room, where there were armchairs and a sofa (often occupied by the students I was teaching), and a small rug that was always edging its way across the stained fawn carpet. Most of the wall space was covered in shelves, partly original to the room, partly built to accommodate my books. Where there weren't shelves there were Spanish Civil

War posters and a large neon-pink print of a Christopher Logue poem.* There were some filing cabinets, one full of notes, the other full of photocopied articles (though one drawer did contain bottles of wine). The green armchair and sofa were reupholstered when I moved into the rooms. I worked at a big oak table with laptop, dictionaries, pens and phone. In later years a second large table in the inner room became almost invisible as rows and piles of books crept across its surface: American poetry from Ashbery to Zukofsky, literary biographies, journals waiting to be read and piles of photocopied poems for practical-criticism classes.

In an alcove just inside the door was the smallest sink in the world, with cupboards over the draining board. The cupboards were full of books, too. There was a large board on the wall covered in cuttings and postcards (mostly of Marilyn Monroe, sent by students to accompany the Eve Arnold photograph of her reading *Ulysses* that used to be on my door). The inner room contained philosophy, psychoanalysis, literary theory, literary criticism and history, linguistics, classics, books in French and German and five shelves of collections of short stories. The first room contained more poetry (from Wyatt to Eliot – more recent poetry was kept at home), Victorian literature and criticism, and what could broadly be described as modernism. Orwell's works occupied two shelves beneath the CD player. A revolving bookcase on loan from the college library held additional books (Frank Kermode, Norbert Elias, the *New*

* It is a four-line poem beginning 'Last night in Notting Hill / I saw Blake passing by . . .'

Princeton Encyclopedia of Poetry and Poetics) and had more papers stacked on top of it. Once there had been a bed in the inner room, but it had been used as a place to store books for so long that in the end the housekeeper took it away and replaced it with another bookcase.

That was my office, my store, my workplace and my home from home for nearly twenty years. It contained my working library of literature, literary theory and literary criticism, philosophy, politics, psychoanalysis, history and art history. I had about the same number of books at home – fiction and poetry for the most part – occupying all the available shelf space. Then came the time when I had to retire. A small Cambridge terraced house like the one I lived in then, even with a library shed or two in the garden, can only hold a certain number of books, and it was already full. I'd had a wooden building, a long, low barn-like structure with a beamed roof, put up a couple of years earlier expressly to house the books I had in college, but almost at once I'd completely filled it with the poetry books and periodicals from the house. I decided that nearly all the books in my college rooms would have to be disposed of. And that would be no hardship, I thought: not really, not with so many libraries, including a copyright library, within walking distance. Silly to hang on to them when there was nowhere to put them except in store, where they'd be inaccessible. So I decided to sell them, all except good editions of literary texts and a few other things that I couldn't contemplate living without, such as some books by Walter Benjamin, Guy Debord, Freud and Lacan, and various other works by philosophers, art historians and literary critics.

Despite having lived within that carapace of books for so

long, I didn't realise what a wrench it would be to get rid of them. I thought at first I'd just sort everything systematically and decide what had to be kept, what could go, what might go, what could go at a pinch, but almost as soon as I started, I realised it would be an impossible task. Each book had its own history, which was part of my history. In the days before the internet made finding books relatively easy, you had to search bookshops, send lists of wants to booksellers and scour their catalogues to find scarce or out-of-print volumes. It could take years. Now each time I pulled a book off the shelf, I remembered when and where I'd bought it. The day I'd finally handed over twenty-five shillings for Spinoza's correspondence. The Bergson with Hubert Bland's bookplate that I found in a jumble sale. The complete run of C.K. Ogden's journal *Psyche*, which he'd bound himself in quarter vellum with his butterfly insignia on the spine, and all the volumes of the Psyche Miniatures I'd picked up here and there over the years.* Books by friends and books by people I disliked. Books full of my notes or jottings on the backs of envelopes. Books bought in Cambridge from the libraries of Raymond Williams, Dadie Rylands, Tony Tanner, Jack Lindsay and other luminaries. Even the most unassuming books prompted recollections. They composed a sort of biography, each one acting like a door in an advent calendar, opening on to some moment in the past.

Still, they had to go. From a dozen shelves of psychoanalysis, I kept nothing but the works of Freud, Klein, Bion,

* The Psyche Miniatures were a series of pocket-sized, essay-length books, edited by C.K. Ogden, dealing with recent ideas in psychology, linguistics, anthropology and the like.

Winnicott and Lacan, alongside Adam Phillips, John Forrester and some André Green and Laplanche. All the other history and commentary and penumbra went, along with books on psychical research, including the two fat volumes of Frederic Myers' *Human Personality and Its Survival of Bodily Death.** A whole swathe of twentieth-century thought went with it: Lukács, Kristeva, Barthes, Sollers, Pleynet, Lyotard, Sartre, de Beauvoir and the complete works of Georges Bataille. And Spinoza, Kant, Hegel, Nietzsche, Bradley, Collingwood, Scheler, Merleau-Ponty, Wittgenstein . . . all gone. No more literary criticism, or literary history, or history, or linguistics. And then there were the sets: Hazlitt's Works, De Quincey's, the Oxford Wordsworth, Coleridge's Letters: they all had to go in the end. (The bookseller, though, declined to take the works of Marx and Engels.)

There were some books I didn't regret losing. A couple of hundred academic volumes called *Modernism and* (this or that). A few inspection copies. Books bought purely for teaching purposes. But that hardly accounted for more than about five hundred. The rest I minded. They weren't a collection so much as an accumulation, but they shared, even embodied, what Walter Benjamin called 'the chaos of memories'. If I'd stopped to try to sort them out, I'd never have been able to part with most of them.

* Myers was a founder member of the Society for Psychical Research, and was interested, sometimes too credulously, in what he took to be manifestations of the unconscious. This posthumous collection of his research into evidence for the survival of some part of the human personality after death is historically interesting but quite rightly was not widely convincing at the time.

I said earlier that there was no more room at home for books. That wasn't quite true. I had extra shelves made in the first of the garden buildings to accommodate some of the books saved from the axe. The rest, texts of poetry from the last few centuries, would have to go on the floor of the second building, the one at the far end of the garden, which housed my poetry library; and forty boxes of books and papers would have to go into store. Walter Benjamin, a great book collector, wrote a marvellous essay, originally a talk, about unpacking his library;[1] I thought of it as I contemplated the prospect of opening those boxes again, wondering whether I'd experience the same sort of thoughts and emotions as Benjamin, though most of the books I'd think of as belonging to collections in the Benjaminian sense were already safely on my shelves.

As a corollary of all this, I've often wondered what it would be like to lose all of my books, the ones I've collected in the course of my life or never parted with, the ones that really matter to me, whether because of their contents, their history, their value or their associations. My Wyndham Lewis, Ford Madox Ford or Mary Butts collections, my 1930s stuff (though I sold my complete set of the Left Book Club* many years ago), first editions by pre-war writers,

---

* The Left Book Club was started by the publisher Victor Gollancz in 1936 to make a reasoned and documented case against capitalism and war, and to show why it was crucial to understand the Nazi and fascist regimes. To do this it published cheap editions, often of specially commissioned books, for a broad audience, hoping to develop a popular front of left opinion. By its peak, just before the outbreak of the Second World War, there were 57,000 members and some 1,500 discussion groups. It ended in 1948.

rarities, oddities, and books of poems given to me by their authors. Not to mention all the poetry books, pamphlets and magazines I've acquired over the last fifty years.

The novelist Rose Macaulay lost all her books, along with the rest of her possessions, when her flat was bombed during the Blitz. When she wrote about it, in *The Spectator* in 1941, she recalled, not without an eye for effect, her first dismay. 'Here was a charred, curled page from one of the 12 volumes of the Oxford Dictionary, telling of hot-beds, hotch-pots, hot cockles, hotes and hotels; there, among a pile of damp ashes and smashed boards, were a few pages from Pepys, perhaps relating of another London fire, a few from Horace Walpole, urbane among earthquakes, revolutions and wars, knowing that all things pass. But no book remains; my library, with so many other libraries, is gone.' Indomitably she started to make lists. She listed ('the saddest list') the books she had had, then she listed the ones she would never be able to replace. Then the ones she hoped to replace. And finally the ones she would replace straight away ('the indispensables'). It's a poignant essay, but also a practical one, gradually registering her coming to terms with the situation, an experience that many of her readers must have shared. There's always a sense of relief mingled with the distress of loss, but it's not always such a relief to recognise it.

The feeling of having to make a mature rational decision that came to me as I confronted the need to get rid of the books turned into something much less controllable when they actually started to disappear. The bookseller sent two very capable men to pack them up. Both were tall, not young, and they brought what seemed like a thousand flat-pack boxes and rolls and rolls of tape. As each box was filled, it was taped up and labelled with my name (I supposed that was what PAT meant) in broad marker-pen letters. When I told the chap in charge that I was thinking of writing about the process, he said he'd like to be described as wearing a beret and with a French intellectual look. They brought packed lunches and ate them sitting in the college grounds. As the shelves emptied, I felt rather sick.

Quite suddenly, through my psychosomatic nausea, I was gripped by a mixture of apprehension, misery and fear. It may have been tied up with thoughts of death (retirement prompting recollection of the phrase 'unburdened creep towards death'), or some terror of displacement or abandonment. I was close to tears quite often as I thought about it. How was I to find space for the right things and how could I let go of half a lifetime's accumulation? The emotions I felt were overwhelming, bound up with my sense of myself and the organisation of my memory and my thinking mind. Ever since I can remember, I've thought through the feel and look of books as a way of getting at the stuff they contain. People I've lived with have tended to comment, sometimes impatiently, on my habit of standing in front of bookshelves with a vacant expression on my face. I have to explain to them that what I'm actually doing is a kind of reading, looking as it were through the spine or the outside of a book to what it contains, remembering the past self that read the book (or that bought the book with the intention of reading it one day) and re-experiencing the feeling of reading it for the first, or the most recent time. There's a latent knowledge or an association of memories that gets released by that, or by the book's smell or its texture or heft, which I find intrinsic to the process of reading.

To explain what I mean, let's imagine a question arises about Heidegger's *Being and Time.* The first thing that happens is I simultaneously see and feel the cloth of my second-hand 1960s edition, before I start to flip through the pages in my mind, stopping here and there because I know the sentences I'm looking for are on the top part of the right-hand page, round about page 110. But I can't now reach up for the book to do the actual research, which is what I would once have been doing as those impressions passed through my mind, because I don't have it any more.* There's something about the authenticity of an encounter with a book that requires *the* actual (not even *an* actual) book. It may be a sort of fetishism, but that's how my mind seems to work best. Proust experienced something similar, and describes it in the sequence of thoughts that assail him when he is in the Guermantes' library in *Finding Time Again.* He explains that 'a thing which we saw at a certain time in our lives, a book which we read, does not remain for ever a part solely of what there was around us; it remains just as faithfully part of what we then were, and can be re-experienced, re-thought, only by the sensibility, the thought-processes, the person that we then were; if in

* At this point, in an attempt to haul myself into the modern world, I interrupted my writing. I found a PDF of a later printing of that edition online, looked up page 110 and found the following: 'Even if we turn our glance in the direction which the arrow indicates, and look at something present-at-hand in the region indicated, even then the sign is not authentically encountered.' Which seemed oddly pertinent.

the library I take down *François le Champi*, a child immediately rises up within me and takes my place, the only one who has the right to read the title *François le Champi*, and who reads it as he read it then, with the same impression of the weather outside in the garden . . .'

While I was trying to sort all these feelings out, and when the first consignment of books had filled the bookseller's van and driven off, I received an email from someone I didn't know, in Sweden. When my late wife, Jenny Diski, was alive she used to write a monthly column for a Swedish newspaper, the *Göteborgs-Posten*, and one of the pieces had been about me and my books and where they'd all go when eventually I retired. My correspondent had, it seemed, been worrying about this for some years. Apologising for what might seem too odd or too personal a question, she told me she couldn't 'stop thinking from time to time about how it ended or will end'. Not so much on my behalf as because Jenny had written 'so beautifully' about it.

It was a strange coincidence and felt too much like a message from the land of the dead for comfort. Ever since I'd started dismantling my office, I realised, I'd been caught unawares by things that weren't there any more. Stretching out my hand to turn on the red Anglepoise lamp on my desk when I'd already taken it home was like missing the last step when you're going downstairs. The jerk of realising that things had changed worked like a momentary revival of the experience of bereavement, which was why it had got so powerfully under my skin. But books are not people, although they do become their readers. It's a lot easier to get used to their absence, even if it takes time.

It used to be my habit to read digressively, taking down

books mentioned or cited in what I was reading and reading them, or reading in them, until they in turn were supplanted by another digressive impulse. (The unpredictability of this process is very helpful to me in my role as editor of the long-running literary quotation quiz *Nemo's Almanac*, enabling useful discoveries of vivid extracts to file away under headings like 'canaries', 'spinach' or 'Westminster Abbey'.) Reading a book about Paris and existentialism recently I kept wanting to follow up ideas, or just read more of whatever the author was mentioning; but the knowledge that I couldn't simply reach for my copies of Sartre or my run of *Les Temps modernes* did at least help me focus on the book in my hands and rely on my own memory. I might at last, in my retirement, I thought, be taking the first steps towards a more organised kind of thinking.

And one of the things this new, organised thinking would address would be the nature of reading itself, the pleasures of the imagination, the satisfactions of thought and understanding, thinking about what books are for and what fiction or poetry can do, the purpose of book ownership, and the continuing life of books whoever claims temporary ownership of them. Some days after I'd sold the final batch of volumes from my shelves, I had an email from a colleague who'd been delighted to find what he called an amazing selection of books in a Cambridge second-hand bookshop. Somebody else mentioned that they had bought the set of Hazlitt's Works. I tried to imagine all the books going to good homes, as I hope they did. Meanwhile, I continued to buy more at a fairly steady rate, even though I still had too many to reread in my lifetime. You don't have to read them all, all the time. The American poet Alice

Notley said once, in response to a discussion about the way poems can find the right time to be read by a reader: 'That's what books are for. You're supposed to have them and read them when you need them.'

Which is a very good reason for having a library. Partly an accumulation of books you've read, but also a collection of all the books you might want or need to read, or reread, or consult, or just look at and remember or think about. When the French literary philosopher Jacques Derrida was asked if he'd read all the many books ranged round his walls, he laughed and said, 'No, only two or three. But those I've read *really* well.' Apocryphal as that story may be, it points to something important: in one's own mental universe there will always be a small number of books that have canonical status. The books themselves may change with time, but their presence means that most of the other books in the library are satellites, or footnotes, ways of extending, illustrating, qualifying or questioning the books you've 'read *really* well'. Libraries, institutional and personal, are more than accumulations of books; they are central to learning, both to learning as a general state and learning as a continuing process, reading and rereading '*really* well'. But in my case, alongside my books now there was also a ghost library, a memory of the books I no longer had, nagging away like a phantom limb. And every so often, a freshly bought copy of one of the books I'd sold would appear on the shelves, or on my desk, like an interloper, a less substantial copy of an authentic original, doing its best to merge its presence with the memory of its predecessor. For some time after my college books had gone, the loss of them was somehow tied up with the death of my wife, sadness about the one infused with grief about the other, but also, by displacing it, helping to make it bearable. Which is why finding a place that I could make into another library, a solid one made from bricks and mortar, and with space for as many of my remaining books as possible, was also a way of reconstructing myself.

It took a few years for the idea of moving to become a reality, and by then it felt as if I was well on the way to being reconstructed. But it was lockdown again soon after we moved, with the curious arrested state of being and time that accompanied the pandemic: the suspension of normal life, the rule of six, minimal social contact and increased awareness of one's immediate surroundings. There was more time than ever to write and think, but I experienced a strange inability to do either, a sort of dragging stasis and mental muddiness, exacerbated by the absence of all those books, in store until the library could be made. I had hundreds of novels and hundreds of detective stories but no poetry and no non-fiction. I felt wrong, unbalanced. So far from finding a new, more organised kind of thinking, I seemed to have lost touch with thinking altogether, although I could still think about the imagined library, about how to organise the books, how to make sense of what was still left from a lifetime's accumulation; though without being able to see them it was not easy to be sure about just which books I still had. Nonetheless, the idea of creating the new library sustained me during that strange period of lockdowns, fear and caution; and thinking about how it would be organised led me to thinking about the place books have had in my life.

That's the main difference between a public library and the sort of library we make as individuals: the personal choices and the random element, books bought on a whim, or inherited, or received as presents, or bought at jumble sales or car-boot sales. More than simply a collection of books, a personal library is the archive of a life. If I still possessed every book I've ever owned, I'd have a record of most of my interests, ephemeral or lasting, and of all the friends and relations and students and strangers who gave me books, and all the notes or letters or tickets or receipts tucked among their pages, and the recollections they'd prompt. As it is, my archive is as full of holes as a piece of Emmental – but a patchy record is better than no record at all; in a way it's just another sort of record, the record of times when I needed to sell books, or cut down on them, or just felt that I needed to be free of the sheer quantity of books everywhere. And anyway, there's no such thing as a perfectly complete library. Even copyright libraries don't hold every book published. Historically, even the greatest libraries have lost books. Whole libraries have been destroyed or dispersed, casualties of war, ideology, fire or natural disaster. The most famous example is the fabled Library of Alexandria, but there have been countless more. In 1070, the Caliph of Egypt sold hundreds of thousands of books from the world-famous Fatimid Library to pay creditors in what the book historian James Raven has called 'one of the greatest dispersals of books ever seen'. Further destruction and dispersals occurred during the Crusades, during the dissolution of the monasteries, and more recently in the Nazi book burnings, China's destruction of libraries in Tibet and the loss of libraries through war in Sarajevo and Baghdad. Nothing can guarantee permanence, which may or may not be a consoling thought.

One of the most famous libraries in fiction, the one belonging to Don Quixote, appears to vanish overnight: Quixote is in bed recovering from a beating, and wakes up in the morning to find his treasured collection of a hundred works of chivalry and poetry gone. In fact the books have been burnt by the local priest and the barber, who think reading romances about knights and maidens has driven him mad, and the room they were in has been walled up, to persuade him into believing it never existed. But the loss of his books doesn't do anything to prevent him from setting out on the misguided adventures in which he believes himself a knight errant; he has simply internalised all the romances he used to read, 'rebuilding his library in his mind', as the polyglot novelist, essayist, historian of reading and former director of the National Library of Argentina, Alberto Manguel says, writing about the loss of his own library, adding that he can now 'better understand what [Quixote] went through and why he set off once again into the world. Loss helps you remember, and loss of a library helps you remember what you truly are.'

I don't think my books have quite had a Quixote-like effect on me, but it's true that what you read affects you and can sometimes make you think differently about things. Many of the books I've read continue to have an existence in my mind, or at least in some distant part of it, and have either had a shaping effect on my thinking or stimulated it, sharpening (or sometimes obfuscating) my relationship to the world and my activities within it. So another way of looking at the gaps in my library-as-archive is as a different kind of archival fact, bearing witness to a decline of interest in this or that topic at different moments in my life. The absence of six or seven hundred of my books of revolutionary history, Marxism, anarchism and allied subjects, for example, indicates the waning of my involvement in far-left politics in my early thirties. (I would really like some of them back again, now I can read them with a less enthusiastic, more detached but still in some sense committed frame of mind.) Reading between the shelves, like reading between the lines, will often reveal more than you expect, and thinking about the books you got rid of years ago may revive memories of who you were then and provide you with a sharper sense of the shape of your life.

All this may seem sentimental to some readers, especially those who deplore the proliferation of unnecessary books, both actual and remembered ones. Back in 1643, Sir Thomas Browne wrote: 'I have heard some with deepe sighs lament the lost lines of *Cicero*; others with as many groanes deplore the combustion of the Library of *Alexandria*; for my owne part, I thinke there be too many in the world, and could with patience behold the urne and ashes of the *Vatican*, could I with a few others recover the perished leaves of *Solomon* . . .' Why bother with superficial or ephemeral works when you could be reading and studying the few that really matter? Browne goes on to say that he approves the desire expressed by 'better heads' than his to limit the number of books, 'for the benefit of learning, to reduce it as it lay at first in a few and solid Authours; and to condemne to the fire those swarms and millions of Rhapsodies, begotten onely to distract and abuse the weaker judgements of Scholars, and to maintaine the Trade and Mystery of Typographers'.[2]

The notion of a limited canon of great literature is a long-standing one, attested by educational syllabi, publishers' 'classics', and attacks on middle-brow, low-brow or otherwise unsuitable works of the sort that have been going on for centuries; but who is to be the arbiter? Who is to dictate which books are to be kept and which condemned? Much better to have too many than too few: we just need to make sure they are as widely available as possible and encourage as many people as possible to read as many as they can. Discrimination comes later.

Although one lifetime is not nearly long enough to read everything we might want to read, it would be appalling if the only books we were allowed to read were books that were morally improving or aesthetically edifying. And even more awful if we were to countenance condemning the rest of them to the fire, the totalitarian approach so vividly imagined in Ray Bradbury's novel *Fahrenheit 451*. We need to read widely and indiscriminately in order to find out what we want to read again or read in the future, borrowing or buying the books wherever we can find them. We need to read in order to continue the process of educating ourselves. And to do that we need libraries, both public and private.

Before the advent of the public library system, at the beginning of the nineteenth century, the twenty-three-year-old poet John Keats ran short of books. He was on holiday on the Isle of Wight with his friend Charles Brown when he wrote to Fanny Brawne on 5 and 6 August 1819 that he 'was alone for a couple of days while Brown went gadding over the country with his ancient knapsack. Now I like his society as well as any Man's, yet regretted his return – it broke in upon me like a Thunderbolt – I had got in a dream among my books – really luxuriating in a solitude and silence you alone should have disturb'd.' He hadn't brought enough books on holiday with him, though, because he went on to tell Fanny that 'This day week we shall move to Winchester; for I feel the want of a Library.' Two weeks later, he wrote to her again, having failed in his quest for books, 'It is more than a fortnight since I left Shanklin, chiefly for the purpose of being near a tolerable Library, which after all is not to be found in this place.' Keats was only twenty-five when he died, but he had already spent much of the little money he had on putting together a library of over a hundred titles. In a letter to the painter Benjamin Haydon, he lamented the fact that he'd lent some £200 (about £12,000 at present values) to various people, which he could better have spent on 'gradually forming a library to my taste', a few months later adding that 'Books are becoming more interesting and valuable to me. I may say I could not live without them.' (Nor could I.)

But then Keats was a poet, and his need for books was probably greater than the average. Are books so important to other people, non-poets, especially now that there are so many other media available – film, TV, social media, the internet? Is reading so important? Yes, I think it is. As I've already said (but it bears repeating), in a world where economic crises, war and climate catastrophe are provoking and exploiting deep social divisions, where totalitarian and undemocratic leaders make up their own claims about causes and effects, where lies and distortions, dishonest PR and indifference to pain and suffering assault us every day, there is a real need for us to know how to read not just books or news items but all the manifestations of language we see every day. They are what mediate, even create, the reality of the world we all inhabit, and if we would like that world to be one in which human beings can be free to live peaceful and satisfying lives, free from hunger, fear and war, we need to know accurately and truthfully, not for ideological reasons or out of resentment or as part of a crowd, just what is happening and why.

Oddly enough, William Wordsworth was worrying about the same thing over two hundred years ago, when he wrote that 'a multitude of causes unknown to former times are now acting with a combined force to blunt the discriminating powers of the mind, and unfitting it for all voluntary exertion to reduce it to a state of almost savage torpor. The most effective of these causes are the great national events which are daily taking place, and the encreasing accumulation of men in cities, where the uniformity of their occupations produces a craving for extraordinary incident which the rapid communication of intelligence hourly gratifies.' (When he talks about 'the rapid communication of intelligence' he means the speed at which news keeps arriving, in an earlier version of contemporary anxieties about social media.)

But knowing things accurately is not as easy as it sounds: too often, people adopt ideas without thinking them through, especially when they're responding to posts on social media. We need to be able to read critically. We need to be able to think for ourselves. One of the crucial elements necessary for this is memory: memory shapes our being and our consciousness and allows us to develop emotionally and intellectually. If all our memories are outsourced to external devices, if memory is treated simply as a need to access information, our powers of judgement are weakened. Reading books is a crucial element in learning how to develop memory and to think for ourselves, to be open to new thoughts, able to test them in our minds, ready to change, to imagine that things might be better than they are, to act accordingly and hope they will be. Critical reading and critical thinking won't change the world on their own, but without them the future is bleak. We need serious thinking and we need imagination. And we need libraries, both public repositories and our own collections: a library is both a physical place, a place for physical books, and at the same time a mental space, a space of intellect and imagination, thought and memory. In the past few years, local authorities, starved of money by central government ideology, have been forced to close hundreds of public libraries. We need public libraries. We need to defend them, and we need to show why we need to defend them. Building a library of one's own is, in a small way, a work of resistance, as well as a work of civilisation.

2

Pleasures of the Imagination

Reading unfolds like a game called 'I' . . .

Lisa Robertson, *The Baudelaire Fractal*

I stood in the coach house, enjoying the idea of the library I was envisaging. It seemed hugely spacious, high at the back and extending in all directions. It had an upper storey too, reached by a vertical ladder and a trapdoor, part of which had once been used as a pigeon loft; but I couldn't afford to make a two-storey library. Money was one of the limiting factors on what I could do; the other was that this outbuilding, like the house, was Grade II listed so I wasn't free to do just as I liked with it. It was a restoration project, really, and as the coach house included a well-preserved stable and loose box, complete with manger and the original stable doors, we would have to work out the best way to keep them without losing too much space. Under the damp, rust, cobwebs and dust the stable looked solid; it might even clean up to be rather striking. The architect came and looked and measured and took photographs and we discussed what I wanted, then he went away to draw up some draft plans for the transformation.

The plans he came up with were imaginative, meticulous and pretty much exactly what I desired but hadn't fully envisaged. A few things needed tweaking, but nothing major. The available space would be quite a bit smaller than I'd anticipated, though, as in addition to the requirement to retain the stable, the place needed serious insulation and that would involve bringing the ceiling level down, raising the floor and bringing the walls in; and removing half the back wall to make the French windows that would open into the new garden my wife, Olivia, was planning meant there would be less wall space for books than I'd hoped. I wouldn't have room for everything I had intended to keep. But there would still be almost 150 metres of shelves, which would hold a lot of books. The plans were exciting, and I was impatient to get started. But nothing could happen straight away: we needed to put the job out to tender, select a builder and then wait until the builder was ready and able to start work. And we were still in the pandemic. As things turned out, it was to be another year before the work began.

All I could do for the time being was dream what it would be like at some point in the future when the world returned to normal, if it ever did, and when all my books would be available again. At the end of his short talk about unpacking his library and about being a book collector, Walter Benjamin claims that 'ownership is the most intimate relationship that one can have with things', not because they come alive in their owners but because their owners come alive in them. I was looking forward to coming alive in my books again.

In the meantime, I could take stock of the books that weren't in store, the ones we'd managed to find room for in the house. Most of those books were fiction. There was a large collection of golden-age and later detective stories, mostly green Penguins and Pan books from the 1940s, '50s and '60s along with a smaller number of reprints. (I'll have more to say about detective stories later.) Then there were two or three thousand more literary novels (many of them first editions, so no good for reading in the bath), several hundred art books, some children's books up on the top floor in the spare bedroom, a couple of hundred cookery books, a number of gardening books, and what librarians would call 'local topography'. The biggest concentration was in my study, where most of the fiction (except the detective fiction) and half the art books lived, and where I spent a good deal of time at my desk or reading.

I still had plenty to read, and I could have spent all my time reading novels I'd never read or had forgotten – but I didn't have my poetry books, or my notebooks, or most of the non-fiction things like history, biography, philosophy or psychoanalysis. These days, my study is a very cluttered room, piles of books everywhere, with books open, books half read on my overloaded desk along with notebooks and reference books, the whole room a record of divagatory reading, frequent distraction, parallel trains of thought and divergent lines of enquiry. But back then, it was as if more than half of my diet had been forbidden me. It unbalanced me. I was writing poems, but I found it unusually difficult to write prose, read non-fiction or even think properly. It may have been a result of dislocation, the move to an unfamiliar place, or perhaps the absence of my books and notebooks, or more likely a consequence of the strange, frightening, restricted atmosphere of the pandemic. It may have been connected to my Covid-related fear of leaving the house, something that continued to affect me long after the pandemic was officially over. But whatever the cause, it meant that without really intending to, I read almost nothing but cookery books and novels (including dozens and dozens of detective stories) for something like two years. I read cookery books a lot – I'm a keen cook – and have done since I discovered Elizabeth David when I was a teenager. The realisation that they didn't have to be just recipes opened my eyes to a whole new world, from which I started to learn about the foods and gastronomic culture of other countries as well as my own. I was fortunate that my growing interest coincided with – was part of – the broadening of British food culture and with the appearance of dozens of excellent books by writers like Jane Grigson, Claudia Roden, Alan Davidson, Arabella Boxer and many others. Along with writers like M.F.K. Fisher and Patience Gray they paved the way for the plethora of good food writing we have today.

I've never wanted to write a novel or a cookery book, but I am interested in what goes on in your mind when you read, and it was impossible not to think, however incoherently, about that while I was reading so much genre fiction. What was it about detective stories that made them so attractive? What happened to me when I was immersed in one of them? Was I enjoying the suspense, waiting to discover who the murderer was, and why? Or was I enjoying other things about them, like the style or the setting or the period? Why could I read books like that but not more serious novels, or poetry, or biographies, histories and other kinds of non-fictional writing? After all, the actual experience of reading, the ways the reader is engaged by a text, must be similar to some extent whatever the book, even though the outcome may vary from one to another.

What goes on in a reader's mind? I've been reading for seventy years but I'm only now coming to think of it as a puzzling activity. Reading novels creates virtual encounters with imagined lives and imagined narratives in order to witness or participate virtually in events that may be interesting, challenging, enlivening, frightening, comical, enthralling or banal, and which may unfold on a domestic scale or a cosmic one or anywhere in between. How we relate to the novels we encounter, if we do relate to them, is dependent on a huge number of factors, ranging all the way from the writer's prose style to the reader's own social preferences, and taking in attitudes to past periods, authorial tone, social conventions, ethical outlook and the reader's interest. But whatever else novels are doing, reading them must also give the reader some kind of pleasure: pleasure must be somewhere in the picture, even if it is complex or conflicted, even if it's sometimes painful.

Sometimes, especially reading a less than wonderful detective story, I realise that what is really interesting me as I read is not the plot or the characters but incidental details of the world of, say, 1934, if that's when the book was written. Things like decor and setting, kinds of food, manners, habits, street furniture, clothes, slang and turns of phrase, political or social assumptions, imperialist attitudes or attitudes to cars, men's assumptions about women or nuances of class distinction. The more genre fiction you read, the more you find out all kinds of trivial information about the past – genre fiction more than literary fiction because it is less self-aware, more innocent, concerned to deliver its story without worrying about the background. Things taken for granted and unnoticed in a novel of 1934 may reveal all sorts of useful information about social life at the time to a reader almost a hundred years later, in the same way as we humans retain impressions from the past that can suddenly and unexpectedly emerge years later to clarify a feeling or help understand a trauma.

Thomas De Quincey compared the human brain to a palimpsest. 'Everlasting layers of ideas, images, feelings, have fallen upon your brain softly as light. Each succession has seemed to bury all that went before. And yet, in reality, not one has been extinguished.' And in a passage that looks forward to the discoveries of psychoanalysis many years later, he describes the power of dreams, especially the heightened dreaming induced by fever or opium, as a 'potent convulsion of the system' in which 'all wheels back into its earliest elementary stage', back eventually to 'the deep, deep tragedies of infancy, as when the child's hands were unlinked for ever from his mother's neck, or his lips for ever from his sister's kisses', impressions that remain 'lurking' below all the other layers of the palimpsest. Elizabeth Bowen offers another truth about memory and fiction when she writes, 'I know I have in my make-up layers of synthetic experience, and that the most powerful of my memories are only half true. Reduced to the minimum, to the what did happen, my life would be unrecognisable by me. Those layers of fictitious memory densify as they go deeper down.'

This mixture of fictional and truthful memory is a

crucial element in our make-up (and that's a telling word in this context). It affects reading, too. We don't always remember what we've read, or not consciously. A friend of mine once decided to write a list of the single most memorable thing he could remember from each of a number of the books he'd read, but he gave up after the first when he discovered that the image of a central incident that had stuck in his mind for years since he'd read the book did not in fact occur anywhere in it. Sometimes it's not the memory of the book that's faulty, but the book itself that revives memories forgotten or repressed. I used to have a very retentive memory, but as I get older it fades somewhat; rather than trying to remember a passage from a book in the abstract, I can get hold of the copy I read, touch it, feel it, look at the page layout and the typeface, then the content usually comes flooding back to me. Books hold memories, libraries hold books: libraries like the British Library or the Library of Congress hold memories for nations, in trust for everybody; personal libraries can be the guardians of individual as well as cultural memory.

Books have their own history, too. Many of my books were bought second-hand, which meant they belonged to other people before I acquired them – sometimes to well-known figures, more often to people who mean no more to me than the names they've left on a flyleaf. Some of them have annotations in the margins, or notes written in the back; some have been handed down from one generation to the next. Some of the notes are interesting, some of the annotations are rude or dismissive, but they all show the history of other readers, other responses, and have the potential to enrich my reading or provoke thought (or more likely annoyance). Sometimes annotations can be historically important, though very few of my books come into that category: reading the marginal notes and comments made by writers, on other writers, or earlier readers, on their books can cast new light on all kinds of areas. The study of marginalia in early-modern books, for example, has brought about a reassessment of the nature of reading at that time, showing it often to have been more of a communal than a purely private activity as one reader so to speak conversed with another via the margins of the page. One's own markings may be like that too, or they may be private responses that, reread years later, may make you feel embarrassed, puzzled, guilty or even proud. When I disposed of the books from my college rooms, I forgot that a few of them had been heavily annotated by me when I first read them, which means I no longer now have access to that aspect of the development of my thinking. There were also a few books that had belonged to critics or writers from past decades, whose notes provided interesting sidelights on their own lives, times or attitudes. Even pencil lines in the margin tell us something about what the reader was thinking.

This is not to encourage the defacement of library books with yellow marker pen or biro scrawls, but to remember that sometimes historical annotations, marginalia, even doodles, which used to be regarded as defacement, can turn out to be historically significant, even important. They act, too, as a reminder that as well as being objects, books can become dynamic collaborations with their readers. The more we know about the stages of writing that precede the finished, published object, the more we begin to realise that the text itself is less fixed than it seems. Is the text the same as the book? In common parlance, it is. But thinking more deeply about it raises what may seem like a silly question: what actually is a book? What constitutes it? Is it the same whatever form it takes? Is a book an object or an idea? How does it accrete its associations? A book can be a story, an argument, a repository, a taste, a colour, a promise, an attack, a dream, a revelation, a disappointment, a memory. (Although sometimes what we remember of a book turns out not to be in it at all, as my friend discovered.) Clouds of association gather round books, blurring our memories of what they contain. Our experience of a book can differ depending on where it's read, in what edition, at what age, even in what language.

I remember when I was a student going to a lecture on practical criticism by Hugh Sykes Davies, who, unknown to me at the time, had been a surrealist poet and novelist earlier in his life; he took us through a couple of extracts from *Antony and Cleopatra* in French translation before he allowed us to look at Shakespeare's original. The exercise worked like a sort of palate cleanser so that when we came to look at the English, we weren't distracted by the mere sense of the passage from examining the way its effects were constructed. I've enjoyed translating ever since I was at school, and I've spent time puzzling over some of the questions it raises, such as the question of what the text of a work actually consists in. What are you reading if you read the same Shakespeare speech in two different languages? My first encounter with *Hamlet*, oddly, was an extract from the Schlegel and Tieck translation in my school German primer. But since I wasn't German, and my understanding of the language was fairly rudimentary, I don't suppose it coloured my later reading of the play. But what if I *was* German – how would it be different for me? What difference does it make if you read Shakespeare in different contexts? Or even in different formats – a facsimile of the First Folio, say, and a copy of a recent paperback edition? Does that make any difference to its meaning?

Many people, many of them writers themselves, have written accounts of their childhood reading, and very often they will emphasise at some key moment in the essay how vividly they recollect the physical nature, the feel and look and even the smell of their favourite books, and how the thought of the story brings back the presence of the physical book, and where they were when they were reading it. I wonder whether you can have the same experience of reading, say, *The Adventures of Robinson Crusoe* if the material form of one book with that title differs substantially from another. You might read it, as I first did when I was a boy, in a small blue hardback, the text abridged; or perhaps in a handsomely bound large volume, full of colour illustrations; or as a pocket-sized paperback; or in a scholarly edition, with explanatory notes and the original spelling; or even in a calf-bound eighteenth-century edition with all the marks of previous ownership it had accumulated over the years. How would the version you read shape your later memory of the book, the feel of it in your hand, the place where you read it, all the associations that might accrue to your recollected reading? Or does the story transcend the context it's read in? Perhaps a book is just a container, though what it contains will impress different people in different ways. The German critic and social theorist T.W. Adorno says, in a slightly tongue-in-cheek way, that 'the ideal reader, whom books do not tolerate, would know something of what is inside when he felt the cover in his hand and saw the layout of the title page and the overall quality of the pages, and would sense the book's value without needing to read it first'. Conversely, supporters of ebooks and other ways of reading on screens argue, like the novelist and translator Tim Parks, that the nature of the physical book is unimportant, insistence on it a kind of fetishism: 'Writing was sacred. In the beginning was the Word, the word written down, hopefully on quality paper. Much of the resistance to ebooks, notably from the literati, has to do with a loss of this sense of sacredness, of the vulnerable paper vessel that thrives on our protective devotion.'

It comes back again to the question of what happens when we read. If my response to a book is different from yours or anyone else's, can we say we've read the same book? Or if we can say that, is it still the same book in our separate recollections of it? What do we look for, what do we seize on, what do we dislike, what do we remember? How much freedom do we have to interpret what we read?

Reading and understanding, reading and interpretation, reading and explanation: almost all the ideas and moments of response that go on in a reading mind as it travels through a book get excluded or distorted or at best summarised when you have to write about the book or think about it, or tell someone what it's about. Otherwise our account of the book would be like the useless Chinese map in the one-paragraph Jorge Luis Borges story, 'On Exactitude in Science', which was the same size as the empire it described. No summary or interpretation or critical essay could ever be fully equal to the minute-by-minute experience of reading; but then a necessary part of reading must also be the process of digestion and incorporation of what you've read into your own emotional and intellectual being. Books, in the end, are made out of language, and the reader's processing of that language construction creates a kind of mental space, a theatre of the mind as psychoanalyst Joyce McDougall calls it, a place where we can allow our emotional involvement in imaginary scenes, situations and narratives to be acted out without repercussions in the real world, often without any conscious awareness of it happening.

As books' material and textual history changes over time, so their interpretation will change, too. Novelists and other writers can only write what it's possible to write at the time, their horizons extending outwards synchronically to all the things people can know and do at any given time (which includes much of the past but replaces it at the same time). Of course authors differ in their own circumstances and knowledge and interests and ability, but there will always be shared epistemic limits to all writers writing at any given time, things it's not possible for them to know. If a character in a novel you thought was by Jane Austen mentioned that they'd come by train, you'd quickly realise that something was wrong. All writing is recognisably rooted in its time. Reading, on the other hand, is different. The conditions of reading vary through time so that – where texts have not become unreadable for reasons of linguistic or cultural change – the book you read in 2025 that was written three hundred years earlier will, for all its continuities, be different in many ways from the same book as it appeared to its original readers, and to Victorian or twentieth-century readers.

This means that books, especially novels, often need to be reinterpreted for new generations of readers who come with different understandings of the world and different expectations and assumptions. Few if any readers of *Mansfield Park*, to cite Jane Austen again, paid attention to the moral implication of Sir Thomas Bertram's wealth deriving from slavery, from his plantation in Antigua, until Edward Said pointed it out. Feminist readings have similarly altered the ways we think about a huge number of novels, including quite recent ones. Questions of race and gender, imperialist and colonialist assumptions, class and patriarchal attitudes all appear differently at different points in history; what is unconscious to one generation appears embarrassing or appalling a hundred years later. Nor should we forget that we too, for all our apparent self-awareness, are still likely to be unconscious of some of our own questionable assumptions. Our dependence on oil, our casual flights and our use of petrol-driven cars will no doubt soon feel obscene to future readers. In short, the literary canon changes. Different writers appear on school and university syllabi, with previously disregarded or undervalued groups such as women and authors of colour bringing a new focus to the study of literature.

Similarly, publishing priorities change too. The make-up of prize shortlists and longlists changes. Classic works in other languages are retranslated to provide more up-to-date or accessible versions. Nothing stays the same for ever, except the basic truth that reading the thoughts of another person extends our intellectual experience by taking us into a world that is not our own. It may provide something to disagree with and argue about, so testing our own thoughts or beliefs; it may improve our understanding, or open a new area of knowledge; it may bring pleasure, it may induce change, it may offer you different versions of yourself, make you imagine yourself adopting new thoughts, taking yourself, consciously or not, to the next stage of yourself. Books contain cultural memory, bear witness to some aspects at least of the past. Reading them can be dangerous, which is why totalitarian regimes practise censorship. Until relatively recently, liberty of reading and access to books, especially fiction, was the prerogative of the elite. Books, apart from those allowed by the powers that be, were potentially subversive. The growth of literacy and the provision of public libraries went hand in hand with democratic movements and the growth of socialism: all are now in perceptible decline, which makes our relationship with books all the more important. And while there is widespread and sometimes free access to texts via the internet, we should remember their susceptibility to cyberattack, power cuts and shortages; ebooks can be taken back by their issuers, too – only in totalitarian states or Ray Bradbury's vision of the future in *Fahrenheit 451* are physical books similarly vulnerable.

Once the architect's drawings were completed and revised, the job of constructing the library went out to tender during the summer, almost a year after we'd moved in. It turned out to be a painless process, and the contractor we selected set a start date in early October. I was getting excited again, counting the weeks until the library was ready, but in September the start had to be put back by three months. Not really a long time, but it meant an extra three or four months without the books in store. I was in limbo, waiting for the work to start, reading novels and vaguely concerned to wonder what went on in my head when I was reading them. During the pandemic, odd things happened to the experience of time as the rhythms of the day were limited to the small domestic round. With no travel, little socialising, fewer expectations and fewer opportunities to make plans, all the ways in which time expands and contracts in the mind with anticipations, anxieties, hopes, regrets and sorrows became overlaid with a sense of endless repetition, permanent stasis; there was a feeling of being on hold, hanging on, maybe looking forward apprehensively to an undefinable future, and always, somewhere in the background, that dull pervasive fear. The ups and downs of lockdowns and partial freedoms only seemed to intensify those feelings. In January 2021, the UK had reported a record number of Covid-19 cases, over 60,000 a day, with almost a thousand related deaths, and the alarm that aroused continued to underlie everyday life for many of us. There was huge uncertainty about what would happen next, and the injunction to 'wait and see' had never felt so ominous. In that context, my diet of detective stories made a lot of sense, as the experience of time in those novels is primarily geared to the final discovery of both the murderer's identity and the reason for the crime, and reading them is driven by a need to know: so long as you are sufficiently interested and motivated to want to discover the answers, the pace of the narrative gives a temporary significance to the passage of time.

In fact, the more you think about novels, the more impossible it becomes to ignore thinking about time. Novels are all about time: they take time, and make time, but the imagined time you inhabit as you read them is just that, imagined, illusory, a fictional time confined within the parameters of the book. Yet it can feel more real, or more exciting, more emotionally intense or intellectually engaging than the real world in which the reader is situated. Time in the novel, the time of the novel in the reader's mind, the time the novel takes to read, the long or short stretches of imagined time the reading gives rise to, all these complex interior responses live alongside the changes reading and books go through in time, in history. Reputation, interpretation, readability, accessibility, both of style and of subject matter, all shift as time passes and society changes. Novels can slip from being interventions in what was once contemporary life to being sharp-eyed witnesses of a lost historical past. This is the primary, even the only interest in many otherwise justly forgotten novels. But for many more, including the best, the modes of reading are inexhaustibly multiple. And from each reading we learn something else about the world, or rather about another view of the world.

Making sense of the world and of one's life within it is an endless task. History, sociology, philosophy, psychology, politics can all offer partial explanations of what there is in our societies and how it came to be what it is; scientific disciplines can tell us about the nature of things, about the earth's place in the universe, the structure of material and the dangers the planet faces from human activity. But useful and essential as all that is, it cannot give us the sense of being that we can get from the arts and literature. That's why personal libraries quite rightly tend to feature fiction more strongly than other things. Information is essential, and these days so readily available through the internet that we all suffer from a surfeit of it. But information without selection and critique is like a relationship without love: everything you need is there, except the central element. And without it, nothing has real value. Scholarly accumulations will help with understanding one or other aspect of knowledge, as long as we don't just go to them for answers but question what we read, embracing doubt and recognising complexity; but fiction (and poetry) can provide a sense of the whole, a way of engaging the imagination, the heart and the intellect that provides an epistemologically different sort of awareness. We all need both. A library that has resources of both kinds of book, both kinds of knowledge, is a spatialised version of the ideal mind we all need access to. Each of us is private; our minds are not accessible to other people in the way they are to ourselves. One of the arguments in favour of reading novels is that they give us the illusion of understanding, even inhabiting, other minds, providing imaginary access to the thought processes, desires, fears and evasions that underlie actions and interactions and allowing us an overview of the ethical world the author is depicting. But while this is one function of novels, it requires a degree of collaboration from the reader. If the primary or sole purpose of the novel you've picked up to read is to provide a temporary escape from yourself and the life you're living, then probably you won't much want to think critically about the moral choices of the characters beyond exclaiming at their mistakes and misunderstandings or feeling satisfied when things turn out well. Which suggests that there are different kinds of reading, and different ways of using imagination.

Elizabeth Bowen described herself reading 'deeply,

ravenously, unthinkingly, sensuously' when she was a child. What she calls 'the overlapping and haunting of life by fiction' for such children goes on until they are ejected from that Eden by 'a bookish attitude towards books . . . inculcated by education . . . Appreciation of literature is the end of magic.' But, she continues, 'What entered the system during childhood remains' unconscious but somewhere in the memory, colouring it for ever. Once out of childhood we can't entirely recapture that profound merging of the two realities, the life and the story, but the pull of the imagination remains and enables the pleasure of reading to coexist with the pleasures of critical thinking. Most writers, asked to write about the pleasure of reading, start off by talking about the books they read and loved in childhood. Almost all the contributors to *The Pleasure of Reading*, a collection edited by Antonia Fraser in the 1990s, and many of the contributors to Dale Salwak's *A Passion for Books*, for example, begin by recalling a favourite book, a trip to a library, the mystique of books on adult bookshelves, or the secret, private, exciting entry into a fictional world. In a letter, Virginia Woolf writes about the pleasure of reading as 'the disembodied trance-like intense rapture that used to seize me as a girl'. Everybody has some memory of the capacity of some book read in childhood to seize and captivate the developing mind, wiping out the surroundings and making reading it a completely private, almost secret experience.

Reading in bed is often remembered as even more intense, especially when it was forbidden, necessarily secret, with torches under the bedclothes (or in Germaine Greer's case, frighteningly, candle ends pinched from the church as she couldn't afford a battery torch). It was my favourite place to read when I was a child, especially if I was ill but not ill enough to prevent me reading. As if the many weeks I had to stay away from school with some illness or other were not enough, I used often to make myself sick or otherwise feign illness so that I could spend a day or two in bed, reading. School was boring by comparison, and for the first few years the reading was unbearably slow. By the end of the first week of term, I would have read through the whole pile of graduated readers in the classroom cupboard, some retold or abridged from Victorian children's books, and would have to twiddle my thumbs while most of the other children were spelling their way through the first and second. I preferred to lie in my bed, or sit by the fire wrapped in a blanket, reading about other children doing adventurous things. It was private, secret, and it felt more real. Alberto Manguel describes it well. 'No one would call out and ask me to do this or that; my body needed nothing, immobile under the sheets. What took place, took place in the book, and I was the story's teller. Life happened because I turned the pages.'

Although falling into imagined worlds can sometimes be escapism (not always a bad thing), it need not be, not by any means. Imagination does essential work in everybody's life, and reading fiction can play a significant role in negotiating the distance between private and social being. Will Self, who regularly claims that the novel is dead, has argued this is the historical condition of the literary novel, but that the 'instant availability of everything that had ever been done' enabled by the internet means that the serious novel can no longer function like that. He believes that for the last hundred years or more, it has been in crisis, and the hyperconnectivity with which the internet has infected our minds has effectively put an end to the privacy needed both to write and to read literary novels, except as objects of (historical and specialised) study. Peter Boxall, on the other hand, has argued that Self is wrong to be so pessimistic, seeing in his conclusion 'a tendency to resist the new forms of democracy enabled by contemporary information technology'. He argues that the precarious position that Self says the novel finds itself in today is actually its permanent condition: the novel, he suggests, 'has come into being . . . in the teeth of a contradiction between the desire for collective being – for the possibility of a fully realised democratic condition in which the law achieves a perfect accord with abstract conceptions of justice and the good – and the refusal of such collective forms, the struggle towards a private or withheld or non-existent space in which the mind might encounter itself outside of the conditions determined by existing cultural forms'. Even in some situations, a secret space, too. But in any case, as there is nowhere not 'determined by existing cultural norms' in one way or another, this is a mental space, a space that needs to be imagined, in a joint activity between author and reader. As Lynne Sharon Schwartz puts it, 'If we make books happen, they make us happen as well. Reading teaches receptivity.' W.H. Auden wrote memorably that 'poetry makes nothing happen', which is probably true as far as it goes. But readers do make things happen. And reading poetry, as well as prose fiction, can stimulate them to action, or at least to thinking about making things happen.

When people used to ask me what it meant to teach a

subject like English, what I actually did all day, I would usually say that I taught people how to read. A glib answer perhaps, but one that's becoming increasingly important. We do all need to know how to read, not only in order to access the sometimes difficult matter of literary art, but also just for day-to-day existence, for negotiating the world we live in, distinguishing truth from falsehood or recognising propaganda, and registering the presence of irony, humour, satire or downright lies. The more you develop the ability to read critically, the more confidence you gain about your own use of language and the more freedom you have from the use of language to have power over you.

The question of the purpose of art has always been a controversial one, and writers have frequently disagreed about the nature of literature and what it's for. When storytelling was a purely oral phenomenon, with familiar tales told to gatherings of listeners, reinforcing a sense of history and cultural coherence, relying on the pleasures of repetition and the significance of mythical or canonical events, it must have meant much the same for everybody. But when each reader of each novel is alone in their reading, free to respond in their own way, to take the story into their own imagination, especially when it's set in the present, the cohesive force is replaced with something different. Being part of a social group becomes more complex. Can literature be a force for social, political or personal change? And if it can, should it be?

There were fierce debates about that for much of the twentieth century, from art for art's sake to modernism, and across various forms of realism from socialist to magical and beyond. Between the First and Second World

Wars, and during the Cold War and after, some writers, particularly poets, wrote explicitly to warn or to rouse or to make people take political sides; others believed with Auden that poetry made nothing happen or, like Philip Larkin, wrote poems regretting that most things had ever happened at all. Others again saw reading simply as an escape from the pressures of everyday life. In the twenty-first century, reading still contains all those possibilities. It can be an end in itself, a form of self-expression, a means to action, an attempt to change people's minds, a kind of knowledge, a communication, an attempt to heighten awareness, increase understanding, give the reader pleasure, or just pass the time.

When you're young, you immerse yourself in reading because you identify so deeply with all the other ways of being you find in stories. For the time you're reading, the imagined world of fiction exerts a more powerful hold on your imagination than the real world does. As I said before, I was a passionate reader. I can't remember not being able to read, and I read everything I could lay my hands on. From about the age of eight I was borrowing three books at a time, several times a week, from the public library, and occasionally buying books for myself. Growing up in the 1950s, I was also reading lots about the Second World War, still very much alive in people's memories. Half my mother's sentences began with the phrase 'During the war, we . . .' I spent a lot of time in the local bookshop, browsing and coveting and, whenever I had book tokens or birthday money, buying books: school stories, adventure stories and loads of War Picture Library comics, with their odd claim 'big 64 pages – don't take less' (how could you? I wondered) and their unsavoury depiction of the German or Japanese enemy.

All the books in the shop looked very different from the books in the library, with brightly coloured dust jackets; even when the library books weren't in library bindings, their jackets were dulled by the sturdy plastic covers that encased them. Also library books often had a notice pasted inside warning the borrower not to return any book that had been exposed to an infectious disease unless it had been disinfected by wrapping in paper and baking in the oven. I was reassured that measles or chickenpox didn't count, only things like scarlet fever or polio, but I still felt a bit uneasy about reading library books when I was ill. I must have been about eleven, stuck in bed with something or other, complaining I had nothing to read, when my father appeared with a pile of books. That was my introduction to more grown-up fiction: there was *My Man Jeeves*, Erskine Childers' *The Riddle of the Sands*, and a fat volume of the complete Sherlock Holmes short stories. 'Start with "The Red-Headed League",' my father told me. I did, and once I'd read that, I carried on until I'd read all of them.

Although I soon moved on to other authors, Dickens and Agatha Christie among them, I was still most deeply affected by the kind of imaginative pleasure involved in fairy, folk and fantasy narratives, especially *The Lord of the Rings*, which I must have read four or five times by the time I went away to school at the age of thirteen. I'd read as many collections of folk tales as I could find, had enjoyed C.S. Lewis's Narnia books until I got to the last one and felt cheated by its transparent allegory. And for years I would hurry home from school to listen to a serial on the radio (or the wireless, as we knew it then). I remember particularly a wonderful reading by David Davis of *The Midnight Folk* by John Masefield; and there was Noel Streatfeild's *Wintle's Wonders** (and as I type that name, I suddenly hear the theme music in my head); I was also keen on Norman and Henry Bones, the boy detectives, and best of all was *The Eagle of the Ninth* by Rosemary Sutcliff (especially because it dealt explicitly with something lost, something of enormous importance and significance). Entry into other worlds, real or imagined, or into the past was what I wanted most of all. I knew it was fiction really, but part of me also knew that something about it was true. When I was eleven or twelve, I read Roger Lancelyn Green's *Tellers of Tales*, short accounts of famous children's writers, the first work of literary criticism I'd encountered, thinking that if I found out about the authors, I might get an inkling of what it was they knew.

So many of the books I was reading then must have problematised the connection between real places and imagined ones, between actual space and psychic space. I wanted desperately to get myself physically into imagined worlds. When, years later, I came to wonder what I was really looking for, I realised that beneath the feeling that haunted me – that powerful sense that the comfortable suburban family world I inhabited was not as real as it ought to be, that something was wrong with it or else something was missing – there lay a genuine reason for it: I should have had an older brother. My mother's first child had died at birth a year or so before I was born (something I was unaware of

* Now retitled *Dancing Shoes.*

until I was an adult, his existence never mentioned during my childhood), but her repressed mourning for him may have been an element in the sense of disconnection I felt. I was certain there must be another, truer reality just under the surface, just round the corner, just out of reach, a place where I would be at home; a feeling that was fuelled by my favourite books, in which children seemed always to be slipping from one world into another, or finding adventure or treasure via a tunnel or cave or secret passage.

Among the blurbs for *The Lord of the Rings* on the back of the dust jackets were comparisons with Spenser's *The Faerie Queene* and with science fiction. I hadn't read any of either, but the idea of them was instantly caught up in the same mystique. When years later I found that Coleridge, writing on *The Faerie Queene*, had said that 'the Land of Faery', with its 'true imaginative absence of all particular place and time', is really 'mental space', I felt a stab of recognition. Then and later, the nearest I came to it was the tingling feeling I sometimes got from poetry.

The first poems I remember were the ones my father read to us by A.A. Milne, the Christopher Robin rhymes in *When We Were Very Young* and *Now We Are Six*; I was particularly fond of poems like 'The King's Breakfast' and 'The Dormouse and the Doctor', 'The Old Sailor' and 'King John's Christmas'. I must have liked the combination of crisis, domesticity, comedy and reassurance that they offered. Some of them I knew by heart, and fragments like 'Alexander Beetle' or 'James was only a snail' became part of everyday conversation. Then, when I was nine, my parents gave me Janet Adam Smith's wonderful *Faber Book of Children's Verse*, which I loved and read all the time, and which showed me the incantatory power of rhythm and rhyme in shaping narrative and thought. It was not really children's verse at all, just a very well-chosen collection of poems that children might find attractive or mysterious or funny or serious, provoking thought and pleasure and helping to build up a repertoire of interior life and imaginative experience. Reading poems also helps to create an awareness of the possibilities of more complex or just different forms of language, and to show that they can be enjoyable rather than just daunting.

Oddly enough, there was one novel that made a particular impression on me, and that I took out of the library and reread many times, called *The Boy in the Ivy* by Linwood Sleigh, a tale of myth, magic and witchcraft encountered by a boy on his summer holiday. Just the sight of its yellow spine on the shelf was enough to fill me with a strange feeling of apprehension and almost erotic delight, until one day when I wanted to take it out for the umpteenth time it was no longer to be found – lost, I was told, and not to be replaced. Years later, when I thought of it, I would look for it in second-hand bookshops, but always without success, until eventually, only a few years ago, I found a copy on the internet, bought it, and read it again. To my surprise, it turned out to be written partly in rhyme (though it was all laid out as prose), which must have been why it had such a special attraction for me. The rhyming bits were the words of a rather odd character called Aiken Drum, and you had to actually voice them, and get the rhythm right, to hear the rhymes. I suspect that if they had been inset as verse, I might have been tempted to skip or slide over them, but because the verse was, as it were, hidden behind the ordinary prose of the story, it was more powerful and more attractive. And more in keeping with the story's purpose of exposing secret and malicious witchcraft.

But for all that poems were an essential part of my childhood reading, it was prose fiction I turned to most often. Looking for other or better realities guided much of my childhood and young adolescent reading. As I got older and attempted to put away childish things, that quest became less important; it retreated as I started to discover more and more possibilities in literature. When I was fifteen and studying for A levels in French, German and English, we spent a lot of time on poetry, as the exams then were rooted in the study of literary texts. I vividly remember the excitement of feeling there was a different sort of knowledge that poems conveyed, something glimpsed but only half known (or if the poem was in another language, considerably less than half known). The main operative elements were a sense of beauty and an unconscious awareness of form, of the work that form can do on the reader's sense of the meaning of the poem. Because it's not only *what* poems say overtly but also *how* they say it that constitutes its meaning: the two aspects are not separable from each other.

Around that time this feeling changed from an emotional conviction to more of an intellectual one, a focus on literature and its secrets, on poetic knowledge. If I could understand poems properly, they would, I was sure, lead me to a vision of a better world, a whole self, or at least to some knowledge of how such a thing was to be found. I remember my earliest encounters with close reading: among the first poems we studied were Hardy's 'Neutral Tones' (containing the extraordinary lines 'The smile on your mouth was the deadest thing / Alive enough to have strength to die') and Gerard Manley Hopkins' 'Felix Randal'; Walter Scott's 'Coronach' was memorable not just for the dirge-like rhythm created by having a final unstressed syllable in every line, but for strange words like coronach, cumber, corrie. When I was sixteen, I was reading poetry by Donne, Keats, Blake, Yeats and Shakespeare, and looking for something I couldn't define and I wouldn't know how to recognise if I found it. I tried hard to see worlds in grains of sand, to identify with sparrows picking about in the gravel, to fathom systems of symbolism, and to follow G. Wilson Knight's semi-mystical readings of Shakespeare. I wanted access to that sense of 'something far more deeply interfused', as Wordsworth puts it, a sense of the numinous of which I'd caught an occasional glimpse.

At university a couple of years later, I turned away from mystical approaches, but in my final year I became interested, in a suitably academic way, in memory, magic and allegory in Renaissance literature, looking for secret patterns of thought beneath the poetic surface of plays and poems, stimulated by Edgar Wind's work on pagan mysteries in the Renaissance, by Erwin Panofsky, and by Frances Yates' work on the art of memory and Renaissance hermetic traditions. Under the influence of Claude Lévi-Strauss, I was also reading anthropologists on myth, and structural linguistics, and I was excited by Freud and Herbert Marcuse, probably because psychoanalytic theory could offer a modern way of understanding the impulses behind Renaissance hermeticism, and because Marcuse extended the scope of Marxism (and therefore Marxist history) to encompass a Freudian Eros. And I was discovering recent

American and English poetry. Through all these pressing enthusiasms, I was trying to get to grips with poetry and rhetoric in order to think about the unconscious, and what 'magic' really meant to the Elizabethans. Was it their way of talking about the 'mental space' of the unconscious?

You can tell from this that I must have been wandering through libraries, pulling interesting-looking books off the shelves and trying them out, taking some back to my room, buying my own copies of the ones that seemed most important (when I could afford them) and adding them to the growing number of books in my own library. If I still had all the books I owned at that period of my life, it would be a good argument against the coherence of the self, but an equally strong argument in favour of the eclectic reading a library can provide. If a narrative is required to give a self the appearance of organic unity, then the multiplicity of my book collection would provide a counter-narrative to that one.

One way and another, though, the search for some invisible key to the meaning of everything seems to have continued like an underground stream through all of my early life, sometimes a trickle, almost drying up at times, sometimes rushing through me in a torrent. At the end of the 1960s and in the '70s it took me to Marxism and revolutionary politics; a bit later to an interest in the history of secrecy, then to a search through second-hand bookshops for long-out-of-print books (mostly novels) by forgotten writers from the 1920s and '30s. When Mary Butts, one of the writers I became most interested in, for both her idiosyncratic prose style and her insistence on a kind of mythic vision or hidden dimension to certain significant locations, writes about a sense of 'living in two worlds at once', or Anna Kavan's protagonist in her novel *Ice* says, 'I had a curious feeling that I was living on several planes simultaneously', I felt an affinity with them without really knowing why. It was something to do with language, something to do with poetry and something to do with the imagination and the unconscious. Literature appeared to hold the answer.

So the books continued to pile up, literally once the shelves were full. And the more books there were, the more the shelves needed to be organised in some way. It's the old problem, how to arrange books in a library; libraries and classification developed together. There's a difference between a library and a mere accumulation of books, or at least there's meant to be, though the line is sometimes hard to draw. Libraries are not only archives; they're knowledge classification systems, however idiosyncratic the classification may be. A French medieval writer, Richard de Fournival, said that libraries were like gardens, with books containing different sorts of knowledge like fruit trees set each in their own place. Books need some sort of organisation if their shelves don't aspire to be libraries: some people arrange them by colour or by size, some by publisher, while others like to shelve them at random, or in the order they were bought; some put like-minded authors together so that they can enjoy the others' company, even if they could never have met in real life. My library, my ever-growing accumulation of books, was never going to have the inclusiveness of a public or academic library, with sections devoted to all the various subjects. But even when I was eight or nine, and arranging my books in my glass-fronted bookcase, they were sorted by size, author, subject and colour. I suppose it was an embryonic form of the slightly obsessive attitude that still governs my approach to shelving my books nearly seventy years later, but nowadays it's done so that I have a better chance of finding the book I want.

Library historians will explain the development of classification systems, and intellectual historians will explain how the classification of knowledge arose in the first place: neither need concern us here. I'm more interested in encouraging people to have libraries. But it is worth saying that there is a literature of libraries, too. Most famously, I suppose, and much cited, there is 'The Library of Babel' by Jorge Luis Borges, but all sorts of libraries – public and private, fictional and real, old and new – crop up as locations where things happen (think of that cliché of detective stories, the body in the library, the title in fact of one of Agatha Christie's books), as resources, as places of mystery, secrets or discovery (think of Aristotle's lost writings on comedy and their significance in Eco's *The Name of the Rose*, which leads to the burning of the library). They may contain secret rooms, moving bookcases, missing wills, treasure maps . . . and they will certainly contain books, which in turn may contain secrets or clues or forbidden knowledge.

The literature of libraries also provides a reminder that libraries in books are made of words, and can escape into imagined dimensions, as when Pantagruel in Rabelais' *Gargantua and Pantagruel* arrives in Paris to continue his studies there and we come upon a list that continues over several pages of some of the books he found in the library of Saint-Victor. The list is satirical and scurrilous, and includes titles such as 'The Churning Ballock of the Valiant', 'Ruboffatorium scolarium', 'The Chimney-sweeper of Astrologie', and 'The Bald Arse or Peel'd Breech of the Widows'. Equally fictional but less pointedly absurd are the books in the library of Lord Sepulchrave, the 76th Earl of Gormenghast, in Mervyn Peake's *Titus Groan*, such as the 'set of the Martrovian dramatists bound in gold fibre', which, like the rest of the books in the library, is destroyed by fire in Steerpike's arson attack. In Borges' story, the library is the universe, containing every possible combination of letters and punctuation marks in every conceivable language and none, past, present and future. 'Everything is there: the minute history of the future, the autobiographies of the Archangels, the faithful catalogue of the Library, thousands and thousands of false catalogues, a demonstration of the fallacy of these catalogues, a demonstration of the fallacy of the true catalogue, the Gnostic gospel of Basilides, the commentary of this gospel, the commentary on the commentary of this gospel, the veridical account of your death, a version of each book in all languages, the interpolation of every book in all books', and so on and so head-spinningly on. The librarians become schismatic, sectarian, desperate and even murderous in their pursuit of whatever ultimate truth they believe the library to contain, somewhere in its unending vastness.

Since public libraries started to close because local authorities couldn't find the money to pay for them, their absence has contributed to falling literacy rates and a decline in reading among children. In her short story collection *Public Library*, Ali Smith intersperses the stories with the voices of other people, telling her what they think about public libraries and what they have meant for them. Together they make a moving and urgent case for the importance of libraries in creating readers, fostering imagination, building a sense of self, offering access to knowledge and providing access too to computers and human assistance for the people who need it most. Reading those contributions brought back vividly to me the memory of my nine-year-old self cycling with my sister up Stanley Road to the library in Hoylake to change our library books, and the excitement I felt as I scanned the shelves, finding books I'd never heard of and books I knew well and books I'd been looking for. Among the books I found there a few years later, as I was embarking on more adult reading, was a 1909 volume by Arnold Bennett called *Literary Taste*, which included lists of books that you ought to have in your own library, as well as advice to the newly literate classes about how to read them. Bennett argued that 'literature . . . is the fundamental *sine qua non* of complete living'. I was inclined to agree with him about that, but his rather declamatory style and a certain old-fashioned feel to the enterprise put me off reading the whole book or following up his recommendations.

Reading the book again now, I'm surprised how good it is, and how many of his recommendations have survived the passage of time since the beginning of the last century, or since Frank Swinnerton's 1938 revision of them for the newly launched Penguin Books. One big change since 1909 has been the huge growth in the academic study of modern literature, which has had a major impact on reading habits and publishing, and has contributed to the availability today of all sorts of once recondite books from past centuries, including essays about books and reading, like Montaigne's, Hazlitt's or Charles Lamb's; others, such as

Robert Blatchford's *My Favourite Books* or Holbrook Jackson's *Anatomy of Bibliomania*, remain to be rediscovered.

I owe a great deal to libraries, both Hoylake and Westminster public libraries (and the old Westminster record library in Charing Cross Road, where I discovered so much about music in my teens), school and university libraries, the old Reading Room at the British Museum, the London Library, the Marx Memorial Library and all sorts of archives in Britain and the USA. Wanting to build up a library of my own, even though it has meant discarding so much of it along the way, has been a constant throughout my adult life, and reading and writing (and translating) have always felt like two sides of the same coin. Proust, writing about his memories of the books that have had an impact on him, explains why he would never be tempted to become a bibliophile. 'I am,' he says, 'too aware of how porous things are to the mind, and how they become saturated with it, for that.' Worried that his original impressions of a book would be erased or overlaid by later ones if he became a book collector, he adds that the new impressions would have 'the same power of resurrection' that memory, untouched by later distortions, can afford him. This is crucial for him, as he goes on to show: 'What we call reality is a certain relationship between these sensations [perfumes, sounds, plans and atmospheres] and the memories which surround us simultaneously – a relationship which is suppressed in a simple cinematographic vision, which actually moves further away from truth the more it professes to be confined to it – a unique relationship which the writer has to rediscover in order to bring its two different terms together permanently in his sentence.' Or to put that in other terms, actually in Nathalie Léger's words, 'When we write – and undoubtedly when we film, dance, or paint – we are at once completely physical and absolutely abstract. Meanwhile ideas are finding their embodiment. And they do it clumsily, secretly.'[1] Ideas find their embodiment in words, but they do it through the writer's body and mind in that dual process.

Proust's great novel is a record of his search for the meaning and form of its writing, exploration, experiment, anticipation and memory coalescing in a single book. As he puts it, 'I slowly became aware that the essential book, the only true book, was not something the writer needs to invent, in the usual sense of the word, so much as to translate, because it already exists within each of us. The writer's task and duty are those of a translator.' We may recognise the truth of this, yet still be less concerned with our own formation than with the possibilities it allows us; and so the accumulation of books, of other people's memories, knowledge and imagination, will continue to be important, both for thinking and for writing.

As I write this, I suddenly hear my father's voice saying, 'It's a bright spring day – you ought to be outside, not frowsting indoors with a book. Put it away and get out into the fresh air', reminding me that there is a world outside the book – but equally that without that world we wouldn't need books or libraries. A library is, after all, a way of finding out about the world, sorting and classifying the written knowledge of it so that we can find it and learn about it for ourselves, as long as the library hasn't been closed down or turned into a café. More coherent, inclusive and impersonal than a library of one's own, those public libraries, more adept at providing unexpected discoveries: but a private collection is rooted in one's own life, and can provide memories and pleasures of a different sort.

3i

Guilty Pleasures: The Body in the Library

The overlapping and haunting of life by fiction . . .
Elizabeth Bowen, 'Out of a Book', *Collected Impressions*

A couple of weeks before Christmas, scaffolding went up all round the old coach house ready for the work on the roof, originally scheduled for four months earlier, to start in the new year. It was beginning to seem that the library was actually going to happen. But when it did start, what happened was largely destruction. The old garage had to be dismantled and removed, along with quantities of junk, which immediately changed my sense of the space available and revealed the potential of the now much larger stable yard. The roof tiles were to be removed while the timbers were replaced and insulation put in place, then put back (fortunately, despite their age, none needed replacing). The other thing that would need to be done at the outset was to knock a large hole through the back wall for French windows opening into the new garden.

It was an exciting but also slightly worrying prospect,

and I wondered anxiously whether everything would work as I'd imagined it. It was winter, though, and it would soon be Christmas. My horizons tend to contract in cold weather, so although I was excited to watch the scaffolding go up, knowing that it signalled the beginning of the process, I was also content to retreat to the comfort of my book-lined study, back in the house.

As a child, I was always happiest in enclosed spaces: small rooms, library corners, bed, dens, bushes, anywhere I could feel surrounded or safely tucked away from the frightening endlessness of open space. In the summers, I used to pitch my tent in the garden and furnish it with rugs and cushions, an orange box to serve as a bookcase and table. There I would spend as much time as I could, undisturbed by parents, siblings and other interruptions, reading and daydreaming. In a way, I've perpetuated versions of that all through my life. There's something about the activities of reading and writing that is exclusive, even secretive, and can still carry an echo of guilt, the feeling that I should be out there doing something, my father's voice going on about fresh air, my own arguing back that I needed to finish the book I was reading. After most of a lifetime earning my living with books, one way or another, I'm still capable of feeling guilty about spending too much time with them, and about needing to possess them.

Guilty pleasure in reading is probably an adult thing, the guilt or shame a consequence of the pleasure. It's nothing new, either: in *Northanger Abbey*, Jane Austen famously felt the need to defend novels against their critics. She imagines a young woman being asked what she's reading. '"Oh! It is only a novel!" replies the young lady, laying down her book, with affected indifference or momentary shame. —"It is only Cecilia, or Camilla, or Belinda;" or, in short, only some work in which the greatest powers of the mind are displayed, in which the most thorough knowledge of human nature, the happiest delineation of its varieties, the liveliest effusion of wit and humour are conveyed to the world in the best chosen language.' But for the next two hundred years it continued to be assumed that improving the mind meant reading non-fiction, rather than the books that Austen claimed 'have afforded more extensive and unaffected pleasure than those of any other literary corporation in the world'. Part of this pleasure is what Malcolm Bowie called our 'imaginative absorption' in a 'writer's words as they unfold in the real time of reading', experiencing the temporality in the writing's dynamics at the same time as feeling the passage of time in the book itself and the passing of time as you read it. It is almost a physical awareness.

All the same, I don't remember feeling guilty about reading when I was a child, except when I was reading Enid Blyton. I didn't feel the slightest twinge of guilt at the sexual frisson I got from reading the Chalet School books – girls' school stories, not in the least erotic to adult eyes but perhaps allowing my eight- or nine-year-old self some way of sharing in the mysterious, attractive, exclusive society of girls. I felt guilty reading Enid Blyton's books because I was forbidden to, though I could never understand the reason for the ban. If my father found me reading one that I'd borrowed from the public library, he would take it from my hands, read out a passage of dialogue, look at me and say, 'You see how bad it is?' which, while it may have been an introduction to literary criticism, wasn't really an adequate explanation. It just felt like another adult prejudice. (Another unexplained way in which my father thought books were bad was if they contained anything that could be described as 'American'. That went along with not being allowed to watch 'commercial' television, only BBC.) Of course, banning Enid Blyton's books only made them more desirable, and I continued to read them whenever I could, guilt and pleasure battling it out and probably intensifying my enjoyment of the stories. I read all the Secret Seven and Famous Five books, and I was particularly keen on the Adventure series – *The Island of Adventure* most of all, which I read several times, enthralled by the feel of the yellow cloth with its pictorial cover design, the mere sight of which made my heart beat faster, and by the sense of a parallel world forever out of my reach.

I often felt frustrated that I didn't live in the right sort of place (or time) for Blytonesque adventures. Writing about his fondness for the Famous Five books in his Cape Town childhood, the playwright Ronald Harwood says that while he liked the 'gentle justice' that always triumphed at the end of each book, it was Blyton's 'ability to share her love of the English landscape' that really attracted him to her. It was that power to evoke a different holiday world that I loved too. We lived by the sea, but it was estuarial, flat and sandy, too shallow and too polluted to swim in. Away from the sea, it was suburban, too populated to be proper countryside. I wanted deep, clean green sea with cliffs, rocks, coves, caves, fishing boats, a harbour and perhaps a smuggler or two. I wanted steep cobbled streets, disused mine workings, mysterious strangers. I wanted remote countryside, a rambling old manor house, ponds or a river, woods, green lanes and history. The pleasure of reading books set in places like that was mixed with my resentment at not having access to their worlds. My parents never died in train or plane crashes or disappeared to India or sent us children away for holidays on our own. They didn't even get divorced. Life was disappointingly ordinary, and summer holidays in Anglesey were as devoid of cliffs and steeply clustered fishing villages as they were of old manor houses and mysterious relations. The real world I had to inhabit felt both drearily familiar and uncomfortably alienating.

That's one of the things about reading, especially reading fiction, once you're past the age of total immersion and reading with an adult consciousness: you inhabit at least two worlds at once. One minute you're immersed in nineteenth-century London or 1920s New York, the next you're looking out of a train window at suburban houses or distant hills. And while you're reading, you may also be remembering earlier parts of the book, or events or people from your own life, or any of the fragmentary thoughts and memories that float around below the surface of consciousness. For the French critic Roland Barthes, these contradictions are central to the pleasure as well as the process of reading. Rather than being a seamless, immersive experience, adult reading is mostly an interrupted process, with different degrees of attention. We read a bit, look up, think about things, go back, skim, skip, jump, reread, reflect – our sense of the text, of the book we're reading, is being retrospectively constructed all the time. The knowledge that we are in two or more worlds at once complicates our sense of the boundaries between fiction and reality, and might make us more aware of the different degrees to which we are present to ourselves in our everyday life. It's all part of the experience of the book.

On the other hand, Alan Sillitoe, describing the way reading can also occupy the whole of attention without hindering introspection, writes that 'a good book, an absorbing story, stops time, gives further distance to eyes that look inwards. And the greater distance in, the greater distance out.' Children can immerse themselves so completely in a book that they lose contact with their surroundings, living entirely in their imagination. The acute pleasure of this kind of reading can create real disappointment when it stops, though, and you're returned to boring, everyday life until the next time you can pick up the book, or plunge into the next one. I can remember my sense that there was always more to everything than any single book revealed; in quest of that totality, or some sense of completeness, I needed to read *all* the Biggles books, and *all* the William or Jennings or Billy Bunter or Rosemary Sutcliff or Arthur Ransome books. And there was still disappointment when there were no more to read: I never got to experience the feeling of completeness I was looking for. I can remember with painful clarity the years I waited to get hold of a copy of the one Arthur Ransome book I hadn't read, *We Didn't Mean to Go to Sea*. The library didn't have a copy (and I didn't know I was entitled to ask for it); I only knew of its existence from the back panel of the dust jackets on other volumes in the series, and so it had accrued an almost mystical power and an almost mythical aura. When I was finally given a copy, for my eleventh birthday or Christmas, I approached it with a terrible feeling of flatness and anxiety, sensing that however good it was, it could not provide the intensity of pleasure I wanted; it was bound to be a disappointment after I'd looked forward to it for so long.

Books can be disappointing in themselves, too, which is one reason why people enjoy the predictability of some kinds of genre fiction. Comedies and romances tend to have happy endings, and detective fiction usually ends with the discovery or apprehension of the murderer. (Imagine how it would feel if Hercule Poirot just shrugged his shoulders at the end of a book and said he simply had no idea whodunnit, and we were left with that.) Roland Barthes was scathing about writing that wasn't seriously engaged with the business of writing, but he was wrong to dismiss genre fiction so quickly. Reading it is not just escapist entertainment; it can be thought-provoking and unsettling, too. Different sorts of pleasure, but none of them needing to induce guilt.

Yet hostility to popular genre fiction has always been around, one way or another. George Orwell worked in a second-hand bookshop in north London for a while, and wrote a short reminiscence about it in 1936, managing to be patronising, sexist, snobbish and dismissive in the space of a few sentences. 'Roughly speaking,' he says, 'what one might call the average novel – the ordinary, good-bad, Galsworthy-and-water stuff which is the norm of the English novel – seems to exist only for women. Men read either the novels it is possible to respect, or detective stories. But their consumption of detective stories is terrific.' He goes on to call detective stories a 'torrent of trash'. Ten years later, in 1945, Elizabeth Bowen wrote an essay, 'Out of a Book', for a short-lived periodical called *Orion*, in which she castigated lazy, immature readers (of both sexes) for not shedding the reading habits of childhood. They are 'the disreputable grown-ups who snap up shiny magazines and garner and carry home from libraries fiction that the critics ignore. They read as we all once read – because they must: without fiction life would be too insufficient or the winds from the north would blow too cold. They read as we all read when we were twelve; but unfortunately the magic has been adulterated; the dependence has become ignominious – it becomes an enormity, inside the full-sized body, to read without the brain. Now the stories they seek go on being children's stories, only with sex added to the formula; and somehow the addition queers everything. These readers, all the same, are the great malleable bulk, the majority, the greater public – hence bestsellers, with their partly artful, partly unconscious play on a magic that has gone stale.' However, she concludes by saying that 'the only above-board grown-up children's stories are detective stories'.

I've always been keen on detective stories, though I don't think they do have quite the children's-story quality that Bowen ascribes to them. But enjoying them used to be seen – maybe still is in some quarters – as a waste of time. I'm thinking of Edmund Wilson's essay 'Who Cares Who Murdered Roger Ackroyd?', full of the intellectual's patronising attitude to popular fiction (or 'low-brow' fiction, as it was known), or the less intemperate but similar view expressed by Raymond Chandler in 'The Simple Art of Murder'. Somerset Maugham was more enthusiastic in 'The Decline and Fall of the Detective Story', though he is of the opinion that nobody will be able to follow Dashiell Hammett and Raymond Chandler. 'I believe the detective story, both the story of pure deduction and the hard-boiled story, is dead,' he says. 'But that will not prevent a multitude of authors from continuing to write such stories, nor will it prevent me from reading them.'

What Maugham and the rest did not see was how inventively other writers would develop the genre, how fertile it would be, how variously and surprisingly not just detective fiction but other genres too would continue to flourish and renew themselves. As is now widely recognised and applauded, except by a few polemicists like Lucy Ellmann, who claims that 'writing genre fiction of any kind is a cop-out. (Would it *kill* those people to write something fresh and new? Something honest and original? Something beautiful even?) But, of all the genres, from horror, sci-fi, cli-fi, po-mo, and chick lit, to travel, sex-and-shopping, speculative, supernatural, fantasy, historical, adventure, thrillers, war stuff, spy stuff, mob stuff, monsters, UFOs, etc., etc., nothing sinks lower in celebration of human lousiness than crime fiction.'

To be fair, her main beef is that many of the books she's talking about are deeply misogynistic, with women more likely to be present as victims of violence than as independent characters (has she forgotten Miss Marple, or Gladys Mitchell's Mrs Bradley?),* and she's only attacking genre fiction. She seems unaware of the ways that category bleeds

* Miss Marple is a familiar figure, but Beatrice Bradley is less well known. She figures in about sixty detective novels by Gladys Mitchell and is a psychoanalyst of a rather reductive, old-fashioned sort, and a dedicated but amateur detective (though an occasional consultant to the Home Office). She is rich, brisk, outspoken, three times widowed, and much more likeable than she sounds.

into 'serious' and 'experimental' writing these days. The disparagement of genre fiction can extend to every kind of fiction, too, although in the last decade or two that kind of assault does seem to be disappearing, perhaps because pleasure itself has become more acceptable.

All the same, people have long been made to feel ashamed or guilty for experiencing this sort of pleasure. As recently as 1980, the writer Brigid Brophy gave a talk to librarians in the course of which she speculated why people felt there was something shaming about reading novels, regardless of whether they were good or bad, frivolous or serious. 'All the arts provoke the puritans,' she concluded, 'because they give and often openly profess to give pleasure . . . The source of the shame people feel when they are caught reading a novel is, I think, that a novel has a strong textural resemblance to those shaming things we have all had, though we may not admit to having had one since the age of six, namely daydreams, whether of the erotic variety or the even more shaming vainglorious kind.' She is relying here on Freud's paper on 'Creative Writers and Day-Dreaming', in which he draws a parallel between daydreams and what he calls 'the less pretentious authors of novels, romances and short stories, who nevertheless have the widest and most eager circle of readers'. Although he says very little about the experience of reading, he does suggest that writers' modified use of daydreams enables the reader 'to enjoy [her] own day-dreams without self-reproach or shame'. But arousing memories of buried desires, even if the reader is not fully aware of them, may still cause a degree of shame or guilt.

Anyway, to get back to detective stories, whether or not

they create a sense of guilt in the reader they are certainly concerned to locate guilt in one of the characters, usually guilt for murder. It doesn't necessarily imply any psychological depth in the writing, but psychological depth doesn't seem to be necessary for the release of psychological tension in the reader, or at least for some unconscious sense of involvement in something mysterious. I suppose it's because detective stories are not viewed as serious literature that they are associated with reading in bed, in hospital, during convalescence or on train journeys. 'Since this trouble with my back, I've read all the detective stories there ever were, I should think,' says a character in Agatha Christie's *Peril at End House*. 'Nothing else seems to pass the time away so quick.' I read a lot of them, and always have, since I was about eleven and read Christie's *Lord Edgware Dies*. I've always enjoyed them, especially books written between the early 1920s and the mid 1970s, an extended range of the genre's 'golden age'; partly because I loved reading books set in the fairly recent past, in my parents' or grandparents' time, partly because I liked the more literary approach of writers like Margery Allingham, Dorothy L. Sayers and Michael Innes (books by all three findable on my parents' bookshelves). Not that that has stopped my reading more recent writers too: P.D. James, Minette Walters, Jason Goodwin, Nicci French, Sarah Caudwell, Mick Herron, Bill James, Kate Atkinson and loads more. I've read a huge number of them over the years.

In 1957, the psychoanalyst Charles Rycroft described reading detective stories as 'in a way the opposite of having psychoanalytic treatment. The motive underlying one is to deny insight and underlying the other is to gain it.' This might be true of the characters inside the books, but it probably isn't so true of the experience of reading them. If insight is restricted to insight into oneself, there isn't much of it, at least not much immediate or direct insight. Maybe some uneasiness or a niggling sense of something, but on their own they probably won't do a great deal to help us know who we are. But they do offer a degree of insight into the world outside, the world that forms the books themselves.

Writing about Agatha Christie's popularity, John Lanchester argued that the reason she's still vastly more read than her contemporaries is partly that she is less invested in her subjects, and therefore less likely to break 'the containment field of the detective genre' by making ideological points that jar with modern readers, attracting a kind of 'readerly dissent'. There's a degree of truth in this, but it relies on a particular experience of reading, one in which the spell cast by the narrative keeps you from thinking about anything except the mystery itself. Then of course whatever breaks the spell will be annoying, especially if it means you have to think about outdated social attitudes or become too aware of the writer's limited outlook. (In fact, though this doesn't alter Lanchester's main point about containment, I think it's pretty hard to read Christie's books without coming up against quite a lot of unpleasant, outdated attitudes: in that, and in her limited vocabulary, she's like a grown-up's Enid Blyton.) But what if reading within the 'containment field' is not the only way, or the best way, to read detective novels? What if they hold in them more than they can quite cope with aesthetically? They may not be as interesting as some literary novels, but reading them might stimulate all sorts of questions about desire, loss and what we can and can't know in life.

Questions are crucial. Detective stories contain a far greater number of question marks than most other novels, and a greater number of lies and evasions in response to the questions. The pleasure of reading detective stories isn't just, or even mainly, to do with getting the right answer to the primary question of whodunnit – there are other questions beside that one. As is well known, there was a huge new interest after the First World War in puzzles, crosswords, jigsaws, word games, board games like Monopoly, quizzes and suchlike, part of the same cultural context as the surge in popularity of detective novels. It's significant that the emphasis on murder as an intellectual puzzle rather than a tragic, distressing or realistic act of violence emerged in the wake of the First World War, and became increasingly self-referential during and just after the Second. But it's not the puzzle-solving that makes me read them, though that provides much of the narrative drive. It's something else, something related to melodrama and reflected in the theatricality, literal or metaphorical, of the detective fiction of the time, and spilling over into works like T.S. Eliot's *Murder in the Cathedral*.

One reason for the popularity of the genre in its early days was the literal disappearance of so many people in the First World War: a cultural attempt to domesticate death that had taken place on an almost incomprehensible scale, leaving few people untouched by it. Another was the unprecedented series of changes in income, class status and the position of women, uncertainties that raised questions about English society and the place of the individual, especially the middle-class individual, within it. The mix of nostalgia, hero-worship, uncertainty and prejudice displayed by characters in these books, along with varying degrees of awareness of the world around them, placed in a tightly restricted setting such as a big house or a theatre, intensifies these conflicting pressures. (The critic Alison Light has said that Agatha Christie's novels could be read as 'one huge advertisement of the murderousness of English social life and of the desperate need to convert to pleasure all those anxieties which an existence like that of the post-war middle classes could produce'.) There's another kind of questioning at work in the reading, too, which encourages us to read between the lines.

Everybody is always acting a part. 'Everybody has something to conceal', as Sam Spade tells the DA in Dashiell Hammett's *The Maltese Falcon*. That's the principle of the detective story, the idea (in the words of Freeman Wills Crofts' detective, the stolid Inspector French) that 'there's always something behind everything'. The thing about the something-behind-everything is that it's not easy to see what it is. Which is why, in the wake of Marx, Nietzsche and Freud, a hermeneutics of suspicion became so widespread. Things are not what they seem, the world is full of invisible forces, which, whether they're malign or well intentioned, may be unconscious or invisible to the naked eye or masked or hidden or encoded or otherwise out of reach. Even solid physical objects like tables are revealed by physics to be complicated collections of space and moving particles. Practices like literary close reading, psychoanalysis, iconology and ideological critique all followed a similar trajectory, as the extreme politics of the interwar years provided a fertile ground for melodrama, and all kinds of decoding strategies flourished. Detective fiction became a symptom of the need to reassert the possibility of conventional social order and common sense, conducted through a refraction of the kinds of analysis that challenged it. So what looks like a harmless way of spending spare time enjoying a comedy puzzle that culminates in the restoration of order after the revelation of the murderer's identity may conceal a more troubling, less detectable subtext. That's what attracts me about it.

Like almost all literary products, golden-age detective stories embody the characteristics and interests of their authors and – overtly or covertly – the attitudes and assumptions common to their times. Dorothy L. Sayers adds social and cultural snobbery to a conservative feminism; Michael Innes ties a display of interest in neoclassical art, literature and architecture to dreams, nightmare and the grotesque; Margery Allingham's deep love of a semi-fictional and fast-disappearing way of life in rural Suffolk and Essex is intensified by a powerful sense of the existence of malign forces; Edmund Crispin links cleverness with an evasive authorial irony, while Agatha Christie's writing draws comfort and certainty from a conviction that there is such a thing as real, uncomplicated evil. And though everybody quotes from Shakespeare, with Ngaio Marsh the central element and the most pervasive trope is theatricality (appropriately, given that she was also a theatre director), playing on and intensifying the likelihood that everyone in the novel is acting a part.

Marsh, who wrote thirty-two detective novels, was born in New Zealand and lived there most of her life, although she spent four years in England between 1928 and 1932, where she wrote her first novel, and after 1948 divided her time between the two countries. Her novels, too, are set in both places. Her books are very good for thinking about detective stories in general because she tried out such a range of different approaches to the form, always with the same central characters.

She seems to have idealised a kind of Englishness, and her writing was clearly stimulated by English contemporaries like Dorothy L. Sayers and Agatha Christie. She even named her detective, Roderick Alleyn, after the Shakespearean actor who founded the school in Dulwich that her father went to. Although not an amateur like Sayers' Lord Peter Wimsey or Allingham's Albert Campion, Inspector Alleyn is quietly well connected, a younger son who went to Eton and Oxford and then entered the Diplomatic Service but left because he couldn't stick the terms of the Paris Peace Conference; his concern for justice led him to join the Metropolitan Police instead. Like most police detectives in detective novels, though, he works largely alone, or with his stolid assistant, as if most of the rest of the police force didn't exist. Thereafter he proceeds smoothly but not obtrusively up the promotion ladder, though without reaching the heights of Innes' Appleby, who ends up knighted, as Metropolitan Police Commissioner. Naming a character after an actor is a very mild gesture towards theatricality, but the novels themselves take the matter much further. As comedies, they rely on misprision, deception, coincidence and an acceptance of basic improbabilities. Death is hardly serious. The murders do little more than motivate the plot, and the corpses provide a fixed central point for the examination of each character's relationship to the deceased.

Marsh makes a lot of Alleyn's ethical scruples, especially about capital punishment, which he justifies on the dubious grounds that capital convictions are never wrong in England, as Scotland Yard and the rest of the British police never make that kind of mistake. Even when the murderer is discovered, the book's ending sometimes suggests they will get off, or plead to manslaughter, or even be allowed to walk away free, in the interest of justice rather than a strict application of the law. Or they may take the opportunity offered them to do the right thing and spare everyone the indignity of a trial by committing suicide. It depends on the circumstances, and whether they are the right sort of person or not. We know what this implies because Alleyn is very sensitive to offences against a class-based code of manners, dress, etiquette and intuitive tone. His easy familiarity with Shakespeare (something he shares with a surprisingly large number of other detectives) marks out for our approval any other figure who can recognise or, better still, cap the quotations that crop up so frequently in his conversation. It's a mark of civilisation, like playing cricket.

On the other side of the fence, there are recurring indicators of uncivilised behaviour: drug dealing is unequivocally bad, as is alcoholism; phoney spiritualism (even worse when, as in *Death in Ecstasy*, it's coupled with drugs) and superstition is a third recurrent concern. And juvenile delinquency. The powerful feelings at work in their depiction and the strength of Marsh's censoriousness can make the actual business of killing another human being seem almost inconsequential. Beside them, the corpse is just a device.

There is snobbery at work here, an attachment to the old

social order and a critical awareness of the shifts in social status and the social fabric she sees after the Second World War, as marked, though in different ways, as the social changes that followed the First. Lady Lacklander in *Scales of Justice* asks: 'Do you find us [the aristocracy] effete, ineffectual, vicious, obsolete and altogether extraneous? . . . Some of us are, you know.' Marsh admits the truth of this as it applies to individuals, but has a firm belief in the idea of 'degree': so long as aristocrats demonstrate behaviour proper to their privileged status, they are all right, and probably more all right than other sorts of people. And when they don't, there's always Inspector Alleyn to unmask them. Genuine social ease is a powerful marker of moral character in these books. If you haven't got it, if your attempt to belong to a class you weren't born into strikes others as 'slightly off', then you're an object of mild derision, satire or outright, even justified, suspicion. Actual aristocrats don't figure very much in her books: the cast of characters is usually quite varied, even when they're literally a cast of characters, in the novels set in theatres. The settings are varied too, though they have to conform to the genre's requirements of a confined space and a limited number of characters and suspects, with concealed or historic animosities among them. The situations in which the murder takes place and the subsequent drama unfolds are frequently bizarre: Marsh's choices of location include a nursing home, a cult chapel, an artist's studio, a nightclub, villages with grand houses (or vice versa), theatres, a ship, a remote New Zealand spa, a canal boat and, most improbable of all, a millionaire's house isolated on an island in the middle of a lake in rural New Zealand. The need for detective stories to have an enclosed setting for a murder in order to limit the number of possible suspects gives rise at the most extreme to the locked-room mystery, in which ingenuity and improbability are taken to extraordinary levels, as in the novels of Carter Dickson (a slightly transparent pseudonym of John Dickson Carr, also famous for locked-room puzzles); other devices include houses cut off by heavy snowfall (used by all sorts of writers) and murders on trains, aeroplanes, in colleges, schools and cocktail parties.

On the reader's part, there has to be a degree of complicity from the outset, a willing suspension of disbelief, an understanding that most of what looks like reality is actually just licensed by the fantasy. So in Marsh's novels, for example, there are gestures towards the real world here and there in the form of contemporary references, like the reference to the theft of the Duke of Wellington's portrait from the National Gallery in *Death at the Dolphin*, followed soon after by a mention of the Great Train Robbery, and later on by a name check for the theatre director Joan Littlewood. There is also an internal fantasy of reality, something Marsh shares with some of the other writers whose novels feature a detective who continues or develops from book to book, such as Michael Innes: references to earlier books occur from time to time, building up a fictitious 'real' background to the detective's life. It's a device that dates back to Conan Doyle's Sherlock Holmes stories, and which Dorothy L. Sayers uses to construct the romantic satisfactions of Wimsey's burgeoning relationship with Harriet Vane. Margery Allingham does the same with Albert Campion and Amanda Fitton, who moves from a reckless, red-headed tomboy of seventeen to being the self-possessed

Lady Amanda, an aircraft designer, whom Campion marries. Sometimes in Marsh there are references to cases that never happened, but the ones that refer back to earlier books as if they were real have a different feel to them. In *Death at the Dolphin*, for example, Alleyn recognises a man in the lobby of some mansion flats as the bailiff who installed himself in the house of the Lamprey family in *Surfeit of Lampreys*, published twenty-six years earlier ('"God bless my soul!" Fox said. "Your memory!"').

But for the most part, the world of the majority of detective novels is sufficiently distant from real events for them just to exude an aura of the time they were written in, and to provide a window on cultural assumptions, which I think is one of the most interesting and pleasurable things about them. The assumptions may be conscious or unconscious, but both offer ways in to the books' subtexts. There is always a balance, though not always a perfect one, between the believable details of the setting and the atmosphere – zeitgeist stuff, social history – and the artificially constructed plot. The formulaic constraints of the genre, themselves encoding responses to the social and political attitudes of the time, operate to filter and focus social attitudes and what lies behind them, sometimes as an aid to understanding a character, sometimes as authorial comment.

Like many writers of detective fiction, Marsh often uses puns in her book titles. These might be taken as another indication of the need to be aware of a double focus, of something behind everything: *Died in the Wool*, *Singing in the Shrouds*, *Dead Water*, *Photo Finish*, *Clutch of Constables* – all these phrases turn out to have a significance beyond the obvious. Examples from other writers might include Nicholas Blake's *The Widow's Cruise*, or *Heads You Lose* by Christianna Brand; repurposed quotations were often used to similar effect, as in Edmund Crispin's *The Moving Toyshop* or Margery Allingham's *Look to the Lady*; Michael Innes was proud that two of his titles were themselves clues to the eventual revelation of the guilty party. Reading any detective fiction, but perhaps especially Ngaio Marsh's, we are drawn more and more to an awareness of implication, occlusion, obfuscation and ambiguity. 'The mechanics in a detective novel may be shamelessly contrived,' she wrote, 'but the writing need not be so nor, with one exception, need the characterisation. About the guilty person, of course, endless duplicity is practised.' The writing need not be contrived, but it does need to keep the reader's attention and keep the reader entertained and wanting to turn the pages, and this is something that Marsh, for much of her career, was very good at. The writing should be, as she put it, 'as good as the author can make it; nervous, taut, balanced and economic. Descriptive passages are vivid and explicit. The author is not self-indulgent.' She doesn't go in for the kind of self-aware (sometimes too pleased with itself) metafictional humour you find in Edmund Crispin and Michael Innes, even in Nicholas Blake, but she does sometimes allow herself some self-indulgence, as for example with characters' names, like Timon Gantry (a theatre director in *False Scent*), Octavius Danbury-Phinn (in *Scales of Justice*, in which the plot turns on the uniqueness of fish scales), and Carbury Glande (in *Spinsters in Jeopardy*); or with the improbably far-fetched ways murder can be committed.

Most detective writers vary their narrative technique occasionally, as Marsh does, trying out new situations and experimenting with new limitations or perspectives, though in some books she becomes so caught up in baroque scenarios as to be hardly readable. (*Final Curtain*, too much a pastiche of her earlier work, is pretty dire.) In *Singing in the Shrouds*, for instance, Alleyn is on board a passenger-carrying cargo ship, trying to find a murderer. In the absence of any friend or co-investigator with whom to lay out (for the reader's benefit) each part of the process, he writes letters home to his wife, Troy, summarising each stage of the investigation. In *Clutch of Constables*, it's Troy herself who sends letters from the canal-boat cruise she's on to Alleyn, who's in the US, detailing the murderous events unfolding around her, so that he can do his detecting from across the Atlantic. In each case, the letters are intended less for their addressee than for the reader. It all gets a bit laboured after a while. Michael Innes' donnish literary style and sometimes rather heavy-handed or referential wit can also be wearing, as can Edmund Crispin's jokiness (though I do still like the famous exchange in *The Moving Toyshop* when, faced with a fork in the road, a character says, 'Let's go left . . . After all, Gollancz is publishing this book').

Because everybody has something to conceal in detective stories, even if it's of the most tangential significance, everybody becomes suspect. Everybody is lying about something. So everybody has to be investigated, which means that the connections between the main characters become increasingly complicated. Lies mean information withheld, making the investigation more difficult and prolonging it unnecessarily, complicating the detective's understanding of the situation and trying the reader's patience. Information withheld from the reader, even if we know it's being withheld, puts the reader in a position comparable to the detective for as long as the tension holds. Humankind cannot bear very much complexity, or at least not for very long, and since the principal question in a whodunnit is almost always who, rather than why, the connection between murder and motive is often tenuous. With the discovery of who the murderer is, complexity suddenly rearranges itself as simplicity, even the most unconvincing motive readily swallowed as explanation. And yet the process the narrative describes has been full of individual retreat, inhibition and suspicion. Inhibition often takes the form of self-censorship, characters not telling the police or the detective something they feel embarrassed about, protective towards or ashamed of. The mainspring of all detective stories, lies, guilt and concealment fuel the plot. It doesn't matter why; people just do it all the time when they're questioned by police or other authorities, because only the most two-dimensionally virtuous characters don't feel guilty about something.

There's a sense in which all the closed communities in detective stories operate as surrogates for the family, with the intensification of psychological dynamics that implies. We're all under surveillance as children, all guilty of wanting to do things we're not allowed to do. Murder in detective stories is hardly ever the act of a criminal. 'Murderers are just people like us,' says Inspector Richard Ringwood in Katharine Farrer's *The Cretan Counterfeit*, 'We've all got it in us to do the same.' It's usually the physical actualisation of a normally unconscious desire, a temporary, almost theoretical rupture in the membrane of repression that allows us to live in relative harmony with each other. The consequent intensification of a sense of surveillance as the detective searches for the explanatory motive is what makes everyone so cagey and uncommunicative or deceitful. The purpose of the final revelation is to restore unconscious normality, and to remove the anxiety that lurks in everybody both about our own death and about our own murderous capabilities. In 'The Guilty Vicarage', W.H. Auden's well-known essay on detective fiction in which he confesses to being addicted to it, he puts a comparable argument in theological terms. 'The magic formula [of the detective story] is an innocence which is discovered to contain guilt; then a suspicion of being the guilty one; and finally a real innocence from which the guilty other has been expelled, a cure effected, not by me or my neighbours, but by the miraculous intervention of a genius from outside who removes guilt by giving knowledge of guilt.' It's an oversimplification, I think, to talk about the re-establishment of 'real innocence', and one that diminishes the interest of the genre; it's of a piece with Auden's fondness for formulae. He admits he can never read a detective story more than once, and finds it difficult 'to read one that is not set in rural England', which rules out many more than it includes. I would rather let the books work more powerfully on me. Auden says he always forgets a detective novel as soon as he finishes it, which is why in his view they have nothing to do with works of art – but then he prefers not to read between the lines.

There's a degree of congruence between Auden's enthusiasm and the disappointment with the genre expressed by Raymond Chandler, who concludes his essay on 'The Simple Art of Murder' by criticising the American style of detective stories and then going on to offer the following lapidary backhanded compliment. 'Personally I like the English style better. It is not quite so brittle and the people as a rule just wear clothes and drink drinks. There is more sense of background, as if Cheesecake Manor really existed all around and not just in the part the camera sees; there are more long walks over the Downs and the characters don't all try to behave as if they had just been tested by MGM. The English may not always be the best writers in the world, but they are incomparably the best dull writers.' The conclusion is where he and Auden agree, I think. 'But there is a very simple statement to be made about all these stories,' writes Chandler: 'they do not really come off intellectually as problems, and they do not come off artistically as fiction. They are too contrived, and too little aware of what goes on in the world. They try to be honest, but honesty is an art.' My response would be that while they may be too little aware of the way the world really works, this isn't quite the point: their honesty is sometimes unconscious, and their awareness of the world made more visible by its datedness or its nostalgia. The books certainly can work artistically.

John Lanchester argues that what makes Agatha Christie's books work so well is her self-conscious formal and technical ability; the books' awareness of their structural originality within the confines of the genre. Unlike Auden, he believes this means 'you don't mind rereading in the same way you don't mind rereading a poem'. He also observes that the novels represent the changing face of mid-twentieth-century Britain partly because they don't consciously investigate it. This is part of the pleasure, but it ramifies in different ways, as rereading can sometimes show quite clearly. Detective fiction is not just about finding the murderer; the process of reading it incorporates a whole host of additional resonances. The genre operates by deploying an entire rhetoric of expectation, anxiety and uncertainty, the elements of which carry the burden of their social content at different historical moments and make us feel it within ourselves as we read.

Denouements are often anticlimactic, despite the theatricality with which the perpetrator is revealed in a final scene, because all they can do is resolve the generic question. They can't often settle the unsettling peripheral questions that the genre brings with it, which hang around uneasily in the back of the reader's mind. Some writers like to end, as Christie's Hercule Poirot does, with magician-like revelations, all the possible suspects gathered in one room and a dramatic accusation coming as the culmination to a reprise of the whole story. Marsh doesn't do this, though like most other writers she often tantalises the reader by having her detective admit early in the narrative that he knows the identity of the murderer but can't reveal it as he needs more definite proof. There still has to be some kind of cathartic moment, though, some retrospective explanation to dispel the lingering atmosphere of anxiety. Could X or Y really be a murderer, rather than just a suspect? Logically, yes: we understand, and we're relieved. But explanations tend to be aesthetically satisfying rather than truly convincing, which is why Miss Marple's unshakeable belief in innate wickedness works better as a conclusion than vague talk about inheritance or exposure. Nobody wants unexplained deaths around them. More than anything else, readers want to avoid thinking about their own death, and it's one of the primary functions of detective fiction to help them with that.

Death is both the ultimate certainty and an absolute change. In books that rely so much on fixed locations, from the outline of the body on the library carpet to the stately home, timeless village, mews cottage or new theatre, unexplained movement can be frightening. Where did she come from? Where have they disappeared to? It's not surprising that untrustworthy people are often described as shifty. It's the desire to banish this sort of uncertainty that makes most golden-age detective stories comedies in that they conclude with a formal restoration of order. Most of them also contain at least a degree of humour. Pamela Branch even manages to get close to farce in her novels, which share something with Ealing comedies like *Kind Hearts and Coronets* or *The Lavender Hill Mob*. Michael Innes studied psychoanalysis in Germany and Austria in the 1930s, and his early novels are strangely suffused with it, although sometimes unconsciously. In *Night of Errors*, Appleby muses that 'when for practical reasons our imagination must become urgent and working we tend to impose upon reality something of a make-believe world potent with us during our impressionable years'; psychoanalysis also shapes the pleasure he takes in grotesquerie and surreal situational comedy. Edmund Crispin enjoys incorporating comic or surreal moments into his narratives, and both writers make use of self-referential comments or meta-narrative jokes. Gladys Mitchell creates absurd situations and comically exaggerated characters (like the old lady in *The Longer Bodies*, and indeed the whole premise of that book, in which the very rich old lady decides on a whim to leave her entire fortune to the first of her great-nephews to represent England in the Olympic Games, to which end she organises a five-discipline athletics competition in the grounds of her home). And so on.

Nicholas Blake (the pseudonym of the poet C. Day Lewis) said once that writing detective stories was a harmless release of an innate spring of cruelty present in everyone. Comedy is a way of persuading the reader of harmlessness, cruelty and comic detachment being not far removed from each other. There are parallels between those ingredients and the incongruities, cruelty and comedy inherent in surrealism, as witness the most surreal detective novel I know: Michael Innes' wartime story *The Daffodil Affair*, which features the kidnap of a mathematically gifted horse and the removal of a Bloomsbury house brick by brick to South America in the middle of the Blitz. One character remarks to Appleby:

> 'I'm being murdered to further the purposes of psychical research [...] a perfect detective-story motive, and yet we're not in a detective-story at all . . . We're in a sort of hodge-podge of fantasy and harum-scarum adventure that isn't a proper detective story at all. We might be by Michael Innes.'
>
> 'Innes? I've never heard of him.' Appleby spoke with decided exasperation.

The surreal is brought down to earth by the donnish metafiction joke. It's a line that in another, less comic way runs through the genre, perhaps especially in the work of male writers, as metafiction becomes a kind of reality in novels like Blake's *The Beast Must Die* or Richard Hull's ironic *The Murder of My Aunt*, both of which use the form of a journal; or, in the most extreme case, in Christie's *The Murder of Roger Ackroyd*, where (spoiler alert) the narrator himself turns out to be the murderer. Journals can blur the line between author, narrator and protagonist, and, as in *The Beast Must Die*, where the diary is in fact a fiction constructed by the murderer, they can turn the detective into a literary critic. In that novel, Nigel Strangeways realises the truth after he has read the diary and thought closely about its phrasing and the context of his discovery of it, reading the text and reading between the lines for clues in the same way the reader is meant to read any detective story.

It's all very literary. It's not just bodies that turn up in libraries: detectives tend to be alarmingly well read, reeling off quantities of poetry by heart, perhaps because the author wants readers to know that they could, if they chose, be writing something much more serious and intellectually challenging. In Georgette Heyer's *Detection Unlimited*, the murderer is a crime writer, and the detective thinks in terms of the plots of detective fiction, welcoming the book's rural setting with its 'nice' concatenation of village and squire and the rest. And in E.C.R. Lorac's *The Theft of the Iron Dogs*, the Scotland Yard detective encourages an amateur writer to improvise an imagined account of a series of unexplained events. Sometimes the detective is an actual professor of literature, like Edmund Crispin's Gervase Fen (who, seemingly too busy solving murders to actually write books, is perpetually annoyed that the Chief Constable of Oxfordshire publishes highbrow literary criticism). Professors, poets and schoolteachers abound, among the authors themselves as well as the characters. Charles Latimer, the protagonist of Eric Ambler's thriller *The Mask of Dimitrios*, a university lecturer in economics, is one of 'the great army of university professors who write detective stories in their spare time' and 'one of the shame-faced few who could make money at the sport'. This self-consciousness about the genre masks an uncertainty about its purpose – making entertainment out of murder is weird – and allows the narrative itself to become a sort of impersonation, in some cases literally: many writers, perhaps most, adopt a pseudonym. Using diaries is one way of emphasising impersonation. Ngaio Marsh's theatricality is another. Plenty of other writers employ theatrical settings, the machinery of rehearsal and performance, and dramatic structures, as the scaffolding of novels, not to mention borrowing plots from Shakespeare. Josephine Tey's novels, which tend to pivot on people lying by pretending to be someone they are not, have a theatricality of their own. In her *Brat Farrar*, indeed, it is the impersonator who unmasks the murderer. In *To Love and Be Wise*, in which there turns out not to have been a murder, only impersonation by cross-dressing, Inspector Grant finds talking to his actor friend Marta particularly helpful: 'It was true that actors had a perception, an understanding of human motive, that normal people lacked.'

Motive is what moves people, and ostensibly that's what needs to be discovered. But people are hard to read. You can't be absolutely certain, in these books, that they are who they appear to be. They are all actors, and the parts they play are often familiar types, social clichés. But as Miss Marple says, revealing that twentieth-century anxiety about shifting values, 'Every village and small country place is full of people who've just come and settled there without any ties to bring them. The big houses have been sold, and the cottages have been converted and changed. And people just come – and all you know about them is what they say of themselves.' That was in 1950, but the same anxiety is there in books written in the interwar period. Theatricality makes this anxiety central, and it also makes it political.

Politics is essentially theatrical, with the important difference that there is much less time for rehearsal and the script keeps changing. It might at first seem odd that writers who in other areas of their lives were overtly very left-wing, like Nicholas Blake, Christopher Caudwell, Julian Symons or G.D.H. and Margaret Cole, make so little of their political commitment in their detective fiction. There's no obvious reason why that subject matter couldn't be used successfully. Politics certainly crops up here and there in other writers' books, either as melodramatic backdrop or as setting (I'm thinking for example of Ellen Wilkinson's *The Division Bell Mystery*). But when it has social agency, it tends to be baleful. Agatha Christie's *One, Two, Buckle My Shoe* is all about conspiratorial politics, about the maintenance of the (British, or possibly English) status quo, the importance of common sense and the putative threats to it from people on the far left (communism) and far right (fascism – or in the novel, members of the 'Imperial Shirts'), most of whom are immature and frustrated and easily manipulated by the shadowy figures at the top. The question of what we or anyone should be afraid of is played out in a temporary, pastoral world; one in which the corrupt nature of power tips the defence of the status quo into action beyond the bounds of democratic reasonableness, the ends not justifying the means because it involves loss of life. And it's the idea that each life has equal significance that makes Poirot deliver the murderer to justice, even though it creates a risk of political instability. Allowing each person their own life is taken to be a hope for continued resistance to extremism. The novel was published in 1940. In that respect it is partly a product of its circumstances and context; even a contribution to the war effort. But its paranoid view of social change as conspiratorial makes it much more interesting than merely a story about detection and (unusually) judgement.

In another of Christie's novels, *Peril at End House*, the protagonist, Nick, says, 'I love End House. I've always wanted to produce a play there. It's got an – an atmosphere of drama about it. I've seen all sorts of plays staged there in my mind. And now it's as though a drama were being acted there. Only I'm not producing it . . . I'm in it! I'm right in it! I am, perhaps, the person who – dies in the first act.' The dénouement of that novel is pure theatre, literally and metaphorically. It's a reminder that social life (let alone politics) is all about acting, pretending, impersonating and, where necessary, lying. It's much easier to pretend to be someone you're not if you're in a novel or on the stage, especially when it's a matter of social prestige. The period of golden-age detective fiction was one when many people were radically unsure about all sorts of things: art sometimes seemed not to be representing anything any more, paper money was puzzlingly no longer related to actual gold, religion was losing its authority, and there was no longer much certainty around the fundamental issues of what life in society meant or required. The theatricality of detective novels like Ngaio Marsh's is partly a response to that time, intensified by her own involvement in the theatre, but the theatricality of the genre as a whole is not just a matter of historical interest: it's a clue to our intellectual voyeurism and to the reason these books retain their fascination. We're all grown-up versions of desperately curious infants: we know where babies come from, but we don't know anything about the fundamental question of our death. At least for the duration of the detective story we're reading, our anxious, paranoid curiosity is directed towards finding out why someone else has died. The body in the library is never actually our own.

To go back to less serious pleasures, though, you never know what other bits of out-of-the-way information you might pick up in your reading. I wouldn't know what an oustiti was if I hadn't read Georgette Heyer's *Envious Casca*. When I looked it up, I discovered that was the first (possibly the only?) recorded use of the word in English. It means a device for inserting into a keyhole to grasp the key and turn it in the lock to open the door from the other side. Essential for some sorts of detective story. The word is said to come from the French '*ouistiti*', meaning a marmoset, though I can't imagine trying to insert a marmoset into a keyhole at a critical moment. And you can learn a lot about Istanbul and the Ottoman Empire from Jason Goodwin's five novels about Yashim, the early-nineteenth-century eunuch detective. Then there's another favourite of mine, S.J. Parris' series about the philosopher and spy Giordano Bruno solving politically sensitive murders in the late sixteenth century. Donna Leon's novels give the reader a good sense of Venice. Nor should we forget Christopher Fowler's novels about the London detectives Bryant and May. I could go on, too, listing all the atmospheric geographical and historical settings that different writers have used, but the list would be almost endless.

And I could go on about why Margery Allingham is such a good writer, and with such extraordinary subject matter, especially in her last books: Christopher Fowler has described her prose as 'allusive, colloquial, witty, bravura stuff – a window to a London mindset now completely lost'; or why I find Dorothy L. Sayers unsatisfactory, or why Mary Kelly is sometimes so brilliant, or why Beverley Nichols' five detective novels are worth reading. And I've said nothing at all about Michael Gilbert, Anthony Berkeley, E.R. Punshon, Freeman Wills Croft, Leo Bruce or Mary Fitt. And nothing about American writers, nothing about Dashiell Hammett or Ross Macdonald or Raymond Chandler or Rex Stout or Ellery Queen or Elizabeth Sanxay Holding or Elizabeth Daly or Hilda Lawrence or Chester Himes or Ed McBain or Cornell Woolrich or James M. Cain or Horace McCoy or David Goodis or Kenneth Fearing or John Franklin Barden or Erle Stanley Gardner or Patricia Highsmith. And nothing about French or Italian or Belgian (Simenon!) or Scandinavian writers. But all of them are well worth exploring. Most important of all, I've almost completely ignored writers of the last forty years: I'll just mention two, in both of which the old conventional division between good and evil is, to say the least, blurred, virtue often disguised as its opposite, or vice versa, especially where the government and its agencies are concerned. Mick Herron's *Slow Horses* novels are not strictly speaking crime fiction as they deal with goings-on in the security services, but they qualify because I like them so much, and because they play so knowingly with the formulae and expectations of the genre (as exemplified by, say, John le Carré). Their primary protagonist, Jackson Lamb, is now well known to many through the TV adaptations, but brilliant though these are, they can't replicate the texture of the writing, the political satire, the humour, the whole relationship between reader and authorial voice that makes the books so enjoyable.

It's the texture of the writing, too, which is so important in my other choice, the Harpur and Iles novels by the pseudonymous Bill James. There are thirty-six of these idiosyncratic police-and-crime novels, together constituting a *roman-fleuve*, a kind of extended serial portraying the public and private worlds of Assistant Chief Constable Desmond Iles and Detective Chief Superintendent Colin Harpur, and a changing cast of criminals involved in drug-dealing and when necessary killing, as they try to keep a moderating hold on the drug business in their city. These are not detective novels, as there is little that isn't known to or guessed by both the reader and most of the characters: I suppose crime fiction would be a better term. But unlike the usual police procedurals, we see things in these novels as much through the eyes of the criminals as through those of the police, the latter pragmatic in their approach, more concerned to keep the streets and the drug-dealing peaceful than to remove the business. They are also animated by wry humour. There is very little, if any, narrative voice or overt authorial presence, just a switching between the interior monologues of whoever is present in each scene, most of the narrative coming through the eyes or mind of characters who make up a gallery of oddballs worthy of Dickens. What little authorial narrative there is is by and large free of judgement, mostly restricted to catch-up information (like

Panicking Ralph's scar, or Iles' flirtation with a Jean Gabin hairstyle). Some characters die violently, some continue against expectation, the nature of the immediate problems changes but the fundamentals don't; there is no clear-cut sense of good and bad, just relatively OK and not OK, in the permanent struggle to manage the threats to a moderately quiet life. These novels are almost the opposite of the classic detective story as, since we see everything through different consciousnesses with their different interests, biases, misunderstandings and areas of ignorance, we are often left uncertain about who was responsible for a killing or some other event: it's the consequences for the leading characters that matter, a sort of informal justice economy. There's also a kind of dual temporality at work: time passes as the sequence continues, but the event time of the novels – the changes of criminal personnel, changes in the environment – passes more quickly than the domestic time of its main protagonists (Harpur's children, for example, age hardly at all), and both temporalities exist alongside the reader's awareness of their own real-time position. Part of the pleasure of reading lies in recognising the co-existence of these different timescales. (The pleasure of suspense relies on it.) Long before he embarked on these novels, Bill James (under his real name of James Tucker) wrote the first critical book about Anthony Powell's twelve-novel sequence *A Dance to the Music of Time*, and he has clearly learnt a lot from Powell about technique, while choosing to set his own novels in a very different section of society.

3ii
Guilty Pleasures: Bodies in Rutshire

> I sometimes feel a little uneasy about that imagined self of mine – the Me of my daydreams – who leads a melodramatic life of his own, quite unrelated to my real existence.
>
> Logan Pearsall Smith, *Trivia*

The history and nature of reading is now a substantial area of study, a sub-discipline in its own right, embracing contributions from education, social science, neuroscience, history, literature and the arts, but less attention has been paid to pleasure and the many potential elements of pleasure that a book can provide, both simple and complex, short-lived and prolonged, familiar and fresh. Solid joys and lasting pleasures may be the province of the great writers, the ones we return to for profound thinking about the ethical dimensions of a civilised society, but there are plenty of circumstances where we as readers turn to less demanding but otherwise rewarding books, books we can read for pleasure without feeling guilty. Take the novels of Jilly Cooper, for instance: the enjoyment of books like hers is often regarded as a 'guilty pleasure', rather like Salman Rushdie's famous 'naughty but nice' slogan in advertisements for cream cakes, with the implication that 'educated readers' ought to know better than to guzzle books like hers when they could be reading Proust or Jane Austen, *Madam Bovary* or the *London Review of Books*. Just precisely what the accusation of guilt and pleasure is about, though, needs examining rather more closely. It seems different from my childhood experience of the forbidden world of Enid Blyton, and probably goes back to some puritan idea that pleasure on its own, unconnected with moral improvement or hard work or the benefit of other people, is a waste of time and bad for you.

In Jilly Cooper's novels there is a noticeable (and moral) presence of the author in the text, the reader drawn into a somewhat two-dimensional world of daydream and wish-fulfilment, but it's done openly and with a degree of tongue-in-cheek self-awareness that precludes feeling guilty about sharing the author's pleasure in the sexual, competitive or romantic shenanigans that permeate the narrative. If the reader does experience conflicted feelings of pleasure or curiosity, shame or guilt at their delight in the way things turn out well for the good characters and badly for the bad in this comedy universe, Cooper's novels weave it all across a broad canvas with a knowingness that generates an air of good-humoured tolerance in which we are freed to investigate our own feelings of unease.

And anyway, guilt-free pleasure, including intellectual pleasure, isn't only to be found in serious novels, the sort that constitute what in English literature used to be called 'the great tradition' – novels by Jane Austen, George Eliot, Henry James, Joseph Conrad. Genre fiction, as I've been arguing, also offers serious pleasures as well as the pleasures of escape. But apart from her 1979 book *Class*, which Laurie Taylor set for many years as 'essential reading' on his second-year social-class course at York University, Jilly Cooper's work is not, so far as I know, much studied in universities. When I was still teaching at Cambridge, and happened to be reading her novels, people's reactions sometimes made me feel as if I'd gone off the rails in some way, revealed my true interests, lost touch with literary values, become a parody of my intellectual self. But if you set aside for a moment any assumptions generated by raunchy cover pictures, breathless titles (*Score!* or *Wicked!* or *Jump!*) and publicists' emphasis on wall-to-wall sex, you do find something well worth reading and thinking about seriously, namely pleasure. There is a particular pleasure in reading about pleasure: pleasure delayed and deferred, guilty pleasure, the pleasure of repetition and indeed the problems of it.

The novels are not gritty or realistic, nor do they take themselves very seriously. They all, especially the series of hefty Rutshire Chronicles, delight in the entertainments of upper-middle-class rural life. The point of view always seems to be comfortably located there, admiring the aristocracy, mocking the awkward aspirations of the nouveau riche, sending children to public schools, riding to hounds, fonder of horses than of reading, dividing the working class into the deserving poor and the probably criminal, and committed to the conventional gender roles that comedy has traditionally worked to uphold, even when the novels are described as 'wickedly subversive'. They have increasingly huge casts of characters and a propensity for subplots worthy of Trollope or Dickens, usually hinging on sex, class or institutional power, or sometimes all three at once. 'I must say I do have a sneaking guilty hankering for dominant males myself,' Cooper wrote in 1977, and nothing much seems to have changed since then as far as the main thrust of her fiction goes.

The best-known figure in her novels is the most dominant of males, a character created from a mixture of Mr Rochester, Clark Gable, Casanova, the late Alan Clark MP and – apparently – various dashing and extant English role models. Rupert Campbell-Black, wealthy landowner, sometime world-champion showjumper, sometime Tory MP and sports minister, exuder of brio, glamour and charisma, is an all-round amoral charmer and shit, immune to scandal and opinion and the envy of lesser men. (Tony 'didn't know which he resented most – Rupert's habitual contempt, his ability to sleep anywhere, his effortless acquisition of women . . .') There's also the capacity he shares with a goodish number of other characters in these novels to swallow catastrophic quantities of alcohol and still function ruthlessly and efficiently. The confidence with which he holds to his priorities is well illustrated in *Riders*, the first book he appears in. His fiancée, Helen, spends all her savings on an Augustus John drawing of a horse for his wedding present. She gives it to him, goes to answer the doorbell, and when she comes back fifteen minutes later finds him looking at the drawing with satisfaction.

'That's better.'

'What?' said Helen. Then, noticing a pencil and rubber in Rupert's hand, gave a gasp of horror. 'What have you done?'

'Redrawn the near-side hock. Chap simply hadn't got it right.'

What makes him a tolerable and even engaging character (apart from his partial redemption in *Rivals* by the almost believable love of an almost unbelievably good woman) is the way the first word of Cooper's 'guilty hankering' permeates the textual atmosphere, moderating or complicating the picture. Wish-fulfilment fantasy and caricatural exaggeration are all very well, but within the rococo extremities of the narrative lies a strong sense of justice and of the acceptable limits of transgression. There are good pleasures, in various degrees, wrong but permissible pleasures, and unequivocally bad pleasures. The distinction between 'high' and 'low' culture may have ceased to matter in some areas, but a version of it continues to be important within the generic world of these novels. Habits of speech, dress or manners are regularly used to establish both the class and the genuineness of characters; social pretension is always gently mocked, but overt mockery is only allowed to the most unpleasant, and usually results in a comeuppance. The whole thing is tempered by the 'good-natured assumption' that Rosemary Hill has identified in Cooper's *Class*, that 'everyone is a snob about something and to that extent we are all ridiculous'. There is mercifully little of the product placement that makes some airport fiction, for me at least, hard to read; instead the books rely on occasional mentions of a small stock of high-end and trustworthy brands: scents tend to be Jicky and Miss Dior, prodigally applied; apart from Château d'Yquem, Moët and Krug, wines are seldom named; and clothes are mostly there for their ability to transform the wearer and reveal their true beauty.

And in a crisis even they can't make up for the absence of true, socially sanctioned love. 'Nothing – not the secret trysts, nor the ecstatic love-making nor the vats of scent and Moët, not the diamond brooches, cashmere jerseys and the slithering slinky satin underwear – made up for not being able to sit beside Drew's bed, holding his hand and willing him back to consciousness.' Only the showy, pretentious or villainous are flagged up by the visibility of their labels, their Louis Vuitton luggage, their Rolex watches or their Lamborghinis. There is always a basic set of assumptions about good behaviour, rewarded quite often with the sort of happiness that has lots of money discreetly in the background.

A comfortable level of cultural awareness spills from the references to (mostly nineteenth-century) classical music, Old Master paintings and the quotations from Milton, Wordsworth, Yeats, Shakespeare and others; these are used sometimes as a ground for jokes or for comic effect ('the marriage of true mindlessness'), and sometimes to provide a cultural texture or textual culture shared with the reader. The huge amount of research that goes into these novels means that specialised knowledge needs to be explained, which is done unobtrusively enough, though occasionally the explanatory information we're given threatens to become a little forced or wooden. Sometimes, too, the author or one of her characters (usually Campbell-Black) delivers a homily about something, usually to do with racing. But most of the homiletic content is not context-specific, and is satisfactorily contained within the narrative, as in one brief scene that culminates in a character's recognition that 'Kindness is the greatest aphrodisiac.'

The author's presence is more successfully felt through the continuous permeability of the language to puns and other forms of verbal humour; these are generally placed in the mouths of any character who happens to be around at the time the pun or the joke occurs, making us feel that the author is always benignly present in the text and rather enjoying herself: the names of horses and minor characters – Touchy Filly, Blank Chekov, Roving Mike, and a porn star's brood mare called Wages of Cindy – are almost relentlessly jolly.

In the course of her earlier career as a journalist and columnist, Cooper created and perfected a characteristic style that could be descriptively precise, insightful, witty, and quite cutting when she wanted it to be, though never without the support of humour. A particularly deft portrait of Margaret Thatcher, written the year after she'd become leader of the Conservative Party, opens: 'The fuchsias in Mrs Thatcher's front garden in Chelsea drooped patriotically from lack of water.' The heat and drought of the summer of 1976, the leader's authority and the mix of voluntary and involuntary obedience in the horticultural detail are contrasted a page later with the momentary glimpse, as Thatcher leans forward, of 'the Arctic gleam of a very white bra'. Cooper has an eye for Thatcher's likeable side and for her disciplined self-denial and she doesn't let either quite win out.

These 1970s *Sunday Times* columns, based increasingly on her own rollicking domestic life by Putney Common, are full of ideas and entertaining anecdotes, many of which provide material for the later novels. Set pieces or casual asides, most of what she wrote relies on the quotidian comedy materials of social class, sex, marriage and children, matters that have always been at the heart of her work. At the same time as writing the columns she was publishing a series of short romances, rewritten from earlier publication in magazines. They were tightly structured, agreeably predictable wish-fulfilment narratives named for their heroines – *Imogen*, *Harriet*, *Emily* and so on. Relatively uncomplicated in outline, they chart the tangles and misprisions on the way to true love, but for all the romance clichés, they are clear-sighted; the characters may be two-dimensional but the emotional timbre is more subtle. After extending and complicating the prelude for as long as possible, often involving lots of sex with the wrong partners, they leave the protagonists and the reader poised on the threshold of final satisfaction, enjoying the expectancy, with timeless happiness guaranteed.

Although even here there may be an unconscious hint of a more trammelled and complex vision of pleasure and guilt. Take the last lines of *Harriet*, just after the marriage proposal:

> 'We've eaten all the gingerbread,' said Harriet ecstatically, 'and now we can enjoy the lovely, lovely gilt.'
>
> 'Exactly,' said Cory, and he began kissing her . . .

The lovely guilt-free gilt is more than just decoration; it's the promise of a future in which everything is settled, idyllic and justified by everything that's led up to it, a tableau in which time has stopped its depredations for ever and ever.

The pleasures of fantasy can have a therapeutic value, despite (or because of) their refusal of realistic thinking, their comedic optimism. It's not necessarily escapist to want to escape reality for the length of time it takes to read a book, as I can testify from my own experience: I had never read anything by Jilly Cooper until quite late in my life, but when some years ago my wife was ill with cancer, dying in fact, and I was distraught, unable to focus or concentrate, finding teaching difficult, a copy of *Rivals* was pressed into my hand. I was told it was just the thing I needed, I must give it a try. I was sceptical and reluctant to, as I thought, waste my time. But I was soon grateful for it. It was exactly the sort of narrative for me at that moment: absorbing, distracting, elegant enough, silly enough and, in a strange way, affectionate and calming. And so were all the other novels, which sustained me through those sad and difficult months. After Jenny died, I carried on reading them until there were no more to read. Then I turned to the journalism, collected in a dozen or more paperbacks in the 1970s and '80s, and almost as many again since then, after which there was nothing to do but wait a couple of empty months for the next novel to appear. I'd become an enthusiast.

When it did, I was momentarily disconcerted by two things when I opened my copy of *Mount!*: first, the cast of major characters occupied nine pages, followed by five more pages listing the animals (four pages of horses). In the face of this my resolve almost flagged. Then there was a prologue, set in 1786. I felt the ghost of Georgette Heyer hovering about, but I persevered through a few more pages of slightly tongue-in-cheek melodramatic backstory, poised somewhere between useful rationale and the evocation of 'too many sightings of pale riders on dark horses and howling white mastiffs'. It was a relief to return to direct descendant Rupert Campbell-Black in his office 'in the west wing of the same pale gold Queen Anne house'.

The loving description of this and other country houses in the earlier books reflects the cultural and political changes of the last fifty years, changes that among other things brought about the marketisation of the English house as a design brand, selling a concept Patrick Wright described as the world of Brideshead, 'a countervailing and predominantly rural world based on private values and culturally sanctioned hierarchy, where history is venerated as tradition and culture is based on ancestry and descent'. The absorption or rejection of newly acquired wealth and Thatcherite notions of success by the established representatives of 'Brideshead' values provides the more or less aspirational background to the narratives. New money tends to be dodgier than inherited wealth, unless it comes, as it sometimes does, in the form of a kind, unpretentious, self-made millionaire with a heart of gold, socially out of place but finally finding love with the right woman after an unsuccessful marriage to a social climber or a trophy wife. (These recurrent characters seem almost to constitute a private *hommage* to the type.) A house like this, with grounds and woods and a lake, is a required feature in all sorts of recent English fiction, but here the semi-industrial racing yard, a complex of stables and cottages and paddocks and offices and lorry parks and a stud farm, makes it a modern, working Arcadia, and one decidedly populated with egos.

Jilly Cooper's novels exhibit plenty of variety in subject matter, as horse-breeding, flat and National Hunt racing, showjumping, polo, TV franchises, the art market, jump racing, secondary schools, orchestras and even football provide the narrative setting for the novels. Competition – naked, unbridled and frequently underhand – is at the heart of all of them and extends into the ramifying subplots as competition for money, sex and love. Cooper's increasingly plethoric plotting has not always been entirely successful; a novel like *Score!* needs so much exaggeration that in the end it loses itself in Grand Guignol, with an almost Wagnerian attempt to mingle whodunnit, thriller, Gothic and romance into a *Gesamtkunstwerk* of all the genres.

The earlier novels keep exaggeration to the level of style, but as the series progresses, each new novel seems to have a larger and more complex set of characters than the one before, a consequence of bringing more and more local people into the spotlight, as well as of the passage of time and the multiplication of generations. In *Riders*, Rupert Campbell-Black is a young man. In *Mount!* and *Tackle!* he is in his sixties (but 'still Nirvana for most women'). In the meantime, the novels' field has expanded to take in nearby villages and their inhabitants, children, grandchildren, schoolteachers, the other big houses in the locality and the huge cast of animals I mentioned earlier. This Dickensian inclusivity makes it harder to keep control of the plots without drawing on commensurately Dickensian melodrama: the villains in *Mount!* are bad on a very large scale indeed.

Deceit, blackmail and sabotage culminate in attempted murder. Historical fantasy repeats itself, the second time descending not into farce but into comic resolution.

This is one of the problems with writing about pleasure. Like pleasure itself, the description of it needs to be ratcheted up to stop repetition becoming dull and the appetite sickening and dying from an excess of the same thing. Cooper recognised this herself in an interview she gave when *Wicked!* came out in 2006: 'I'm terrified of repeating myself – there are a limited number of ways one can do it, aren't there? There's a lot of almost getting to bed, but not much getting to bed in this book.' The fundamental narrative pleasure at the heart of all these books is the old-fashioned one of finding true love, but as they become more and more expansive and incorporate a greater range of genres, the need to control the plot reaches an almost hysterical pitch. Pain plays a greater role, violence intensifies and what was delightful threatens to become absurd (as it finally did in *Score!*). The subsequent novels try to pull away from that abyss. The extent to which they succeed is partly down to the writing itself, and the sheer verbal exuberance, the jokes and puns, which create enough distance between reader and plot for some emotional slack still to be taken up. The random lateral connections set in play by the puns defuse the narratives' overdetermined grotesqueries, as does the regular appearance of girls who are precociously wise, perceptive and articulate, writing PR copy or Rupert's newspaper columns, or drafting articles for the *Guardian* at the same time as revising for their A levels. They seem to operate as surrogates for the younger Jilly Cooper – good-natured, sharp-witted, intelligent and acutely funny, with a penchant for the subversion latent in linguistic echoes and associations.

Cooper shares a fondness for both wordplay and wise children with Ali Smith, (girls like Brooke in *There but for the* or George in *How to be both* or Rose in *Gliff*), but while there are similarities in the way they behave and the fun they have with language, their presence in the text works in quite opposite ways. Smith uses her precocious girls to direct our attention to the tumbling abundance of verbal wit, not just for its own, and truth's, sake but for the unstructured pleasure it opens up, as an anarchic vision of freedoms. In a world of language, the pleasure of language-play leads towards an awareness of radical possibilities and unpremeditated choices, while the pleasures in Cooper's text are essentially conservative ones, wordplay for the pleasure of it, but as an end in itself. Smith's girls are part of a world in which language creates the possibility of exploding out of expected roles, developing or metamorphosing into something better or more exciting, more in tune with one's personal feelings and intuitions. The comedy of Cooper's novels is more conventional, relying on a myth of unchanging values, with an unchanging human nature at the core of society.

There are two different sorts of comedy here: the comedy of misrule and disruption and the comedy of re-established order. The former shows how we can transform or metamorphose into whatever we want, in the same way as words and rhymes can shift their shapes and change identities. The latter argues for fixed values. We have no choice, the novels say, but to discover and settle for these true values if we are to find happiness, especially if it's destined to be found in a pale gold Queen Anne house in the Cotswolds.

The counterparts in the emotional life of some of the later novels are the underdog animal heroes (can horses be underdogs?). A horse called Mrs Wilkinson, cruelly maltreated and abandoned, is rescued in *Jump!*, and goes on eventually to win the Grand National, becoming the moral focus of village and racing life on the way. She returns in *Mount!*, but mostly as the dam of Master Quickly (sired by Rupert Campbell-Black's Love Rat), who overcame a sabotaged bridle to win the flat racing World Cup. The aims that underlie characters' choices in the novel are not as important as the means by which they achieve them. And how people choose to treat animals is a touchstone of their humanity, as well as a central element in the emotional texture of the narrative. Animals sometimes behave in an almost human way too, which reinforces this. As a focus of human emotions, expectations, suspense, hopes and fears, they form a shadow emotional drama behind the main story, a sort of chorus acting as sounding boards or parallels, or simply pushing the plot forward. Dogs and horses, and the occasional goat or cat, provide an implicit moral counterpoint to the main narratives, one that exists at the same level of detachment from the narrative as the verbal wit.

Here it becomes clear what animals and people share in this world. As readers, we are directed at every turn. We don't have a choice about liking the likeable characters any more than the women in the books can choose not to desire Rupert. The emotion-driven narratives don't leave room for choices: we are moved by the pleasures of desire or the attractions of virtue to like the right people, just as we're moved by the pleasures of revenge or dislike or hatred to delight in the downfall of the wicked. What was seamlessly present in the shorter early novels continues to take its place in the polyphonic or orchestral structure of these later ones, in which Cooper, again like Dickens, can flaunt the heart she wears on her sleeve.

Animals in this world are a living and entertaining demonstration of the virtues of loyalty, perseverance, big-heartedness and love, as well as being given to destructive pleasures like eating the dinner, chewing up clothes or impregnating the wrong mare. Rupert Campbell-Black is asked in a TV interview:

> 'Who are your heroes? If you could choose, who would you like to meet in an afterlife?'
>
> For a second he seemed to have some difficulty in speaking: 'I'd like to see Badger again,' he muttered.

Badger was his black Labrador. Jilly Cooper has long been a campaigner on behalf of animals: it was her book *Animals in War* that inspired the Animals in War Memorial, located outside Hyde Park near Brook Gate, commemorating animals killed in wars and conflicts. The smaller of the two inscriptions on the monument reads, poignantly: 'They had no choice.'

There isn't much dwelling on moral choice in the books: Jilly Cooper's is a simplified, circumscribed, imaginary world, without the moral complexity of a Henry James or the ethical problematics of an Iris Murdoch, but it has many pleasures of its own, and the capacity to stimulate thinking about a variety of subjects, including the complexity of pleasure itself. Genre fiction is often taken to be inferior because its pleasures are easily come by and essentially ephemeral, like the pleasure of cake. But there's an art to it, when it's good, and Jilly Cooper's books, classic detective fiction, thrillers – all sorts of genres – can be supportive, nourishing readers' hearts and minds through the pleasures of reading and imaginative thought, and along the way defeating the impulse to feel guilty about reading for pleasure rather than the possibly more dubious end of self-improvement.

4

Forgotten Writers, Rare Books and Books to Change the World

No place affords a more striking conviction of the vanity of human hopes than a public library; for who can see the wall crowded on every side by mighty volumes, the works of laborious meditations and accurate inquiry, now scarcely known but by the catalogue, and preserved only to increase the pomp of learning, without considering how many hours have been wasted in vain endeavours, how often imagination has anticipated the praises of futurity . . .

Samuel Johnson, *The Rambler*, No. 106 (23 March 1751)

One night in my early twenties, I woke up at about three o'clock in the morning to find myself in the lavatory of our first-floor flat, attacking my landlady's wood-effect wallpaper with a knife and a spoon, convinced that reality, the real truth about everything, was to be found behind that patently false surface. It was more than embarrassing to have to explain the damage the next day, first to my wife and then to the landlady (who regularly inspected the bathroom and lavatory), but that sleepwalking dream was an indication that I still somewhere had a conviction, which had been reinforced by my childhood reading and obviously still continued to fuel my imagination, that there was a hidden truth of things lurking out of sight behind the everyday world we lived in and were aware of. I don't think I ever believed consciously that there was any kind of controlling principle, let alone purpose, underlying the universe or the world or the society I inhabited, but I did have a sense that there was a meaning that had so far eluded me, and that literature – some books at least – might grant access to it or give me glimpses of it. It was the reason for my student interest in Frances Yates' writings on Renaissance hermetic thinking, for my love of Freud and psychoanalysis and Philip K. Dick's novels and poetry. I was twenty-four years old and I felt very deeply that I was missing something.

I was a secretive child and adolescent, given to self-protective fictionalising and lying, preferring to keep myself private and imagine myself inscrutable. As I grew older, I lived necessarily in a more social, adult world, and distanced myself from childish feelings. So the discovery that I was digging in wallpaper for a hidden reality came as a surprise, but not one I took seriously until years later; at the time I was too busy, partly with my job (until I gave it up) and partly with all sorts of activities to do with politics or poetry. At Cambridge I'd started a poetry magazine with my friend Nick Totton, then after I graduated I'd taken over the editorship of another, *The Curiously Strong*, from the poet Fred Buck, another friend, who'd returned to his native America. That magazine ran for twenty more issues, and by this point I was in the middle of it. I'd bought a second-hand Gestetner duplicating machine, and as well as enabling me to produce the poetry magazine cheaply and distribute it for free, my ownership of the means of production was partly responsible for my also becoming editor of a small-circulation newssheet, *Rank and File Tech Teacher* (later it became a properly produced magazine, with the brisker name of *Tech Teacher*), a radical paper for the left-wing movement within the union I belonged to – I was teaching English and general studies at a south-east London further-education college – the Association of Teachers in Technical Institutions (ATTI, now part of the UCU). Involvement in the union led to my election as branch secretary and a delegate to the London region, to being a delegate to the Greenwich Trades Council and then their delegate to the Anti-Apartheid Trade Union Committee, and thence to the National Committee of the Anti-Apartheid Movement. All this politicking and my extensive reading in Marxism and left-wing history also led to my joining the International Socialists and becoming actively involved in revolutionary politics for a few years.

Naturally a good part of my activism had to do with books. In fact, I think a lot of my enthusiasm for revolution came from my reading, although the widespread youth radicalisation in the late sixties, with the spectacle of the American war in Vietnam and the new wave of feminism, were the necessary context. Apart from editing the *Rank and File* paper, I started selling Pluto Press books* and

* Pluto Press was an extremely good radical publisher, broad-minded in its approach to the revolutionary tradition but always producing stimulating and well-designed books.

International Socialist pamphlets from a bookstall I would set up at meetings or to sympathetic individuals at work and to friends. I read extensively in Marxist history and theory, trying to find a workable synthesis of revolutionary politics, poetry, phenomenology and psychoanalysis. I read history, too, which I hadn't really studied at school, and went to lectures on urban history at the Architectural Association. I read writers like André Breton, Leon Trotsky, Fredric Jameson, Merleau-Ponty, Foucault, Kristeva, Althusser, Christopher Hill's *The World Turned Upside Down*, Walter Benjamin, Freud, Lacan, E.P. Thompson, John Berger and Juliet Mitchell, as well as everything I could find by Philip K. Dick. I was reading poetry from Shelley to Brecht, Breton and Tzara, Tom Raworth and J.H. Prynne, lots of contemporary and current poetry, and I was involved with the Poetry Society, where for a while I was the events organiser.

Behind everything I thought and wrote, though, there was still a sense that I was looking for something lost or hidden, some key or some piece of knowledge that would allow everything to make sense as part of a pattern. There seemed to be something in common between that feeling and the Marxist idea of false consciousness, the idea that the alienation inherent in work in a class society creates an ideological distortion in people's minds so that the true state of affairs and people's true interests are invisible to them. I wanted to find a way to experience the totality of the world, rather than continually feeling that everything of real significance was on the other side of a veil. I was also reading a lot about theories of language – sociolinguistics, Chomskyan linguistics, Sapir and Whorf, Basil Bernstein,

Saussure, Shklovsky, the Prague linguists, Roman Jakobson and the Russian formalists, and Kristeva. I hoped that one day I would be capable of formulating an explanation for one of my central preoccupations in those years: why wasn't it obvious to everybody – as it was to me – that the capitalist system was wrong, unjust and in urgent need of radical change? What stopped people seeing what was in their own best interest?

That period of engrossing politics lasted four or five years, at which point I began to express serious disagreements with the way IS was going (it became the Socialist Workers Party). As a result, I, along with a number of others who felt the same way about the organisation, was expelled. That turned out to be a good thing, as our first child was about to be born and I was therefore much less keen to be going out to meetings every evening and most weekends. I was also unsure about what I really wanted to do. I'd given up my job at the further-education college after two years, spent a year on the dole trying to write and decide on a career, then slipped back into part-time teaching, and doing consultancy work for the Open University. I planned then to do a PhD, but fatherhood meant I needed to earn some money. Then, some six months after my son was born, I got my first commission for a translation, a book about the French Revolution by the anarchist writer Daniel Guérin. A popular abridgement of a longer scholarly work, it argued that the period between the fall of the Gironde in May 1793 and the execution of Babeuf four years later saw the unfolding of the first modern class conflict. For months I spent hours sitting at my desk with the infant Jacob strapped in a sling to my front, typing up the translation, reading books about the Revolution or looking up unfamiliar words or expressions, until I'd be interrupted by the crying baby or the need for coffee or whatever else had to be dealt with. My wife and I were sharing childcare, and as well as translating, I was still teaching part-time, writing poems, writing occasional reviews, and thinking about the kind of politics I wanted and how best to integrate the political elements into my writing.

Years later, I read Edward Upward's wonderful trilogy of novels that make up *The Spiral Ascent* and discovered that I was by no means the first to want to find a way of writing that incorporated a unified theory of everything into the defining field of revolutionary Marxism. Nor did I possess the clarity of moral purpose that inspired him, being already in at least two minds about the revolutionary project but still hoping to combine pessimism of the intellect with optimism of the will. But it did have the effect of strengthening my interest in all the writers who'd shared a vision of a better society, like those who'd been in the Communist Party before the Second World War, and especially those who'd been on the revolutionary left but also fought against Stalinism, like Victor Serge, whose novels, especially *The Case of Comrade Tulayev* and *Birth of Our Power*, are very much worth reading. Upward's three novels, *In the Thirties* (1962), *The Rotten Elements* (1969) and *No Home but the Struggle* (1977), reconstruct the personal and political history of Alan Sebrill, a poet struggling to write in a way that would reflect his political thinking and be equal to 'modern life' without, as he puts it, 'the over-richness of twentieth-century bourgeois modernism', which means getting rid of 'literary allusiveness, clotted imagery, deliberate ambiguities'. He wants his 'first aim . . . [to] be truthfulness rather than poetic richness'.

Written retrospectively – like Proust's *In Search of Lost Time*, to which it owes a debt – and therefore aware of the fact that the hopes of the 1930s would be badly disappointed in the post-war world, the trilogy has to strike a balance between objectivity and irony. It does it supremely well. There is no other work like it: Doris Lessing's five-volume sequence of novels *Children of Violence* (1952–69), which narrates a Lessing-like character's involvement in politics in the post-war period, is significant but much less dialectically complex and much less self-aware. Hindsight dominates the narrative, and the imagination of a better world eventually finds its primary and explicit outlet in prophecy rather than in hope or continuing commitment.

Poetry and politics. How to write one without being divorced from the other? I spent a lot of time experimenting, pondering and wondering. I explored all kinds of utopian thinkers, and a few more pragmatic ones. I read widely in poets who I thought had faced similar questions. I've mentioned the surrealists and Brecht already. In the United States, I discovered, there had been a loose grouping of poets known as the Objectivists, some of whom had been active in communist politics in the thirties. George Oppen, whose work I'd known since the end of the sixties thanks to the poet Anthony Barnett, had stopped writing and publishing for some sixteen years to devote himself to political organisation, and Louis Zukofsky worked at a more complex intellectual fusion of Marxism and poetics in his long poem *A*. Of the two, I preferred Oppen's poems, which were shorter and less knotty and somehow less obvious, but his long silence didn't help me work things out for myself. I was continuing to write poems, though not with Oppen or Zukofsky as a model, but I wasn't very happy with them. I also collaborated on two pamphlet-length sequences with Martin Thom and Nick Totton, both done quickly and published as poetico-political interventions, the first at the 1977 Cambridge Poetry Festival, the second partly driven by thinking about fascism at the time of the anti-National Front marches in the summer of 1979.

At the same time, I was teaching English A level at evening classes and for young school leavers – Chaucer, Shakespeare, Dickens, Hardy, H.G. Wells, some mainstream modern poets who were not to my taste and Wordsworth, whose work I liked very much indeed. It was enjoyable and interesting work but not wholly satisfying, partly because part-time teaching was precarious and poorly paid, partly because I was spending as much time as I could in the old British Museum Reading Room following up other more pressing interests, in French theory, literary history and philosophy. It was a wonderful place to work (although the blue leather chairs could be comfortable enough to make me fall asleep in mid afternoon), the reading desks that radiated outwards from the central circle of the great catalogue somehow more conducive to study than the open-office-like arrangement in the new British Library. In her memoir *Paper Houses*, the novelist Michèle Roberts describes what it was like to be employed there and explains one component of the atmosphere of which I was unaware: 'Scholars [employed by the Museum] dwelt in their own hidey-holes. George Painter, the biographer of Gide and Proust, worked above the North Library. Mr Nixon, the world-renowned

Renaissance binding expert, had a secret cubby-hole behind the public gallery and its glass cases. They concealed themselves behind the walls of ordinary activities. They led a secret life in the Library's unconscious mind.'

The idea, however fanciful, that a library can have an unconscious mind is a perfect figure for the way you can discover things you didn't know you needed to know, never as much in control of your curiosity as you believe yourself to be. Appropriately enough, I also worked my way through the works of Aleister Crowley, the infamous magician, 'Great Beast', writer and self-styled prophet of the new religion of Thelema. He proselytised for his version of magick, which he defined as 'the Science and Art of causing change to occur in conformity with Will' and which involved rituals, often sexual and orgiastic; but despite finding numerous, if often short-lived, enthusiasts to back him, his popularity waned as he turned out not to be able to do much at all in the way of actually causing change or summoning powerful demons, and eventually he died in poverty. I was interested in Crowley partly because he kept on cropping up in the lives of writers I was researching, partly because he wrote and published poetry (which I found largely unreadable, though historically interesting) and partly because he fitted into my continuing sceptical interest in occultism. He'd been admitted to membership of the Hermetic Order of the Golden Dawn just before the turn of the century, where he'd fallen out with other members, including W.B. Yeats. Twenty years or so later he founded what he called the Abbey of Thelema in Sicily, which for a while became a notorious site of pilgrimage for the committed or the curious.

My other reason for reading Crowley was my growing interest in the life and writing of Mary Butts, one of those out-of-print writers from between the wars who'd fallen into complete obscurity. The poet Andrew Crozier recommended her to me one day, and I set out to find her books and read them. She was interested in what she thought of as occult forces (which I tried to think about in terms of the unconscious), providing an additional and unusual element in her already idiosyncratic, opium-fuelled modernist writing, and she'd spent three months at Thelema in 1921. Her output wasn't huge, just twelve titles. A trilogy of English novels, *Ashe of Rings*, *Armed with Madness* and *The Death of Felicity Taverner*, two historical novels, three volumes of short stories, *The Crystal Cabinet* (an autobiographical account of her life up to the age of twenty), two pamphlets, *Traps for Unbelievers* and *Warning to Hikers*, and a short book called *Imaginary Letters*, in which she analyses her semi-maternal unrequited love for a gay Russian exile in Paris, Boris, who takes her money, lies and gets drunk until she finally cuts him off, in unsent letters to his mother.

One thing I discovered about tracking down information on forgotten writers – or at least this used to be the case before the internet came along – is that there have almost always been earlier, unsuccessful attempts to enthuse people about them. Mary Butts, it turned out, had been friends with almost everybody in literary and artistic circles between the wars, and is mentioned in dozens of memoirs, letters and diaries. Yet it was hard to catch more than a glimpse of her from any of them, as if there was no need to say more than that she was there because everyone must know all about her. Her books had found supporters, mostly too late to benefit her – she died young, in 1937. But one later enthusiast was the American poet John Ashbery, who'd been recommended her stories by a co-worker during his brief stint at the Brooklyn Public Library, and who in 1965 had published the one piece of biographical writing I had found about her, a short introduction to her work and a selection from her then unpublished journal, in his magazine *Art and Literature.*

What attracted me to Mary Butts was not just her interest in the occult, but her insistence in her writing that the surface of things, and indeed things in themselves, could be indications or expressions of other deeper currents at work in us and in the world. That interest in what we might call non-rational knowledge is something she shares with the surrealists, with Yeats, with the ghost stories of M.R. James (which she loved) and with other early-twentieth-century writers, including T.S. Eliot of *The Waste Land*. In fact, she regarded Eliot's use of Jessie L. Weston's work on the grail legend – acknowledged in his notes to the poem as one of his influences – as trespassing on her own territory, feeling herself to be the proper conduit for that work. She was invested from childhood on in myth, ritual, power and fear, found many of her interests amplified in the work of Jane Harrison and the Cambridge Ritualists, a group of classicists influenced by anthropological ideas, and writes with a sharp-edged conviction that her works are a pursuit of truth, often of something lost or threatened by the modern world. At the same time, they are very much of their period, bohemian, sexually alert, intelligent, mystical, a kind of modernist pastoral. It took me some years to find copies of all her books, and I sometimes had to sell the best ones to keep the wolf from the door, but eventually I succeeded, adding a collector's sense of satisfaction to the pleasure I already took in her writing.

She later became one of the central figures in my PhD, along with her first husband, John Rodker, and her friend Douglas Goldring. They were an odd and absorbing trio of writers, and I was excited because nobody seemed to know about their work and their interconnections. As they got older, they became more divergent in their outlook and their writing, but they all started from a position of deep opposition to the dominant English culture of the first two decades of the twentieth century, with its philistinism, sentimentality, militarism, imperialism and hypocrisy. Naturally, they were opposed to the war, and strongly opposed conscription when it was introduced in 1916: as Rodker wrote later, 'we would not be involved [in the war] . . . Instead we drank ourselves C3, drugged, fornicated, turned night into day, violently, desperately, anything to destroy ourselves rather than be involved'. Goldring and Rodker were conscientious objectors, Goldring spending the period 1916–18 in Southern Ireland and Rodker, after his arrest for evading conscription, in prison in Dartmoor and London until he escaped. Mary Butts had done a course in social welfare at the London School of Economics and worked for a while for the London County Council Children's Care Committee in Hackney and for the pacifist organisation the National Council of Civil Liberties.*

Although none of them was involved in revolutionary

* This was a different organisation from the NCCL, now known as Liberty, which was founded in 1934.

politics, all would call themselves socialists in their youth, and Goldring remained a committed left-winger throughout his life. Of his dozen or so novels, *The Fortune* is about the Easter Rising in Dublin in 1916, and the need to reject war and build a new civilisation, while *The Black Curtain* takes its cue from the hope of a new society inspired by the Russian revolution of 1917. *The Fortune* had difficulty finding an English publisher and was published by Maunsel in Dublin. Fifteen years later it was published by Desmond Harmsworth with a new preface by Aldous Huxley, who praised it as 'the earliest fictional account of War-time pacifism' and for its description of the effects on 'an impressionable mind' of 'the germs [of war propaganda] that were floating in the mental atmosphere between 1914 and 1918'. (My copy, though, has a reader's disgruntled pencil comment on the dedication page: 'The only real interest of this book is the utter "wrong-headedness" and delusion of the "Bloomsbury" religion of writers in 1930, as subsequent history has proved.') All of Goldring's books – he wrote about fifty altogether: novels, poetry, plays, travel, biography, memoir, criticism and essays – are still out of print.

I had become hooked on the excitement of discovering out-of-print and forgotten writers who it seemed to me ought never to have been forgotten. Gilbert Cannan was another. I can't now remember how I came across his work – perhaps in Henry James' 1914 essay on 'The New Novel', in which he singles out Hugh Walpole, Cannan, D.H. Lawrence and Compton Mackenzie as the four most interesting English novelists. Cannan was prolific, publishing poems, translations, plays and essays as well as sixteen novels – some forty volumes in the space of fifteen years.

Some of the novels are fictionalised accounts of his life or his friends – *Mendel*, for example, perhaps now the best known, is a portrait of the painter Mark Gertler. Three involve Bertrand Russell, thinly disguised as 'Melian Stokes', notably in his role of pacifist in the First World War in *Pugs and Peacocks*, and those were the ones that captured my interest, extending my knowledge of depictions of conscientious objectors and containing descriptions of a very recognisable Garsington Manor, with fictionalised portraits of Ottoline Morrell, D.H. Lawrence, Aldous Huxley and other people I was interested in cropping up in their pages.*

Reading memoirs, journals, letters and diaries by writers and artists from the period was the best way to find out more about the social groups that fascinated me, I found. By the early 1980s, I was living in Cambridge, teaching in London two days a week and translating academic books and articles. We now had a second child, Johnny, but he was at nursery and Jacob was at primary school so I could regularly spend days in the university library, working on translations or following up my own researches. My notebooks started to fill with names and book titles that in those pre-internet days had an aura of mystery about them. How would I find out more? Where should I look for information? How far could I follow things up? I became adept at using all sorts of reference materials, at skimming dull books for the single mention they might contain, at guessing who

* Cannan was often a guest at Garsington Manor, Lady Ottoline Morrell's house, where a number of Bloomsbury pacifists worked on the land during the war. It was a centre for literary and artistic figures, and a magnet for affairs and gossip.

else might have written something that would give me more information about whoever or whatever I was researching that week. Good luck and random finds both played a big part, books discovered in second-hand bookshops and on the open shelves of the university library. I enjoyed the experience of a constantly renewed curiosity, slowly building up a much denser picture of the literary culture of the interwar years, filling in gaps in my knowledge and finding more and bigger ones. Very gradually I was able to start reconstituting the broader texture of writing and publishing in the period.

The other sources I found helpful were literary periodicals. Little magazines were important, especially in the period between about 1910 and 1960. Some were well produced and long-lived, and often supported by rich backers; others were hand-to-mouth affairs, ephemeral and, consequently, in some cases very hard to find. I started to collect as many as I could, gradually putting together complete runs and trying to find out more about the names I found in them, often struck by a brilliant poem by somebody I'd never heard of. Literary culture, like horticulture, thrives by composting – only a very small percentage of the writers in those magazines had books that were still in print, and many of them never published any books at all, a situation exacerbated by the number who were killed in the war. Yet many of them struck me as not just promising but genuinely good, and their neglect unjust.

Even at the best of times, of course, publishers can only keep a relatively small number of writers in print, and as both the canon and fashion change all the time, it's easy for writers to become forgotten. Some come back into favour, new generations of readers and writers discover new forebears, and publishers like Virago, Persephone, Carcanet, Faber Finds and Penguin Classics have been influential in bringing writers back into circulation. Recent years have seen a further increase in the number of publishers reissuing out-of-print novels; there has been a selection of John Rodker's work but nobody yet has reprinted anything by Gilbert Cannan or Douglas Goldring. And Mary Butts, whose *Armed with Madness* was published in Penguin Classics in 2001, is now out of print again in Britain, though most of her work is available in the USA. Carcanet has been a properly and idiosyncratically adventurous press for certain authors, including Rodker and Butts, and especially for poetry, but one publisher can only do so much.

The focus, for understandable reasons, has lately been on republishing women writers and writers of colour. It's good to see attention paid once more to Sam Selvon, Una Marson, Peter Abrahams and C.L.R. James, to Sylvia Townsend Warner, Anna Kavan, Ann Quin, Brigid Brophy and many others. But more are still waiting – Sarah Campion and Bryher,* for instance, could both do with a new audience.† Bryher wrote fifteen novels, two memoirs (one,

* Annie Winifred Ellerman adopted the name Bryher (after her favourite Scilly Isle), partly to escape being associated with her father, one of the richest men in England.

† Amazon quotes the blurb from a US reprint of two short novels by Bryher, which runs, 'Bryher's novels have a strong place in the history of lesbian and transgendered writing. This volume is sure to be a useful tool for modernist studies, women's studies, and queer, gay, and lesbian studies.' This tags the novels as student essay fodder, which does her writing and her reputation a disservice by reducing them to a 'useful tool'.

Days of Mars, about the war years, 1940–46, in London) and some other non-fiction and two early books of poems. Sarah Campion was the pseudonym of Mary Rose Coulton (later Mary Rose Alpers), daughter of the prolific historian G.G. Coulton; she wrote a dozen or so novels including the anti-war *Thirty Million Gas Masks*, two set in Nazi Germany, and a detective story, *Unhandsome Corpse*. Another writer due a critical and publishing revival is James Hanley, most of whose fifty-three books are out of print. The only one most people know is the often reprinted *Boy*, probably because of its prosecution for obscenity in 1935; Penguin in 1992 republished *The Furys*, the first of his series of five novels about 'the downfall of a whole family excepting one, and that is the woman. That woman is heroic, powerful, exercises a tremendous influence over her family', as Hanley described it. But many of his other books deserve to see the light of day again, especially his Blitz novel *No Directions*.

Ideally, I suppose, nothing would ever be unavailable, but the logistics of that, which would mean many multiples of the British Library, let alone the quantity of materials it would use and the space the books would occupy, would be out of the question. Ebooks may seem like an attractive solution so long as you don't mind not having the actual book-object in your hands, but, as the recent cyberattack on the British Library has shown, electronic storage is extremely vulnerable, as well as difficult, time-consuming and costly to restore when it goes down. There's also the problem of electricity generation itself in a world changing as rapidly as ours is. And as I pointed out earlier, many libraries, including the national collection in the British

Library and other copyright libraries, have stopped acquiring physical copies of many new books.

I don't like the phrase 'heritage publishing', which has crept into publishing jargon. Heritage is not the same as history: heritage may be what you warm to, but history is what you learn from. Back in the 1980s and early '90s, in the Thatcher years, the writer and historian Patrick Wright conducted what felt like a one-man campaign against the insidiously spreading notion of 'heritage'; he was concerned about the politics of national identity and the Thatcher anti-left project of 'modernisation', the full dire consequences of which can be seen everywhere around us today. He explained in a later interview how when the 'wider questions of national identity came to the fore, and were repeatedly ignited by policies such as privatisation, a lot of new ideological fall-out settled over what may still have seemed relatively innocent debates about architecture and history. It seemed to me quite clear that there were forms of memory and consciousness of history that had to be questioned in their influence on the present.' In an article in the *Independent*, Neil Ascherson, another critic of the idea, characterised Wright's argument as 'not just that the past was being prettified but that "heritage" was often being presented as an alternative to modernisation – a trick to bolster right-wing ideology or conceal national decline . . . the use of the word "heritage" as a term of obligation, binding people not only to respect relics of the past but also to understand them in one prescribed way as "national symbols", is not spontaneous. It is a form of manipulation, devised by politicians and quangocrats to make the tatty, dishevelled building-site of the present look more imposing.'

He's talking about the attitudes to historic buildings, theme parks, pastiche architectural styles and the creation of a myth of the past, not about literature, but there is a comparable danger in the repackaging of the past as well as a value in reassessing what has been forgotten. The dark green livery of Virago Classics, with paintings reproduced on the cover, tended towards a claim that all the books in the series were equally important elements of a neglected heritage, and although the project of republication was welcome, the lifestyle implication flattened the variety of the writings; and the elegant uniformity of Persephone books, modulated by the wallpaper or fabric designs on their endpapers, likewise appeared to offer a guarantee of a certain kind of 'heritage' quality. Both the idea of 'national heritage' and its offshoot in publishing are elements within a broader movement in the last fifty years, which began as a reaction against modernism.

The reputations of most of the forgotten writers I found most valuable, most exciting, have been victims of that reaction, and their work is only now beginning to be recognised again and, in some cases, reprinted. Hugh Sykes Davies' extraordinary surrealist prose-poem-narrative *Petron* (1935) has never been reprinted, and his three novels are similarly hard to find; Joseph Macleod's poetry has been brought back into print by the Waterloo Press, but his work is still too little known. It's a chicken-and-egg situation: it's not economically viable to publish a book until there are buyers for it, but equally the work needs to be available in order to create the demand. This is especially true of more experimental or idiosyncratic writers, who tend to attract belated or even posthumous recognition. At the other end of the reprint spectrum, there are the grand projects of collected works, designed to make annotated and properly edited editions of an author's entire output available to scholars and those who have access to the sort of libraries that can afford to stock these sets. For example, Oxford University Press is currently engaged in projects to publish the works of Wyndham Lewis, Ford Madox Ford, William Empson and Evelyn Waugh; Cambridge University Press has published scholarly editions of the (more canonical) works of writers like D.H. Lawrence and Joseph Conrad, and is in the process of producing an edition of Henry James. I hope that having produced a reliable edition, the publishers will make some at least of the newly established texts more cheaply available in paperback form, as sometimes does happen, though predictably and ironically it tends to be the already familiar ones that get republished.

As the first signs of spring were appearing, the tiles were all back on the restored coach-house roof, with at one end the weathervane smartly repainted. A small digger was at work in the library garden excavating the new pond. Ideally I would have made the library a two-storey affair, but that would have meant putting in a staircase, and insulating and wiring, plastering and lighting the upstairs, as well as building more shelves, and the single-storey library we'd designed was quite expensive enough already. But with the roof now clean and insulated, the building was beginning to look renewed – despite the hole in the wall (providing entry and exit for the digger, and the stone slabs that would be laid in a circle round the pond in due course) that would eventually become French windows in front of what would be my desk. I was starting to envisage the library as it would be in the summer, with the shelves in and everything finished. And I was beginning to think about which books would go where, already realising that they wouldn't all fit in.

It felt as if I'd spent all my life accumulating and discarding books: if I still had all the books I'd ever bought, I think there would probably be fifty or sixty thousand of them by now. Back in 1984, I still had a long way to go, but the pursuit of forgotten writers had already led me to spend so much time in second-hand bookshops all over the country that one day in the spring of that year, in a sudden fit of thoughtless enthusiasm, I decided to stop my FE teaching and reinvent myself as a second-hand bookseller. I was in my early thirties and saw it as an escape from the obligations imposed by work, even the part-time work I was doing. I was lured by the imagined freedom of self-employment and the pleasure of spending more time among books. It was an impulsive decision, but it was also the logical outcome of a decade or more looking for books on my own account. At first I just used to visit bookshops, jumble sales and the like whenever I had the opportunity. Then sometime in the late 1970s I discovered booksellers' catalogues, which brought a new level of excitement to my searches. I'd always liked getting things through the post, and opening a catalogue and reading through the books on offer was a new pleasure altogether. There were associated anxieties, too: if there was a book I wanted, would I be in time to order it or might it already have been sold? The vagaries of the post and postal delivery times meant I might have received the catalogue later than other people, or even if I hadn't, I might still be pipped at the post by someone who rang the dealer five minutes before I picked up the phone. Then I discovered that you could make a 'wants' list and circulate it to likely booksellers, who'd contact you if they found any of the titles you were looking for. As I gradually became a more serious and sophisticated collector, I also drew closer to the business itself, which made me think I knew enough about it to make a living at it.

I didn't.

I had done no preliminary planning at all and thought I could get all the advice I needed from my friend Ian, who'd been a bookseller for some years and who generously lent me my start-up capital of £300. On my first day in my new role, I cycled into town, to the market square, to take a look at the book stall. There was nothing much there, but as I was leaving, I spotted a stall selling odds and ends of bric-a-brac, which also had a single row of books, about ten altogether. I nipped over to have a look and one title caught my eye immediately: Lawrence Durrell's *Pied Piper of Lovers*, his first novel, never reprinted. It wasn't a very nice copy, having come from a wartime aerodrome library originally, but even so it was worth a very great deal more than the fifty pence I paid for it. I took it home, calculating that if I could find a title like that just once or twice a month, I'd probably be able to make a reasonable living. But like the first time I played poker, when a couple of hands into the game I came up with a royal flush when there was almost no money on the table and three of the other hands had already folded, it was something that never happened so perfectly again.

It does illustrate the excitement of the trade, though. The pleasure a collector feels at discovering an elusive book is exciting, but there's something both purer and more corrupting in the realisation that a lucky find is worth significant money. On the relatively few occasions when that happened during the ten years I continued my business, I felt it mainly as a way of – literally – buying time for other activities. (Or in the latter years of the business, as a way of relieving pressure on my overdraft.)

I never had a shop of my own, and I always specialised in books that dealt with areas I knew about, often marginal or recondite ones, rather than in books I knew I could turn a profit on, so to that extent I was never a proper (nor a very profitable) bookseller. I became a member of the Provincial Booksellers Fairs Association and set up my stand at PBFA book fairs (where for the first couple of years I traded with Ian Alister as Alister and Patterson), travelling round the country from Edinburgh to Bath, as well as doing the monthly fair at the Russell Hotel in London. The first fair I did, before I started travelling about, was a much smaller-scale event, the Cambridge book market, and I couldn't have started anywhere better – the other dealers were friendly, helpful, welcoming and good company. In the pub at lunchtimes, I quickly became immersed in a new world, a world of anecdotes, warnings, advice, and stories of good buys, rare books, legendary and quirky booksellers. It was a whole new subculture, but I never really felt quite at home in it because I was always more interested in reading books than in buying and selling them.

One of the other reasons I couldn't really become a proper bookseller was because I was busy doing other things – translating books from French, looking after my children and doing a small amount of teaching for the university. And as I say, I was usually more concerned with the content of the books I stocked than with their value as objects. Dealing in the kinds of books that were scarce in any condition, I didn't have much opportunity to pick and choose or wait for a copy in a mint dust jacket, and anyway they tended to be the kind of books that had been passed from hand to hand, not always carefully, and showed the marks of it. For my first few months in the trade and for my first catalogue, I sold poetry and modern first editions, but when the poet Peter Riley, who dealt in similar areas, moved to Cambridge, I didn't want to be competing with him for local resources so I switched to a focus on left-wingery and modernism, fiction (and some non-fiction) by left-wing authors after about 1880, political pamphlets with contributions from recognised writers, works of social reform, novels with a political background, radical pamphlets (especially the Communist Party and the British Union of Fascists), the Left Book Club and the Spanish Civil War. I loved the fringe, crossover, ephemeral things – not exactly literature, but not not either – writers contributing to political pamphlets, or writing them, or writers' work in other guises, like the cartoons that David Cornwell (better known later as John le Carré) contributed to the magazine *Oxford Left* in the 1950s. And I was keen on minor writers, writers nobody knew much about, except their highlights if they had any, including those I discussed earlier like Mary Butts, Douglas Goldring, Jack Lindsay, James Hanley and Sarah Campion. Of course, the fact that nobody much knew about them meant that nobody much wanted to buy them, except occasional penniless graduate students and underpaid academics.

I carried over into bookselling the principle I'd always had as an ordinary (if slightly obsessive) book-buyer, which was also the advice Susan Sontag gave to Edmund White: 'When you see a book you want, buy it instantly because you may never find it again.' As a bookseller I should have been buying the books that I was pretty sure other people would want, but then I've always hated doing what people expect me to do. So the books continued to accumulate much faster than I sold them, until eventually I'd turned my £300 float into what was theoretically many thousands of pounds' worth of books, pamphlets, periodicals and ephemera. But as one bookseller used to remind me, they might as well be worth nothing until they were actually sold. I also extended the range of the periodicals I was looking for, making up sets of magazines like *Horizon*, *The Criterion*, *New Verse* and suchlike, happily bringing together my collector's impulse and my bookseller's optimism. I made other collections, too, all of which I sold successfully (though now I wish I still had them): among them there was a complete collection of the Left Book Club, including the magazine *Left News* and lots of ephemera, a social credit collection (actually I don't miss that), and a collection of pamphlets and manuscripts by Robert Blatchford, the revolutionary socialist editor of *The Clarion* newspaper and author of the very successful *Merrie England*, an argument for his somewhat idiosyncratic vision of a socialist England. There was also a run of the Clarion Cycling Club magazine.

I learnt a great deal from being a bookseller, but sometimes at a cost. It was harder in those pre-internet days to discover what a book was, by which I mean how rare it was, what sort of price it went for, what its history might be. I spent long days in the Cambridge University Library, looking up titles in bibliographies, book auction records and other reference works. I pored over my by now sizeable accumulation of booksellers' catalogues. But I still made plenty of mistakes, selling books for much less than their true value. I occasionally felt ambivalent about putting a price on knowledge, as I thought of it, but salved my conscience by selling too many books at something close to cost price to academics, writers or librarians who really wanted them.

Everything changes. With the advent of the internet, two important things happened: booksellers started to list their books on AbeBooks or one of the other bookselling sites; and with the changing nature of the marketplace, combined with rising rents, lots of second-hand bookshops closed down. One consequence of that change was that I could search online for any title and see at a glance how many copies of it were for sale. Discovering the scarcity of books that had once been common, I slowly became aware of something I ought to have realised when I was bookselling, namely that the availability of books is generational. I took it for granted that the old Penguins and Left Book Club books and hardback novels from the 1930s that I wanted would always be around in jumble sales and bookshops and market stalls, but of course they came from the shelves of people who'd been young in the 1920s and '30s. It took me too long to work that out – now, when it's much too late to do anything about it, the books that used to cost twenty or fifty pence cost twenty or fifty pounds.

One of the great pleasures that is vanishing along with second-hand bookshops is the joy of discovery, of finding books you didn't know about or books you've been looking for for ages, running your eyes along shelf after shelf of dusty, out-of-print volumes until you're stopped by something that looks interesting. As Marius Kociejowski puts it in his memoir of a life in bookselling, 'bookshops are magic places: somewhere, in one of their nooks and crannies, there awaits a book that will ever so subtly alter one's existence. And with every shop that closes so, too, goes still more of the serendipity which feeds the human spirit.' It's not just your eye that's doing the work, either, as the feel and sometimes even the smell of the book can be important too, something you can't know about if you're buying online, however full the bookseller's description (which is sometimes not full at all, and all too often inadequate or misleading). There's simply no substitute for holding the book in your hand and inspecting it yourself: that way you can see the details of publication, look for tears or marginalia, maybe find letters or pressed flowers among the pages, if you're lucky recognise a signature on the front flyleaf as that of a significant previous owner, even the author. I once found a fifty-pound note in a book, used as a bookmark and then forgotten.

Books are always objects, as well as texts. That's why it's important that they be properly described by booksellers in online inventories and sale catalogues. Their condition is important, the difference between 'almost very good' and 'about near fine' is considerable, 'good' is almost bad, 'fair' is awful and a 'reading copy' is probably not one you'd want to read except out of desperation. Then there are the book's associations, such as ownership or presentation inscriptions, significant annotations or marginalia, or the complete absence of any marks at all on pristine first editions in crisp unmarked dust jackets. Many collectors want to get as close as they can, in some intangible way, to the author, by acquiring the earliest copy of a book, even a proof copy, or else one that has some tangible connection to literary or social history, like a dedication inscription to another writer (the more famous the better) or a well-known public figure. Part of the art of selling books is in creating a context for them that increases their value, or finding an angle that makes the book something more than at first sight it appears to be. This might involve showing that a central character was drawn from life and casts some revealing new light on its original, or detailing some unique set of circumstances surrounding a work. There's a novel by Shane Leslie (once a name to conjure with) called *The Cantab* that made a small scandal when it was published because it was a *roman-à-clef* and most of the university characters were not very well disguised; it had to be withdrawn and a revised version issued in its place. One day I found a copy of the original edition for fifty pence. It was cheap because it had ink annotations plentifully scattered through its margins; when I examined them closely, though, they turned out to be keys to all the real-life figures the novel's characters were based on, making that copy unique and extremely useful to anybody wanting to research the scandal it provoked. It is now in an appropriate Cambridge archive. Sometimes, too, there are extraneous but related circumstances that provide an aura of significance to an item – I once sold a copy of a 1950s Cambridge poetry magazine not so much because of the poems it contained but because it was the issue at the launch party of which Sylvia Plath first met Ted Hughes, the memorable time when she bit his cheek and drew blood. Books accrue associations in all sorts of ways, including through the way the bookseller describes them: a very minor element in a book, or even the presence of a minor character in it based on a relevant figure, can be enough to increase its desirability by just tipping it into a collectible category like 'weird fiction' or 'Bloomsbury', and therefore appealing to a whole new set of potential buyers.

George Orwell wrote a brief essay about the time he spent working in a second-hand bookshop in the 1930s, and concluded that although he'd had 'some happy days' there, he would not, on the whole, like to be as he puts it 'a bookseller *de métier*'. He comes up with various reasons for not wanting to do it – the customers, the dust, the hours of work – but goes on, 'the real reason why I should not like to be in the book trade for life is that while I was in it I lost my love of books. A bookseller has to tell lies about books, and that gives him a distaste for them.' He stopped buying books, and lost all the pleasure he used to have in bookshops and country auctions.

I don't know why Orwell felt obliged to tell lies about the books he sold. I don't think I ever did, even when I was desperate to sell something, even though book fairs could be very boring, especially on the second afternoon of a two-day fair when a bit of invented backstory for a book might have livened things up. Since I never had a shop (though I kept a small stock in somebody else's), I never really had a chance to test Orwell's experiences for myself. I certainly stopped going to so many bookshops, but that was because

I bought more books from book fairs and catalogues and from house calls than because of a distaste for bookshops or books themselves. And in the decades since I left the trade, I've enjoyed going to the second-hand bookshops that still remain and have continued to buy books at a fairly brisk rate. I've certainly never lost my love of them. My only regret is that I can't now afford to buy copies of some of the books that passed through my hands then – the Hogarth Press edition of T.S. Eliot's *The Waste Land*, Ezra Pound's *A Draft of XXX Cantos* published by Nancy Cunard's Hours Press, first editions of books by Ranier Maria Rilke and Tristan Tzara, portfolios by Wyndham Lewis – but that's life. They're all way out of my price range now.

I used to sell quite a lot of books to academics and to libraries, especially rare book and academic libraries, and as the years went by, my own interests and my bookselling interests converged so much that I eventually decided that I'd be happier, though probably no richer, if I gave up trying to sell books and devoted my time to reading them instead. I was also tired of driving about the country when I could be spending time with my children (the youngest, Jamie, was fast approaching primary-school age). So I became a PhD student. As well as finding forgotten books by 'minor' writers in order to read them, I'd become increasingly concerned to work out why they had been forgotten in the first place, why they'd fallen out of print, out of favour and off the shelves, and I wanted time to research those questions properly. Of course by the time I started my PhD, in 1991, many of the out-of-print writers I'd been looking for over the years were available again. Virago had pioneered the reprinting of books by women back in the 1970s, and by now the dark green wrappers were a familiar and ubiquitous sight; later Persephone Books with their elegant grey livery would follow suit, and since then many other publishers have been allowing readers to discover forgotten books and writers too. It was both very cheering and slightly galling to think that after I'd spent so much time scouring the country for second-hand copies, the books I'd taken years to find were now for sale everywhere. But in fact I'd just been one tiny element in a very large movement of reclamation. It was a protest against the idea that had become orthodoxy, that only a small number of classic writers were really worth reading.

Back in the nineteenth century, editors and critics were fond of recommending 'the best books' to new generations of readers, especially those from newly literate social strata; and anthologies like Francis Palgrave's *Golden Treasury of the Best Songs and Lyrical Poems in the English Language* attained huge popularity. In the early twentieth century, when English literature was becoming a new subject of study in universities, lineages of canonical authors were becoming further entrenched. Away from the university syllabuses, Arnold Bennett and others carried on the tradition of recommending work to autodidacts in books like the immensely popular *Literary Taste*, which I mentioned earlier. Among the many upheavals of the late 1960s and early '70s, students and others were asking radical questions about why so many writers, especially women and working-class writers as well as writers of colour, seemed to be absent from literary history (or from art history, or the history of music, or indeed from many areas of employment). The idea of literary value was changing as the literary culture of the past and the present was being reshaped, just as the History Workshop movement was championing history from below, history as it affected and was made by actual working people, rather than the conventional focus on high politics, high culture and a view of society based more on social homogeneity than class conflict. That orthodox thinking was entrenched in university English courses when I was a student in the 1960s. I was actively discouraged from reading or writing about Virginia Woolf, let alone exploring any lesser women writers or any more contemporary figures.

So the writers I'd discovered in the years after my degree were partly a reaction to its limitations, and in this I was unwittingly joining a new wave of readers. Not only readers, either: opening up the canon to include women was also happening in art history, with interventions like Linda Nochlin's 1971 article 'Why have there been no great women artists?' and Griselda Pollock's 1988 book *Vision and Difference*, and there was a similar development in music, first with the early music revival and the renewed interest in period instruments, more recently with the expansion of the catalogue to include the many women composers who had been marginalised and forgotten in a male-dominated world. It was partly owing to the new wave of feminism that this was happening, and to the enthusiasms of the new left, but there was also a growing recognition that no work of art arises on its own, it's always part of a culture in one way or another, and that culture gives rise to a great number of artists. When people started to look laterally at cultures, rather than vertically, they moved from tracing influences through a tiny number of 'the best' writers or composers over time to exploring their contemporaries, expanding the canon and revising categories like importance or originality. The result has been a hugely enriched awareness of the range of cultural production at any given time.

Having studied almost no writing by women during my three years as an undergraduate at Cambridge, I had set out in the early seventies to educate myself, reading everything I could lay my hands on. At the same time I was trying to bring together my commitment to the revolutionary left and my conviction that there was value in the writings of poets and novelists conventionally dismissed by the left as reactionary, writers like Ezra Pound and Wyndham Lewis. I was reading all the left-wing writers I could find, teaching motor vehicle mechanics and recent school leavers, drafting a book (never finished) on class, sociolinguistics and English teaching, and becoming more and more deeply involved in politics. All of which was the necessary background to my involvement over the next three or four decades in the rediscovery of forgotten writers.

The intense activity of political commitment diminished after a few years, giving me more time to feel haunted by the way novelists and poets I admired had vanished from cultural memory. So many writers seemed invisible, because they were forgotten or misrepresented or just out of fashion, that I became determined to rediscover them all. During the decade I spent in the book trade, I read an enormous number of out-of-print or forgotten books from the 1920s and '30s, which changed the way I thought about literature so radically that going back to university to write a PhD seemed a perfect opportunity to sort out my ideas. I was vaguely aware, too, that there was a personal element in all this. My own writing as a poet, and my activities as a poetry publisher and magazine editor, occupied a small and relatively ignored niche in the culture. My work as a translator was also mostly invisible. So the questions I wanted to address, such as why writers get forgotten or overlooked, how the mainstream canon is formed and perpetuated, and what happens to the works that have been rediscovered by publishers like Virago and Persephone, resonated with my sense of myself and what I was doing with my life, or at least with that part of it.

What made the PhD possible was a change in the rules of the grant-awarding body, the Arts and Humanities Research Board (now the Research Council), to allow older applicants, a change for which I shall always be very grateful. The cut-off age up to that point had been twenty-eight, I think, and when I applied I was over forty. The grant wasn't enough to contribute properly to the household income, so I continued to do some bookselling and translating while getting to grips with my topic and catching up on the developments in literary criticism that I'd missed during the past twenty years. The time spent in the Cambridge University Library during the years I was bookselling meant I'd learnt how to use it as a research facility, finding out about authors and publishers and trying to discover details about specific books, as well as getting background information on them. PhD research didn't have the same urgency or endpoint (or potential profitability), but it was something I'd always imagined doing and had put off for years; I also had a vague hope of getting an academic job at the end of it.

The research work at least was made easier by the number of scarce books I now had in my own collection. I hadn't settled on which writers would figure in my thesis, but the central questions were clear: what were the factors governing the formation of the canon, and why did some very good writers come to be excluded and forgotten. There were plenty of candidates to choose from: I was particularly interested in writers like the ones I mentioned earlier: Gilbert Cannan, Douglas Goldring, Mary Butts, John Rodker, James Hanley, Joseph Macleod, Hugh Sykes Davies and, though he was controversial and often disparaged rather than forgotten, coming back into print thanks to the American publisher John Martin and his Black Sparrow imprint, Wyndham Lewis. One obvious element in the process of canon formation is ephemerality, short-lived popularity, and while they say a week can be a long time in politics, publishing fashions can seem pretty ephemeral too, especially when they are reflecting political changes. The rapidity with which left-wing writing was marginalised in the Cold War is a case in point, and something some of the writers I was interested in clearly suffered from. It was a reminder, if one were needed, that all books are subject to the vagaries of political attitudes, however indirectly. The most flagrant examples, like book burnings, or authors and their books being cancelled, are entirely visible, but the great network of small decisions, shifts in beliefs or values, changes in taste and fashion or morals and politics, almost unnoticeable as they occur, can have long-term consequences for a writer's reputation.

One crucial thing at stake here is memory. The internet, googling and the proliferation of social media provide a continuous barrage of information, far more than we can ever take in, far more than we need, and a consequence is that we no longer feel a need to remember things. When any piece of information is a phone click away, why bother to remember it? 'I think how little we can hold in mind, how everything is constantly lapsing into oblivion with every extinguished life, how the world is, as it were, draining itself, in that the history of countless places and objects which themselves have no power of memory is never heard, never described or passed on', writes W.G. Sebald,[1] in an echo of Thomas Gray's 'Elegy Written in a Country Church-Yard'. Even with the proliferation of trivial records in social media, what people know mostly dies with them. Media accounts may group photos together to offer you created 'memories', but the more of them we have, the less real social or historical memory we seem to possess. Yet we need that kind of memory if we are to have a temporal perspective, to learn from the past, to have an understanding of history in the broadest sense, to know what political and social choices might or should be made. Information is not the same thing as knowledge: most information is freely available, but knowledge has to be learnt, made your own, and this often requires reading and rereading, as well as reflective thinking. We have to learn how to read for knowledge, especially now that so much seems to be designed to hinder access to it, and the use of social media, AI and the internet is weakening people's capacity for attention and concentration and fostering groupthink, all of which contributes to the rise of false beliefs, dangerous opinions and hasty actions. It also underlies the resurgence of the far right, which is another product of everything 'constantly lapsing into oblivion'. Libraries and individual book collections are part of the process of transmitting knowledge;

without them it is dangerously altered and weakened.

I spend a certain amount of time these days curating my library, by which I mean categorising the books and putting them in (roughly) the right place, looking for books I'm sure I have but that I can't find, reading booksellers' catalogues and looking online and in auctions for books that I need to fill gaps of one sort or another. Some of the sections of the library are definitely not 'collections', but a few of them – poetry, poetry magazines, particular twentieth-century writers – certainly are, and it is in the nature of collections never to be complete, though sometimes I lose interest in adding to them. I'm not fanatical, either. It would be nice to have dust jackets for some of the books that don't have them if the jackets are attractive or otherwise interesting, but dust jackets for rare books are even rarer than the books themselves and are commensurately expensive. Dust jackets and the other elements of book production are, in their way, important, though at most they can only complement the contents of the book; but they can do that by offering a kind of aesthetic and historical knowledge, with the book itself as object providing a commentary on the poems or fictions it contains. Not long ago, I saw in a catalogue the striking and elegant dust jacket for John Sommerfield's 1936 novel *May Day*. My copy of the novel is a bit tatty but it only cost me fifteen pence, back in the late 1970s; the copy with the fine dust jacket cost something approaching a thousand pounds. I didn't buy it.

5

What Poems Know

> Joe Brainard reportedly said on his deathbed, 'The best thing about dying is that you never have to go to another poetry reading.'
>
> Edmund White, *The Unpunished Vice*

Outside the coach house, the library garden was taking shape. The flagstones were laid, making a circular area around the pond, edged with the original beds. The pond itself was now lined and ready to be filled with water. Inside, everyone was still waiting for the lime plaster on the walls of the old loose box to dry, but it kept raining, day after day; the builders had to bring in a heater to try to speed up the drying process. For the time being, nothing else could be done inside. When the weather allowed, work continued on exterior tasks. I was anxious to see what would happen next, but it was a slow business for a while. The space left for the library was smaller now all the layers of insulation were in place, and I began to worry that there wouldn't be as much room for books as I'd imagined. The wiring for the lights and the plugs hung in loops or from holes in the wall or stuck up through the floor. But I could now envisage what the space would look like eventually, with shelves and books and furniture in place.

The secondary room contained the old stable, with its doors and manger and other fittings, all of which were listed and had to be retained; the idea was for the stable itself to become a reading space, while the rest of the room, the old loose box area, would be shelved. The main room, which would have French windows and a glazed door, was pleasantly light, and you could see out onto the garden. When it was shelved and painted and ready, this would house all my poetry books and my runs of poetry magazines. Before we moved, I'd been used to reading poetry most days, but the books had been in store now for nearly two years. I could read plenty online, but that was no substitute for sitting comfortably with a book in my hands.

Reading poems is perhaps the most intense kind of reading in some ways, and yet oddly it can also be the least intense. It's not intense in the way reading philosophy is intense, as you try to muster enough concentration to follow an argument, see its implications, struggle with its reasoning or assess its conclusions; the strain of trying to understand and assess each stage of a philosophical argument requires serious focus. But the aim there is to extract unambiguous meaning and test it with one's own thinking powers in order to discover some kind of truth. Poetry is different: it isn't paraphrasable, there isn't a straightforward meaning that equates to the poem's words, and its truths are elusive, aesthetic and affective as much as intellectual. Also poems usually need to be read more than once and in different ways, varying from the most analytically scrupulous to the most passive, from line by line to the poem as a whole, alert to both intellectual and affective responses. And of course there are big differences between the way we read long poems like *Paradise Lost*, *Don Juan* or *The Cantos* and the way we approach short lyric poems. But both work to a greater or lesser extent in ways different from prose, different in how they use figurative language, in the operations of ambiguity, in the workings of form, and in the kinds of pleasure they arouse. And although poetry these days tends to be associated with self-expression, emotional states and anecdotal narrative, that is to deny much of its potential, as well as a large slice of its history.

Poetry can take many different forms, of course, and the most popular is not always the best. The ideas about poetry that tend to dominate discussion reflect traditional, conventional writing, the sort of thing that is taught in schools, anthologised and published by mainstream publishers. Against or alongside that there is a thriving performative culture, with 'spoken word' poets and hip-hop and rap drawing audiences who want something different from those who go to poetry readings by GCSE stalwarts like Carol Ann Duffy or Simon Armitage. The trouble is, the way some poets are treated in educational syllabuses, in newspaper reviews and on the radio suggests that there is only one way – their way – of writing poems, which obscures the work of writers who don't fit the idea of poetry that this view disseminates.

It's a view whose essential features are something like this: a poem should be based on a memorable incident or feeling, something the reader can relate to, and it should be made distinctive and elevated above the ordinary by using descriptive similes and metaphors that implicitly and explicitly extend the experience depicted in new or surprising or unusual ways. Subject matter and the feelings associated with it tend to be the focus, with less attention given to the form the poem takes. Where formal features are noted, they are often misunderstood, or made to fit unthinking rules, such as 'enjambement creates a feeling of fragmentation' and so on. This would be OK as a minimal account of how some poems work if it didn't stand in the way of later development, but it's very limited as a vision of the potential range and scope of a poem, as even a cursory look back over the last few centuries reveals. There has been a tendency for the last seventy years or so to think of literature, and more especially poetry, as a meditation on personal things, events or anecdotes, guaranteed by a sort of authenticity of individual experience (something that increased with the rise of identity politics), but it should be – it is – far broader and more capable than that view allows.

Poetry is not just an instrument for evoking, expressing or describing emotional states or observed realities, nor is metaphor on its own an adequate mechanism for the work that poetry is capable of doing. It has a capacity to address even the most complex sorts of awareness of our being in the world and our knowledge and experience of it, sometimes in the process becoming hard to understand and requiring repeated reading. But so-called 'difficult poetry' is seldom wilfully obscure. It may be complex, and it may require two or three readings or even more before it becomes fully comprehensible, but that's part of what poetry is, what it does. The straightforward readability of a poem partly depends on when it was written: the meaning of words shifts over time, verbal expressions fall out of use, rhetorical structures lose their force and so on. Yet so long as the broad outline is comprehensible, the rest can be picked up or looked up where necessary. When reading old poems, your mind has to be in at least two places at the same time – in the world of the poem and in the present moment. The two temporalities can speak to each other, tracing lineages, suggesting connections, providing histories, and by doing that revealing some of the complexity of the present. Something similar is true of contemporary poems, too.

One thing that strikes you if you flick through anthologies is that there are almost no subjects people haven't written poems about. There are long (sometimes very long) narrative poems like *The Odyssey* or Chaucer's *Troilus and Criseyde*, epic religious poems like Dante's *Divine Comedy* or Milton's *Paradise Lost*, philosophical poems (like Mark Akenside's *The Pleasures of Imagination*), theological poems, historical poems, instructional poems, poems about cider-making (John Philips' *Cider*, 1708, is a long poem that manages to be accurate, detailed *and* instructional), satirical poems (like Byron's attack on Robert Southey in *The Vision of Judgement*), love poems, nonsense poems, meditative poems, descriptive poems, topographical poems, scientific poems, poems written to or about particular individuals, eulogies, elegies, biographical poems, autobiographical poems (like Wordsworth's *Prelude, or the growth of a poet's mind*), novels in verse (like Elizabeth Barrett Browning's *Aurora Leigh* or Vikram Seth's *The Golden Gate*), allegorical poems (like *The Faerie Queene*), poems of advice or warning, political poems – the list is almost endless, as are the many and various forms the poems take.

To some extent, a poem will dictate how it's read because of all these variations. In other ways, readers, and the time and context they are reading in, make up the poems they read. The kind of close reading of poems I'm advocating, which focuses on writing rather than performance, sometimes called practical criticism, derives from the work of I.A. Richards and his student William Empson,* and might be seen originally as a strand within modernism responding to its more self-conscious verbal complexity and a more exacting focus on the meaning of meaning. Richards, when he was lecturing in English at Cambridge in the early 1920s, was interested in the psychological determinants of the way his students approached poems, and in order to study this, he gave them copies of a number of poems presented without any indication of author, date, subject or type of poem and asked them to write down their responses anonymously for him to collect the following week.

Introducing the results of his experiment in his book *Practical Criticism* in 1924, Richards wrote that 'The most disturbing and impressive fact brought out by this experiment is that a large proportion of average-to-good (and in some cases, certainly, devoted) readers of poetry frequently and repeatedly *fail to understand it*, both as a statement and as an expression.' Often the poems were distorted by the preconceptions the students had, many of which they weren't conscious of; one of the things we can learn from Richards' experiment is the importance of making ourselves

* And probably also from the critical writings of Robert Graves, especially *A Survey of Modernist Poetry* (1927), written with the poet Laura Riding.

aware of our own preconceptions and expectations when we read a poem, and trying to put aside the ones that aren't relevant.

The first requirement is to be open to the poem, and to let its words act on you, and to think about how it creates the effects it does. The second is to recognise that it is a product of its time, and to find out what that means for the way the poem is written, and for what it means. The third is to be prepared to look things up. I often look up words to find out whether their meaning has shifted over the centuries, what their etymology is and what other meanings they may have apart from the one I first think of. Words are after all what poems are made of; words have histories and poems try to say something new. Or to put it another way, in order to escape the limiting horizons imposed by habit and the conventional expectations of the possible, we have to be able to see things differently, rearrange perceptions, think in fresh ways; and one way to do this is to read writing that embodies that distance from the normal. Writing that tries, in Ezra Pound's phrase, to 'make it new'.

Not that people need to jettison all their habits of thought: plenty of them are sensible and right, but some are not. Some are prejudices, some are just what other people have said, while some are out of date, inadequate or untenable, or just plain wrong. And the more rapidly the world and society change, the greater the need to be open to the new and at the same time capable of making informed responses to whatever's going on. If 'reality' is composed of language, and if our perception of the world can only make itself known through language, then language must become the means to see through the comfortable and easy barrier of common sense and all the inherited attitudes it embodies, and be set to work to think critically about the world, even in poems.

You can like a poem straight away or, equally, dislike it straight away, but either way it's always helpful to find out why. Then, if possible, disregard that initial emotional response and concentrate on the poem itself, its mechanisms and meanings. And then when you're fairly clear about how the poem is doing whatever it is doing, and you have a sense of the way in which the time it was written shapes or limits its expressive possibilities, and perhaps a sense of the poem as something more complex, less clear-cut than it seemed at first, return to your original response and reassess it. You may feel the same way about it as you did to start off with, but now at least you should be able to give better reasons for it.

Words can be slippery, though, and the poem may continue to resist your reading, or at least resist being pinned down to one version of itself. Poems may be ambiguous, they may alter their meaning according to their context, they may arouse contradictory feelings or associations, they may be unfamiliar or outdated. Words are the material of poems, but poems often work by drawing on thoughts and feelings we're not fully aware of. Both poems that appear to be crystal-clear and those that appear to refuse any coherent meaning involve the reader in ways that need to be teased out, brought to the surface, recognised and incorporated into a fuller reading. The expectation that poems should always be straightforward, should 'say what they mean' and say it clearly and memorably, is short-sighted because it misunderstands language and the mind. We live in language and construct our world with it, adapting our understanding to what we can say and in the process often reshaping reality to fit with our own articulation of it. 'What is the language using us for?' asks the poet W.S. Graham, pointing out that we are not totally in control of language when we use it, or when we read it. Language exists outside us; it is something we all have to learn, and it is more extensive and complex than any of us can understand completely. It has, you might say, a life of its own, and that life is most visible in poetry.

Poems, like all works of art, can know more than their authors know they know; they can escape from the control of their creators because none of us knows everything that goes on in our minds, or anything (by definition) that goes on at the deepest level, in our unconscious. A while ago I heard a pianist talking on the radio about the feelings he experienced when he played a Chopin piece on Chopin's own piano. 'Certainly,' he said, 'a lot of emotions are triggered by memories we've never had.' Or, we might add, by memories we can't access because they're unconscious.

So for all sorts of reasons we may see things in a poem that the poet had no awareness of at all. Not just the semi-instinctive things like word patterning that help to hold the poem together, but aspects of its meaning, as in William Blake's assertion that Milton in *Paradise Lost* was 'of the Devil's party without knowing it' because of the poetic energy he endowed Satan with. That is an extreme example, perhaps, but we all have unconscious conflicts and repressed desires, and they can only make their way into consciousness through dreams and art, disguised by visual and linguistic puns and tricks, where they can be safely unrecognised unless they are subject to analysis. 'Consciousness,' says the art critic Adrian Stokes, 'is a brisk dream of the unconscious within: the dream of utmost substitution or distortion, made vivid, made real by continuous contact with the actuality of the not-self.'

If poems, then, escape their creators' control, how far do our own fantasies and preoccupations shape our reading of them? Does that mean that any interpretation is as good as any other? No, because there are limits: Blake's poem 'The Tyger', for instance, cannot be read as a poem about a rabbit, but the meaning that the poem uses the figure of the tyger to construct is less definitive, more open to interpretation, which can then be argued for and be found more or less justifiable on the basis of the workings of the poem itself and what we can know about its personal and historical context. The tyger's 'fearful symmetry' is given its sense of mystery by the repeated use of questions and by the metaphorical use of scale ('In what distant deeps or skies / Burnt the fire of thine eyes?') and powerful manufacturing techniques (hammer, furnace, anvil). The result is a beast, and its creator, more abstract and mythic than any actual tiger could be. At any given time, there will be limits on what can be thought, what is known, how language is used, so the more we are aware of this, the more exact our reading will be. Yet in the long run, that may not be what matters most, or not to most readers. Poems that are any good need to be readable long after they were written, and what they offer to readers will necessarily change as language and the culture change. So there is a degree of leeway in interpretation, depending on who is doing the interpreting and in what context and for what purpose.

I began by saying that poems can be ambiguous, complex and contradictory, or simple, direct and straightforward, long or short, strictly formal or unstructured, but they are never the same as writing that isn't poems, because the kind of thinking that poems enact is different, and therefore the kind of knowledge to be had from them is different, too. It might be helpful at this point to take a poem and see how it works, and what kind of thinking the poem is doing.

First, William Blake's poem 'London', from *Songs of Innocence and Experience*. It's a powerful and moving vision of conditions in Blake's city in the late eighteenth century: the misery of the people, the culpability of institutions like the Church and the monarchy, people's acceptance of servitude, and the corruption of love. But if that were all, it wouldn't need to be a poem: it could be a speech or an essay or some other form of prose utterance. So what is gained by its being a poem? How does it work?

In the form in which Blake first published the poem, it was engraved in cursive script and surrounded by hand-coloured images: at the top of the page, a rather grown-up and concerned-looking child leads an old, blind man along a dark street, lit by a slanting shaft of light; he has a long white beard and walks with the help of crutches. Both figures, in some copies of the book, have faint haloes. Lower down on the right-hand side, a kneeling figure warms his hands at a billowing, smoky fire.

LONDON

I wander thro' each charter'd street,
Near where the charter'd Thames does flow.
And mark in every face I meet
Marks of weakness, marks of woe.

In every cry of every Man,
In every Infants cry of fear,
In every voice: in every ban,
The mind-forg'd manacles I hear

How the Chimney-sweepers cry
Every blackning Church appalls,
And the hapless Soldiers sigh
Runs in blood down Palace walls

But most thro' midnight streets I hear
How the youthful Harlots curse
Blasts the new-born Infants tear
And blights with plagues the Marriage hearse

Reading the poem for the first time, a reader would ideally have as relaxed and open a mind as possible, just letting him or herself receive what the poem has to offer, feeling the substance and the movement of it in their body as well. After that will come several more readings, taking the opportunity to think about anything that felt difficult or knotty or particularly striking. After that, having got a fairly clear sense of what the poem is saying, it's time to look at what makes it work, its material effects and its conceptual development.

The first word, the pronoun 'I', is an invitation to the reader to identify with the person of the poem, or at least to see things through those eyes, bringing us closer to the experiences described as he (could it be she?) wanders through London streets. To begin a poem with wandering, especially around this time, is usually to evoke a pleasant state of receptivity, often in natural surroundings (as for instance in Wordsworth's 'I wandered lonely as a cloud'); here, however, the ambivalence of 'charter'd', which carries a primary sense of licence and freedom with an overtone of control, is followed by observation of universal misery. The repetition of 'charter'd' and the repetition of the 'ar' sound in the repeated 'mark', along with the alliteration on 'm' and 'w', foreground the sense of treadmill-like captivity, even further emphasised by the way 'mark' shifts from a verb to a noun. The grammar is simple, the rhythm and the ABAB rhyme regular, and apart from the layered significance of 'charter'd', the vocabulary is easy to understand. A further sophistication to the symmetry of the rhymes is that ABAB is counterpointed by a grammatical ABBA of noun verb verb noun.

The second stanza reverses the grammatical pattern of the first by leaving the main verb, 'I hear', to the end, after the five-times-repeated 'every'. The sound of the word 'hear' echoes 'near' in the first stanza as well as its rhyme, 'fear', and cements the soundscape, which begins with the different cries and continues for the rest of the poem. After the shrinking horizons implied by 'fear' and 'ban', the complex and memorable 'mind-forg'd manacles' introduces a new level of thinking into the poem, the relation between actual captivity, figured in the metonymy of 'manacles', and the psychological limitations imposed by an ideology of acceptance and self-restriction. Yet it also introduces the possibility of rejecting those 'manacles', because however iron-like they may be, metaphorically, they are also not real but forgeries, 'mind-forg'd'.

At this point, the poem pivots, using the phrase 'I hear' twice, despite its only appearing once, as grammatically it has to introduce the clauses beginning 'how' (a word that comes to seem more and more like 'howl' as the poem progresses) that follow in the third stanza. The figurative language thickens now, developing a non-literal sort of meaning beside the literal sound of more cries, as the wretched climbing-boys used by chimney sweeps are an affront to Christianity: the churches are 'blackening' literally because of smoke from chimneys, and figuratively because they are morally culpable for allowing little children to be so ill-treated; and the word 'appalls', ironic in that the Church is not appalled or dismayed by it, but etymologically complex in that it also bears a sense of weakening and, in contrast to 'blackening', making pale. The 'hapless Soldiers sigh' may be a sigh of resignation, or a dying soldier's last breath figured as his lifeblood as he defends privilege and royalty: the coherence of the figurative language is reinforced by the almost anagrams ('paragrams' as Saussure calls them) of 'appalls', 'hapless' and 'palace', the shifting a-p-l pattern creating a sense of kinship among the three words. Also, whether by design or not, the first letter of each line spells the word 'hear', which as we've seen is otherwise missing from the stanza, and points us forward to the intensified aurality of the final lines.

The structure of a poem's argument is one of the basic elements in the way a poem works, and this is no exception. From the wandering and observing at the start, to the increasingly pressing sounds, to the insistent 'But most' at the beginning of the final stanza, the intensity increases, providing the right sort of intellectual and emotional pitch for the horrors of the concluding lines. And as if in accompaniment to that, the 'st' sound in 'most' and its reversed 'ts' recurs in 'midnight streets', 'Harlots', 'Blasts', 'Infants tear' and 'blights'. The darkness, the oxymoron of 'Marriage hearse', the child harlot's curse assaulting the weeping newborn, everything that blights and plagues the city streets, all flesh out the marks of weakness and woe the poem draws attention to in its opening lines. In another case of pattern repetition, 'blights' and 'Blasts' harken back to 'blackning' and 'blood' in the previous stanza.

So syntax, the shapes and sounds of words, the structure of argument, the nature and degree of compression or condensation in the figures of speech, the patterning of sound, rhyme and rhythm, the alliteration and repetition, all contribute to the poem, whether or not Blake was conscious of the effects he was creating. And I've said nothing about the pace of the poem, its gaps, pauses, pitch, volume, inflection, cadence, degrees and placing of stress, which would require a much-extended analysis. Nor have I said anything about the causes of the wretchedness Blake depicts in the poem, about the historical moment of its composition, its mode of publication, its place in Blake's work and a hundred other possibly illuminating things. I think these matter. It was one of the great limitations of close reading as practised in universities, especially in the USA, in the 1950s and '60s, during the Cold War, that poems were treated as ahistorical entities, self-sufficient organic wholes that needed no biographical or conceptual or historical or indeed etymological context in order to be fully understood. Blake's poem has an immediate context as one of the poems in *Songs of Innocence and Experience* (though not one paired with a poem in *Songs of Innocence*), and it also needs to be set within the broader historical context of the radical movements of the 1790s that he was involved in. It might also be rewarding to think about the history of the kind of poem this is: regular, four-stress, four-line stanzas, a kind of ballad metre and a common form for poems and songs for several hundred years.

One of the things that makes this poem so powerful is the presence of the observer, the 'I' of the poem, and it raises a question about what is often called poetic voice. There is a widespread attraction to poems that seem to speak with a personal voice, often anecdotal or confessional poems, poems that tell a story, that deal with dreams, wishes, sorrows and other life events so that the poem is, in the popular, and often narrowing term, 'relatable'. Such poems have their place, but it is a mistake to think that they represent the whole scope of poetry, or that the personal voice is all there is to them. As the British poet J.H. Prynne forcefully puts it in his essay on 'Mental Ears', textuality, the written word, changes language. 'It is indifference to the alterative effect of textuality that causes [professor of English] Derek Attridge to write, following the consensus, that "Poems are made out of spoken language". I believe this statement to be decisively not true, unless it is also to be believed that tables and chairs are made out of living trees.'

Spoken language is essentially ephemeral, while written

language has a claim to permanence. This obvious truth carries interesting implications: it means, for example, that the text of a poem may well echo or follow or invoke or remind us of earlier poems or other written sources, often without the writer's conscious awareness. There are a host of paralinguistic features, too, which we need to bear in mind, and which become more perceptible when the poem is read aloud: rhythmic structures, patterns and degrees of emphasis, shifts of tone, intonation, pitch and loudness, how quickly or slowly a phrase or line or stanza is read. The alert reader hears the echoes in the poem's text or picks up on the etymology of a word and the poem develops a history of its own. (This applies to prose, too: as Proust or one of his characters wrote somewhere, 'A great writer should have in-depth knowledge of his dictionary, and be able to follow a word through the ages in the works of all the great writers who have used it.') Working with language means working with its history, as its past is always already embodied in its present and therefore in us. The voice of a poem can never just be the speaking voice of the poet, however vivid the illusion of speech may be.

Take this poem by Thomas Hardy, written in 1912–13 after the death of his first wife, from whom he'd long been estranged but whom he felt obsessively haunted by in the period after her death:

THE VOICE

Woman much missed, how you call to me, call to me,
Saying that now you are not as you were
When you had changed from the one who was all to me,
But as at first, when our day was fair.

Can it be you that I hear? Let me view you, then,
Standing as when I drew near to the town
Where you would wait for me: yes, as I knew you then,
Even to the original air-blue gown!

Or is it only the breeze, in its listlessness
Travelling across the wet mead to me here,
You being ever dissolved to wan wistlessness,
Heard no more again far or near?

Thus I; faltering forward,
Leaves around me falling,
Wind oozing thin through the thorn from norward,
And the woman calling.

Particularly worth noticing here, especially when read aloud, is the rhythm, the stress pattern, the way the sense of the words relates to the regular metrical structure of the poem. This is set at the start as dactylic tetrameter (four-stress lines, going dum-di-di, dum-di-di), with the falling cadence at the end of lines one and three of the first two stanzas creating the sense of an echo. But having established this insistent rhythm, Hardy goes on to complicate it, or rather to make it awkward in lines two and four of the third stanza, where an atypical quantity of stress has to fall on 'wet mead' and 'me here'; and again in the last stanza, where the reader needs to insert two silent two-beat rests, one after each of the first two words, and where line two has only three stresses instead of four. The metre is restored in the third line, only to return to three stresses in the final line, forcing a stress on 'And' that reinforces the poet's need to have it both ways, to hear the ghostly voice of his dead first wife, and at the same time to recognise that what he hears must be the 'Wind oozing thin through the thorn from norward'.

Yet although we may know the biographical story that lies behind the poem, we may not be justified in identifying the poem with the poet. The poem is called 'The Voice', and the sound patterning and the homophones, the parts of the poem that strike the ear, are important, too. The sense of the ghostly woman's presence is intensified first by the phrase in the first line, 'Woman much missed', which sounds like 'much mist', and then by the ethereal epithet 'air-blue', both of which hover between solid and airy bodies, as does the 'Wind oozing thin', where the bodiless wind is given substance by the viscosity of 'oozing'; it's also there in the repeated 'you' sounds in the second stanza in 'view' and 'knew', and echoed in 'oozing'. That's the obvious voice, the subject of the poem; but there is another voice, too, the voice of the poem, which also creates a voice for the poet as a sort of fictional character within the poem.

It's an interesting effect of the first-person pronoun in some poems that while we may temporarily put ourselves in that position, as if we identified with it, we also see the 'I' as a distinct, separate person. We are, as it were, in two minds at once. This is especially so in a poem like this one, where the 'I' is reflecting on its own experience, questioning itself at the same time as it evokes the voice it keeps hearing, bringing together past and present in a present that is itself both past and present (an effect reinforced by the poem's own verbal memories of earlier poems by other writers). By the end of the poem, when the 'I' is seen 'faltering forward', a lone figure among the falling leaves and the 'oozing' wind, this self-projection has become figurative as much as literal, and the voice of the poem – its cadences, rhythm and tonality – has become the site of feeling. This last stanza echoes Shelley's 'Ode to the West Wind', where falling leaves also figure the leaves of paper the poem is written on; the word 'oozing' might remind us of the 'last oozings' of the 'cyder-press' in Keats' 'Ode to Autumn', or if we turned to the *Oxford English Dictionary*, we'd see that Washington Irving wrote of 'The wind oozing through the rat-holes of the old mansion', showing that Hardy's expression has a history, too.

So is this last stanza self-description? Is the self of the poet the person described or the haunted, uncertain questioner we encounter as we read, or a construction of the poem's own voice? Or does it contrive to be all three, so that the question of whose voice the poem's is is beside the point?

If the effect of the poem is to show the simultaneous presence of two contradictory beliefs – that the writer can hear his late wife calling to him, and that it is the wind – then the art of the poem is to make us share this contradictory mental state, at least for the duration of the poem. Poems don't have to be singular assertions – they can often make you hold several different or contradictory potential meanings at the same time. Some poems even make this semantic lability central to the way they operate.

Contrast the two poems we've been looking at with 'In First Tuft', a poem from J.H. Prynne's 2020 booklet, *Passing Grass Parnassus*. Here there is no evident narrative to hold the poem together; instead there is a shared presence of a variety of wildflower names within an experience of sound-patterning in which words shift and morph into other words, creating an unstable texture through the weaves of which the poem's apparent referents emerge evanescently, then disperse like smoke. Here's the poem in full:

IN FIRST TUFT

So be it bell bee lift medick black reliquary
fumitory cloven zigzag agree proud bee scout
provoked teasel, we'd hawk orange sleeping
licit brighten maybe buck past night eye win
shadoof arrested honour honied gathered thorn
apsidal mantle; bee better supple wax oddment
reside around torment until tillage phrasing
candour in first tuft. Will to be absconded,
bit over frugal step foot bird gibbous seek
to wade speed sweet braid brigantine western
grass-wrack oh willow lighten one obol fescue
half scruple rueful strife lost foil sunken
flag yellow alchemic, well to speed, spelling
alex and erstwhile milder dewfall flow gentle
vernal enjoy unravel, glove wolf to foxy off
must to travel figment worth welsh popularise
astonish crop to stretch. Stitch, worshipful
dropwort walking basset mallow elbow winding
ill-met crane billet chalk hill, fugal would
sorrel sorrowful meadow scented entreat sweet
fasten shaded if rift, listed thrift on hold
bed strewn mown tufted edgeways led by nature
hardly felt, the kind you are, square spear
new-mint tway robert herb blood fortune meet
fate hay rattle settle; white bryony bees
terse creeping wrack grapple miller dusty.

It's clear that this poem is not syntactically conventional, that it doesn't make the kind of sense we are used to in normal forms of literary discourse, but at the same time it makes an emotional and intellectual impact through combinations of words, and the reader can see that emphases and potential linkages also occur through sound-patterning. The most obvious pattern is the presence or semi-presence of flower names or phrases derived from them: black medick, fumitory, zigzag clover, hawkbit, buckthorn, eyebright, whin, lady's mantle, tormentil and candytuft in the first sentence, hay rattle, white bryony and dusty miller in the last, some more obscure in form than others. The poem's obscurity is not like the obscurity of a cryptic crossword: the only thing that looks like a crossword clue occurs in line 14, where the phrase 'alex and erstwhile' contains the hedgerow plant 'alexanders'; much of the rest of the poem's text seems to have been suggested by the names of flowers and turned to other uses, so 'figment worth welsh popularise' in the next line takes its cue from figwort and Welsh poppy but converts the literal and material into other potential meanings, which in turn contribute to the accumulation of possible thought-routes through the poem. The poet Peter Larkin, in an essay on Prynne's use of flowers in his poetry, says that 'Flowers once seeded in language rapidly spring up as flowers of language (*flores rhetoricae*), innately metaphorical but figures of thought as well as speech. We may start by thinking about these named or ghosted flowers as a kind of thinking.'[1]

Next, we might notice that the poem begins 'So be it', suggests later that the 'Will to be' has 'absconded' and concludes (almost) with 'led by nature / hardly felt, the kind you are, square spear / new-mint tway robert herb blood fortune meet / fate' (the unfamiliar 'tway' derives from the twayblade orchid, with the 'blade' bit transformed into 'blood', the old name 'twayblade' meaning 'two-leaved'); the effect of these three fragments is to induce a sense of passivity or acceptance in the text of the poem, and therefore in the reader, in which to receive the other elements of this semantic encounter. If we read the poem without worrying too much about description, narrative or coherent consecutive thinking, we might find that some words or phrases carry greater emotional intensity than others and that our response to them is commensurately more significant. Words like 'torment', perhaps, or phrases such as 'rueful strife lost' or 'blood fortune meet' may stand out; equally the apparent lament of 'oh willow', often found in old songs, may provoke a pang of sorrow, or curiosity about sorrow, while 'milder dewfall flow gentle / vernal enjoy unravel' may stimulate a pleasanter response as well as echoing lines by Robert Burns and William Wordsworth.

Further probing could reveal that all the letters in 'vernal' can be found in 'unravel', which also rhymes with 'travel', or that 'hay rattle settle' sounds like 'hey diddle diddle'. There are some terms associated with movement, both human and animal (especially bees) – lift, step, wade, speed, sunken, flow, unravel, travel, walking, winding, led, creeping – and at least one word that seems out of place, namely 'shadoof', which unambiguously means 'A contrivance used in the East for raising water for irrigation purposes, consisting of a rod or pole working upon a pivot, at one end of which is fastened a bucket and at the other a weight to serve as a counterpoise' (*Oxford English Dictionary*). On the other hand, 'shadow of' would fit better, and I can't help feeling something like that shadow lurking behind the shadoof. The poem doesn't rhyme in any usual way, but there is a fair amount of rhyme and near-rhyme and sound echoes in it, starting with 'reliquary / fumitory'. The echo of 'ill' in 'until tillage' is picked up in the next line with 'Will', and that constellation of sound returns later in the poem with 'ill-met crane billet chalk hill' (the crane deriving from the plant cranesbill), creating a cross-linkage that at the least helps to hold the poem together. Sometimes these poems make use of the division of a word into its component elements so each element carries its own semantic weight, as in 'brim / stone' or 'rock face cramp on time' in 'Downcast In Case' later in the sequence; the meaning of the word 'brim' is normally absent from 'brimstone' and 'cramp' is similarly inert in 'crampon'; but here they introduce a sort of double focus, and the 'rock' and 'face' in 'rock face' are allowed to be verbs as well as nouns or a compound noun.

At this point, a reader might well ask questions like: Does any of that matter? Does it contribute anything? Has all this been done consciously? To which the best response is probably 'We don't know yet: we'll have to wait and see. Carry on reading.' A reader might still be niggled, though, by whether they need to know enough about flowers to recognise them, or to know what a shadoof is, or a reliquary. What if you're missing things? You can look up unfamiliar words in a dictionary or online, but it can be hard to accept that not really knowing what's going on in the poem is an important part of a first reading because it allows all the contrivances of verse – the allusions, the sound-patterning, the rhythms, the line endings, the way the pace of it moves, even the idiosyncratic syntax – to impress themselves, consciously or unconsciously, on the reader's ears and mind. It also allows the reader to accept their own uncertainty rather than meeting the poem with definitive ideas about meaning, rather like Keats' account of what he called 'negative capability', the state of being 'in uncertainties, mysteries, doubts, without any irritable reaching after fact and reason'. Each subsequent reading will clarify the poem's effects, perhaps reveal new ones, and raise questions, some of which may be usefully answered with the help of the internet or reference books. Attending to the effects – emotional and physical as well as intellectual – the poem has on you as you read it allows its different dimensions to emerge and shape themselves in your mind; 'enjoy unravel' then 'stitch' and 'grapple', to quote from the poem. Because this poem can't be fitted into conventional sentences or a conventional narrative, it makes different demands on its readers; the work of reading it, and the pleasure of reading it, lies in this collaboration between reader and text, but it would be wrong to think of it as a puzzle that can be solved. It isn't: poems aren't puzzles (unless they're riddles or Anglo-Saxon kennings). Part of the pleasure lies in the unsettling effect of the work, what the artist, director and writer Tim Etchells has called 'a pull into discomfort'; you don't know what to make of what you're reading, and you're not sure if that's because you don't know enough, or can't think properly, or you're in some way out of touch, or there's a way to read it that you don't know about. You have to pay attention, that is, to the effects the poem is having on you and if necessary readjust your thinking to fit it.

Just as paintings can be abstract, so can poems, or at least so can the way the language is used in a poem. It can be abstracted from the representational sense we are used to finding in syntactically grammatical concatenations of words, and fragmented or joined up in unpredictable ways. Unlike in abstract painting there is no absence of represented objects; instead there is an overlay or a plethora of possibilities: syntax that changes abruptly, ghosts of phrases or sentences, bits of rhyme, all shaped by and shaping mood and tone. In some ways, too, poems are like music, a complex of sounds, cadences, rhythms and silences. They are frameworks for thinking, and they themselves can teach you how to read them. People's readings will differ about nuance, emotional response, resonance and the poem's thinking, because readers differ in what they bring to the poem and therefore to some extent in what they take away from their encounter with it, but there will always be parameters of some kind or other to guide interpretation and offer limits to it.

If you're used to thinking of poems as being descriptive or personal expressions made more intense or more complex by the addition of metaphor or novel simile, this can be unsettling. There's a satirical but accurate account of 'easy' poetry in poet and novelist James Russell's story 'Souvenir from a Dream', where one character is lambasting a poet called Mandy Pullen, who writes 'stuff that absolutely looks and sounds like poetry while presenting the reader with little jumpable hurdles to interpretation. You give them the flowers of poesy plus the satisfaction of being able to pluck them to their heart's content. The punter can safely give books of them to one who may become – to whom they want to become – a loved one. Giving poem-books betokens sensitivity, you see.

'The formula here has two main elements. First, pile on imagery, all dressed up in metaphors and similes that look bold but are actually sloppy and approximate, while having the safety net of seeming "surreal" if they badly misfire. These must be like codes with built-in crackability . . . Second, you really must end with an epiphany of some kind, an epiphany with echoing and phoney resonance. It's as if somebody offers you an ice-cube or a cheese grater and says "So what about THAT!", somebody who has worked hard to earn credentials as being on a higher art-intellect plane than you. The huge advantage of this stuff is that it sells. It does the trick.'[2]

That's a parody, of course, but the point it makes is a good one: too much of what passes for poetry suffers from the fault of being essentially a prose story with unexpected metaphors, rather than working through the kind of figurative language that the poet and translator Christopher Middleton describes when he writes, 'I stand by figurative speech, as a time-tested access to truth in finite existence, and more, as speech which tells of the impact of the world upon the body. Figures offer an access – to truth and to death – which might be called physiognomical, because it does not sheer away feeling and randomness, but admits them, whatever the pain, in a purged and dynamic condition.'[3]

There are not all that many poems that challenge the reader in the way that J.H. Prynne's can, but by setting aside preconceptions, allowing the language and the poem's constraints to work on you, you find that the poem, like any other poem, will gradually or maybe even suddenly open up and you'll be able to attend to the thoughts and feelings it arouses in you in that curious exchange that only happens in reading. It may be significant that the three poems I've been discussing come from longer sequences: 'London' is from Blake's *Songs of Experience*, 'The Voice' from Hardy's 'Poems 1912–13' in *Satires of Circumstance*, a sequence of first eighteen then twenty-one poems sparked by the death of his estranged first wife, and 'In First Tuft' is the first of the twenty-four poems in Prynne's *Passing Grass Parnassus*. It may well be that they gain by being read within their full context, or that the context adds a further level of complexity to the individual poems. But context is always pretty much infinitely extendable unless you set some limits.

The main thing is to remember that poems aren't paraphrasable; they don't say anything except what they say: making a paraphrase to find out how the poem works and what its words add up to is like killing a hare to see how fast it runs. The best thing to do is just to let the words enter your mind and see what happens. Then work out *how* it happens. Or as Denise Riley aptly puts it, citing the words of Gerry and the Pacemakers in the early 1960s, 'How do you do what you do to me? I wish I knew'.[4]

I was thinking about all this, especially the relation between words and the kind of reference or affect they carry, and reading books by writers in case they had something interesting to say about it, when I came across a comment by the novelist Amina Cain. She writes, '[I]n my novel *Indelicacy*, when the narrator Vitória is visiting the desert, she says, "I pulled my hair into a loose bun, but not like a dancer would do it." There is no dancer in this sentence, yet I see the dancer.' I think what Cain means is that there is no dancer in the narrative, because obviously there *is* a dancer in that sentence. The word 'dancer' necessarily evokes a dancer, an idea or an image of a dancer, however ephemeral that impression may be; in fact that's the whole point of similes. This is an essential fact about poetry: nothing that is in it isn't there. Every word makes an impression, often several impressions overlaid, depending on the resonances and associations the word rouses in the reader's memory or imagination. And these impressions can continue to transform in the reader's mind as the words that follow redefine or reshape the perception of the words that came before. Reading a poem, like listening to music or looking at a painting, is a process. It inspires thought and, more important, questionings.

In this intimate encounter with language we come up against what we think we know and what we think we are. But I'm not sure my thoughts are ever entirely my own, even the most private or personal ones, not when they take shape in language. ('What is the language using us for?' to cite W.S. Graham's line again.) All kinds of thoughts hover in the cultural ether, in ready-made language, waiting to be adopted by us like clothes we try on for fit, though we can and do also alter our sense of our selves to fit the ideas we meet. That's what culture is to a large extent: the accumulated expressions of past thinking, from thousands of years to just a few minutes ago, which is why truth can be such a difficult thing for people to agree about.

The French philosopher Maurice Merleau-Ponty says

at the end of the preface to the *Phenomenology of Perception* that art (he instances Balzac, Proust, Valéry and Cézanne) demonstrates 'the same kind of attentiveness and wonder, the same demand for awareness, the same will to seize the meaning of the world or of history as that meaning comes into being' as phenomenology does, and in this is part of 'the general effort of modern thought'. It is not necessary to think of poetry as a replacement for religion, as some have argued in the past, to recognise that the aesthetic experience, which includes reading poems, may involve us in a kind of profundity not to be found anywhere else. Like any good work of art it leaves us with a sense that there is more to it than we can reach, something that finds an echo in ourselves so that we try to find the right wavelength to explore it, trying to plumb the depths of the thinking and feeling and perhaps the enhanced sense of being that constitutes our aesthetic experience.

This is not the place to start a disquisition on aesthetics, but I do want to put in a plea for the idea of beauty, not as a set of ideals or a benchmark but as something about a great poem or other work of art that accompanies or delineates our aesthetic experience. It may be to do with the pleasure the poem gives the reader, or its formal perfection, or the framing of its political or ethical convictions, but whatever it is it has the potential to make us feel more alive and more aware of ourselves. It can also make us more aware of the society or the world we live in. Blake's 'London', for example, sparks a sense of outrage and anger at corruption and exploitation, but rather than simply doing that, it sets the reader's immediate response within the measure and power of the four stanzas, offering a glimpse of a possible social beauty to be sought after the overthrow of a tyrannical social order, anchoring the sense of anger in a calmer vision of hope for a better future.

There is an argument here for a surplus, something glimpsed but never fully grasped in reading a poem. 'Writing, whatever else it is doing, is always getting at something that it never quite obtains. There is always something unsaid, something that clings to writing like a shadow.' The writer and political commentator Richard Seymour here is articulating an important truth: because language and the world are not the same thing, because we have to learn to use language, there will always be a degree of approximation in what we say or write, and often an accommodation to what has already been said. The shadow, the glimpse, is frequently denied in the interests of clarity or certainty, but it's one of the functions of poetry (and other literary forms) to reveal its presence, to make the reader feel that there is more than the words apparently say. A gap appears, a distance, a different angle, something that provides an intimation of another way of seeing and induces a sense of estrangement from the clichés and banalities of everyday language and so-called 'common sense'. The French writer and psychoanalyst Julia Kristeva puts this well when she uses the trope of exile to explain what she means: 'Our present age is one of exile. How can one avoid sinking into the mire of common sense, if not by becoming a stranger to one's own country, language, sex, and identity? Writing is impossible without some kind of exile.' There's no sense in just repeating what's already been said and done: thinking clearly, especially in poems, means trying to stand outside the language we live in and through from day to day and trying to use it to see things in a new way.

I'd been thinking about this, and about dreams because you're so often a stranger to yourself in dreams and dreams have quite a lot in common with poems, as has often been pointed out, not least by Freud and after him the surrealists. They both rely on ambiguity and figurative language, for example – dreams because they often express things that have been repressed and can't be shown directly, poems because they want the layering or concatenation of ideas that enable both feeling and cognitive understanding to coexist, to incorporate words, form, feeling and thinking into a single experience that is both intellectual and somatic, conscious and unconscious, known in the mind and in the body.

I was absorbed in the novelist M. John Harrison's 2023 non-memoir *Wish I Was Here* a while back, and was taken by his view of this: 'I like any book or film or group of images that stacks up ambiguities then walks away from them. I'm overly stimulated by that, and indeed disappointed when an argument comes too far into focus. I don't want to be guided by conclusions; they're so often indifferent & boring. I want meaning lodged somewhere I can see it, but not quite get at it, the way it is in a dream.' Glimpsed but not fully known, and not entirely knowable, either, refusing to come completely into focus, like dreams when you try to recapture them, or ghosts. Much of our fear and desire is repressed and unavailable to our conscious knowledge, but still shaping us and capable of constructing dream scenarios that distort or blur the things we want to know. Poems can often achieve a comparable effect, whether or not they draw on dream material or create simulacra of dreams, because the unconscious works by imagination and association and metaphor. There's an idea in some circles, prevalent in the teaching of poetry in schools, that poems are a kind of puzzle and that once you can see the simple fact beneath the fancy metaphor you've solved the poem, when all you've really done is reduce it to a prose paraphrase. As I've already said, there's no meaning separate from the poem: if you unwrap a poem to find the meaning, you discover there's nothing inside.

Like any work of art, poems need you to give them your time, not because they are intrinsically difficult (though they may be) but because it takes time to listen to yourself, to attend to your response and find out what's going on in you when you read a poem. This can be difficult because we aren't used to doing it, but that is precisely why it's a good thing to do. Our heads and hearts are full of second-hand language: it's refreshing to get some distance from it. When I was a child, between the ages of four and ten, I used often to hear voices in my head, ordinary speaking voices but just too far away or too quiet or too blurred for me to catch what they were saying. At the same time I could make my surroundings, including people, become very small. I liked these episodes, partly because they were very slightly scary and partly because they held out the promise of comprehensibility without ever providing it. The voices were always just out of reach, never quite comprehensible, sounding like grown-up conversation, disconcertingly mysterious. They also seemed to repeat themselves, going round and round as if on a loop, sometimes becoming more and more intense until they stopped. I think on balance that I found them more comforting than alarming, but there was a strong element of frustration at not being able to hear any actual words. Instead the babble functioned as patterns of sound and cadence, almost akin to music, like an earworm; it was recognisably adult speech but it was also a form of play, the way children make nonsense sentences when they want to imitate a foreign language, and as it was like play it beckoned me into its world until it faded away and I was back in the real world again.

Before they can speak, children babble, and something of that pre-linguistic childhood pleasure in the sound of words is embedded in much poetry, not just in rhyme and alliteration but in all the instances of repeated or echoed or mirrored sounds in a poem. It's important to pay attention to them because they're an intrinsic part of the poems in which they occur: they are a source of pleasure, and like all the other non-factual elements in a poem they colour the way we read it and shape the kind of knowledge poems give us. It's part of the way poetic thinking and the type of knowing we gain from poetry is different from scientific or factual knowledge. One works by inclusivity, bringing disparate or varied elements together, the other by exclusion of all but the most salient facts. Both are necessary, both need work if they are to be understood. People sometimes argue that difficult poetry is elitist, a term I dislike, related as it is to the populist disdain for specialists and to the thoughtless, in fact greedy idea that everything should be immediately available. Consumer poetry for a consumer society. Elitism, a lazy term at best, implies privileged access to which one is not entitled, whereas the history of poetry is full of examples of poets who have educated themselves by their own efforts, like Blake, or indeed Hardy, as well as writers and readers who have studied more formally. Tackling difficulty in poetry as in any field is interesting and rewarding. Poems can create or demonstrate new thoughts or new ways of thinking, they can make connections between ideas, they can inform, make you more fully aware, and more alert to the global or human implications of factual information.

People are sometimes put off poetry by one of its defining features, its form. Poetry, unlike prose, doesn't fill up the page: it either uses a defined form or invents one of its own, usually based on schemes of rhythm and rhyme, and traditionally related to the poem's topic. Milton, for example, when he came to write *Paradise Lost*, chose to write it in blank verse because, he argued, 'Rime [is] no necessary Adjunct or true Ornament of Poem or good Verse, in longer Works especially, but the Invention of a barbarous Age, to set off wretched matter and lame Meeter; grac't indeed since by the use of some famous modern Poets, carried away by Custom, but much to their own vexation, hindrance, and constraint to express many things otherwise, and for the most part worse, than else they would have exprest them.' He was proud to be the first to restore the example 'of ancient liberty recover'd to Heroic Poem from the troublesom and modern bondage of Rimeing'.[5]

The idea of freedom in poetry, and its relation to constraints of form, recurs as rules are tightened or loosened and as fashions come and go. Take for instance the 'imagist' movement for free verse (or *vers libre*) in the early twentieth century. The leading figure in that movement, Ezra Pound, was battling what he saw as the stifling and conservative conformity of the lyric poetry that was culturally dominant at the time. Along with his fellow poet Hilda Doolittle, who wrote as H.D., and others, he drew on French and classical Greek models and derived his aesthetic argument in part from psychology, defining the image, the central feature of the poems, as 'an intellectual and emotional complex in an instant of time'.

Sometimes, though, the constraints that shape a poem and its form are less visible. Many of the lyric poems of the Renaissance and later are translations or adaptations of Latin or Greek originals, or variations on classical themes like *carpe diem*. Early in the twentieth century, the French writer Raymond Roussel invented a method of translation in which he ignored the sense of the word and translated its shape instead, using the consonants to define the shape of the word he selected.[6] Georges Perec wrote a novel without using the letter 'e' (*La disparition*, 1969, translated as *A void*), and other members of the French group Oulipo have experimented with a huge variety of invented and inventive limiting rules.[7] Poets have always written with constraints of some sort: formal constraints like verse form (couplets, sonnets, sestinas, haiku and all kinds of stanza forms), metrical patterns, rhythm, rhyme and so on, not to mention the more idiosyncratic uses of repetition, or acrostics and anagrams, often as a feature of occasional poems (so for example the first letter of each line of an epithalamion might spell out the names of the bride and groom).

Or sometimes poems are written *against* constraints: one of the central activities of the surrealists was automatic writing, the deliberate attempt to prevent anything getting in the way of transcribing whatever comes into the mind, in the hope of setting down their unconscious thoughts and desires before the repressions of capitalist society distorted, tamed or betrayed the impulse. Immediacy in the service of thinking truth: '*La pensée se fait dans la bouche*' ('thinking happens in the mouth'), as Tristan Tzara, leading Dadaist and surrealist poet, put it. But it turns out there's not so much difference between the two approaches as at first appears. Both aim to avoid the banality of superficial expressiveness, the easy expression in language of the self as a social being, a creation of social language. T.S. Eliot memorably claimed in 'Tradition and the Individual Talent' that 'Poetry is not a turning loose of emotion, but an escape from emotion; it is not the expression of personality, but an escape from personality. But, of course, only those who have personality and emotions know what it means to want to escape from these things.' However, he was wrong to express the process as escape rather than transformation or re-creation. The only evidence as far as the reader is concerned is the poem itself, and poems, however impersonal in their intention and construction, still bear the marks of the poet in their cadence, their vocabulary and the way they do what they do. Frank O'Hara, defending his work against charges of obscurity, once wrote that 'Perhaps the obscurity comes in here, in the relationship between the surface and the meaning, but I like it that way since the one is the other (you have to use words) and I hope the poem to be the subject, not just about it.'

O'Hara is right: the poem is always the subject of the poem. All the contemporary poets I most admire write to find ways to make the poem work, on its own terms, 'to be the subject, not just about it'. I mean poets like the late Tom Raworth, of whom Luke Roberts has written, 'nobody has yet matched the *speed* of Raworth's thought, where "any piece of language / will fuse with any other piece"'.[8] Other poets I would also recommend include the late John James, Lisa Robertson, Denise Riley, Peter Gizzi, Rae Armantrout. There are many more, and a good way to get a broader overview is to look at some anthologies that can give an idea of what has been going on in the publishing margins over the last fifty years.[9]

I started writing poetry seriously at university; though I'd written a few poems at school, I didn't have any confidence in them. In my first term or two, I tried to follow the models that were around, but found that Auden and Larkin and Thom Gunn failed to ignite any spark in me. Ginsberg and Ferlinghetti seemed more congenial, but when I tried writing in their modes, the results felt trivial and silly. Reading science fiction, especially Philip K. Dick but Brian Aldiss and others as well, loosened my imagination, and reading William Carlos Williams and then Robert Creeley allowed me to stop trying to be gnomic or clever and let the language breathe. The poems that followed were better, though limited in scope, and I began to understand that line endings were part of the form of a poem, and that thought had rhythms of its own. I became very interested in the concept of time, an interest that has surfaced again quite often in subsequent writing.

I want to say something here about my compositional practice. It's not unusual for poets these days to include in their texts fragments of language culled from various places elsewhere, to fold into their writing quotations and to produce in various densities kinds of bricolage of other people's work, and I've often done it myself, using snippets of quotation or conversation or memories or dreams in my poems. About twenty years ago or so, I wanted to find a working method that was more schematic, more demanding, and which allowed me to use other people's words to make representations of my thought and feeling. The first product was a sequence of fourteen poems, love poems in fact, composed entirely of words from Thomas Hardy's collected poems, one word or short phrase from each poem taken in the order in which they were printed and chosen because they worked to make the thoughts I wanted to make. That was the main change I aimed to make in the way I wrote – I wanted to *make* poems, not just *use* language, rather as a sculptor like Phyllida Barlow took scraps of materials to make sculptures. Except that I got all my materials out of the one place.

My next project, *The Glass Bell*, used a different technique. I wrote a series of twenty-two fourteen-line poems, three sets of seven, and a PS, thinking about and using Jacques Derrida's 1974 essay *Glas*. The book's three sections, titled Glossalgia (which means a pain in the tongue), Glossolalia (speaking in tongues) and Glossoplegia (paralysis of the tongue), all complications to do with utterance, develop the phonic axis between the ambiguities of '*glas*' (which means 'death knell', literally or figuratively) and the various meanings of the English word 'gloss'. This sets up the basic terms of the poem's material operation, and becomes more emphatic in the third section, where there is a consistent patterning of words beginning with or containing 'gl'. The text itself derives from a rough acoustic translation of the top line (only) of the two columns of the Derrida source text, starting at the beginning and leaving off somewhere around page 100. (I used the 1974 Galilée edition, chastely bound in paper wrappers and printed for the most part in two columns of different font size with occasional incursions from a third column in a smaller sans serif font.) The poem bears no direct trace of the different strands in the two columns, although Derrida's polyvocality is carried through or gestured towards at other levels, as are aspects of the things he's talking about. The first draft of the poem retained the order in which the lines were composed, but in later workings some of the poems altered their place in the sequence, and a few fragments from outside the text found their way into the poems; as a result it is not directly possible to read my text back into Derrida's, although with effort and detective work it could probably be done. Occasionally, though, the practice of acoustic – Rousselian – translation was sometimes varied by the direct translation of a word or phrase; and I sometimes took other liberties.

I'll explain what I mean. The opening line of the first sequence, Glossalgia, begins with a word selected because it can be both French and English. 'Chose' (simultaneously 'thing' in French and 'selected' in English) formally, if ironically, inaugurates the poem's procedure. It replaces '*du reste*' in the opening of the first French line, which reads '*quoi du reste aujourd'hui, pour nous, ici, maintenant*' and '*ce qui est resté d'un Rembrandt déchiré en petits*'. '*Quoi*' becomes 'wire' The first two lines transform the French to read:

> Chose wire today for news to see maintained
> skies [ce qui] resisted down and more remembered
>   [Rembrandt] cheer.

That should give some idea of how the first stages of the composition process worked. It got more complicated as the poem proceeded and other kinds of fluency, reference and allusion were required, but the fundamentals remained the same.

I returned to writing with strict constraints during the first Covid-19 lockdown, when I wrote a sequence of twenty-five poems in various self-chosen forms, called *Home James*, the first word because that's where I was in lockdown, the second because I took all the words from Henry James' novel *The Sense of the Past*, one of the two he left unfinished when he died. I took mostly single words, occasionally two-word phrases, and used them to give body to what I could otherwise only feel as a vague outline of what I might call thought-effects, sensing which words might work, working quickly to catch the thinking as it developed a poetic form. The actual process of selecting the words is opaque to me: I will pick a word or a couple of words from here, another one from there, one from over there, put them together, reject one or two, try others, always trying to bring my blurry thoughts into the proper verbal focus. It was important that the words were not a direct expression of what was in my mind, so that the finished poem would be made of material that was already in the external world, a sort of object, untouched by direct personal expression. This is not to say that the poems do not involve personal emotions, personal feelings; they do, but the emotions get transformed or reshaped in the process of finding the verbal material. Like novels, in fact like all art, poems have to work through some elements of the relation between, in general terms, reality and form, and it's in doing that, in testing the constraints – chosen or discovered – that the poem comes into being. W.S. Graham catches the difficulty of this as he tries to find the right words to type onto the blank paper in front of him: a poem, he says, 'is a public place / Achieved against subjective odds and then / Mainly an obstacle to what I mean.'[10]

6

Reversing Babel: The Invisible Arts of Translation

The limits of my language are the limits of my world.
Ludwig Wittgenstein, *Tractatus Logico-Philosophicus*

The constraints I was writing about in the last chapter are closely related to the constraints inherent in translation; I worked as a translator on and off for thirty years, which intensified my sense of the arbitrary and labile nature of words. In his essay on translation, Walter Benjamin expounds the quasi-mystical idea that there is an ideal version of a text lurking behind whatever language form it takes, and that it's the translator's job to discover it behind the source text and make a new approximation to it in the target text, rather than just translating from the words of one language into the words of another. I don't believe this, but I have generally found it a helpful idea to work with as it coincides with my sense that the process of translation involves a third stage between the two languages where clouds of possibilities swirl around in my mind until the best word or phrase falls into place. Translations are always provisional and incomplete, often inadequate, and never final or perfect.

I agree with Edith Grossman (one of the great translators) that literary translation is a kind of writing, an attempt, as she puts it, to enable the readers of the translated text to perceive it 'emotionally and artistically, in a manner that parallels and corresponds to the esthetic experience of its first readers'. By literary translation, I mean the translation of texts that require more than the mere transmission of information, texts in which the medium and the message are inseparable, writing that could be described as imaginative knowledge, primarily novels and poems but also some essays and autobiography. It is these translations in particular that need to be remade from generation to generation as language changes, even though some 'classic' translations – Florio's versions of Montaigne's *Essays*, the exuberant seventeenth-century translation of Rabelais by Urquhart and Le Motteux, Scott Moncrieff's Proust, Pope's Homer, Dryden's *Aeneid*, Burton's *1001 Nights*, Constance Garnett's Chekhov, Ezra Pound's poems from the Chinese – continue to be read for their own qualities as literature.*

* In some cases, the qualities they are read for definitely do not include perfect accuracy. Scott Moncrieff's translation of Proust is notorious for its howlers, and Pound's poems have only a loose connection to their originals. Pope's translations of *The Odyssey* and *The Iliad* and Dryden's version of Virgil's *Aeneid* both elaborate considerably on the Greek and Latin, but then that was the way people tended to translate at the time. But Florio's Montaigne has the dual virtues of being almost contemporary with the French and being very lively prose, and something similar could be said of Sir Thomas Urquhart's translation (continued by Peter Le Motteux) of Rabelais, which, to

Why translate? First because it's a public service, providing readers with access to works they would otherwise be unable to read, and thereby access to other cultures and other world views, broadening minds and encouraging a kind of hospitality to different ways of life and different attitudes and ways of thinking, and a tolerance that our world stands very much in need of. For a long time, British publishers had a very poor record of commissioning translations, and we still have a long way to go to catch up with much of the world's literature. The British have long been the most insular readers in Europe, with a tendency to regard foreign ideas with suspicion as subversive and wrong, and are only now beginning to shake off those assumptions (though Brexit shows how far we still have to go).

The second reason for translating is because the best translations can sometimes reveal aspects of the writing that remain hidden or veiled in the original. Timothy Mathews, writing about translating Roland Barthes, highlights the positive side of any reader's limited vision; he writes about rediscovering the interplay between what's lost and what's found in translation. 'For it's always both at once: holding on to the idea of an original and letting it go; holding on to what I'm hearing, and that it matters to try and convey

---

quote the 1653 title page, contains 'the five Books of the Lives, Heroick Deeds, and Sayings of GARGANTUA and his Sonne PANTAGRUEL Together With the Pantagrueline Prognostication, the Oracle of the divine *Bacbuc*, and response of the bottle. Hereunto are annexed the Navigations unto the sounding Isle, and the Isle of the Apedefts: and likewise the Philosophical cream with a *Limosm* Epistle. All done by Mr. FRANCIS RABELAIS, in the *French* Tongue, and now faithfully translated into *English*.'

it, while letting go of the idea that what I'm hearing is congruent to the hearing of others; and still less to a writer's original intention.' All translations, all translators, have their own personal relation to the world of language, just as every language encodes a different way of looking at the world. Where a book has been translated several, or even many times over the years, as Michael Wood says, 'we can prefer one version to another, but then we are choosing one understanding over another: either (mostly) the understanding we ourselves have, or (better) an understanding we hadn't thought of before'.

Translators, in fact, are writers. Translating poetry or fiction or essays or even philosophy and theory demands a degree of attentiveness and care for language that brings it very close to original writing. Translation is also the closest kind of reading: a translator needs ideally to be aware of every aspect of the writer's words, from their meaning, associations and implications to the rhythm and tone of the sentences and the ambiguities and allusions in them, and then to try to reproduce all that in their own language. Or at least produce something that's both readable and true to the spirit and body of the original. Three and a quarter centuries ago, Dryden wrote that 'the qualification of a translator worth reading must be a mastery of the language he translates out of, and that he translates into; but if a deficience be to be allowed in either, it is in the original, since if he be but master enough of the tongue of his author as to be master of his sense, it is possible for him to express that sense with eloquence in his own, if he have a thorough command of that. But without the latter he can never arrive at the useful and the delightful, without which reading is a penance and fatigue.' I think that's still true; the delight in reading, the pleasure and sometimes the sheer joy of it, fuels engagement with the difficulties of the translator's work.

There is another school of thought, though, represented well by this comment by the translator Lawrence Venuti: 'The effect of transparency in translation is illusionistic: accessibility or easy readability . . . leads the reader to believe that the signified has been transferred without any substantial difference.' According to this theory of translation, the text should be sufficiently distant from ordinary English to keep the reader aware that she is reading a translation, as not to do that diminishes the reader's sense of a different mode of perception or a different sort of understanding of the world and absorbs the foreign into the new discourse of the translation in a kind of colonial appropriation. Yet however knowledgeable and skilled a translator may be, there is always a mismatch between the original and the translated version, stemming from the fact that languages are inseparable from their cultures and that, as the French philosopher Paul Ricoeur pointed out, with particular reference to philosophical terms but with general application, vocabulary, syntax and 'turns of phrase do not serve as a vehicle of the same cultural legacies; and what is to be said about the half-silent connotations, which alter the best-defined denotations of the original vocabulary, and which drift, as it were, between the signs, the sentences, the sequences whether short or long'. Language shapes cultures and is shaped by them: a cup of tea can be a startlingly different experience in different countries. This seems to me to be enough on its own without consciously creating more distance between the two languages.

My own involvement with translation began when I was fifteen and starting my A-level classes. Despite hardly having done any German before, I'd been placed in the modern-languages sixth form, studying French, German and English, and I had nine or ten weeks to learn enough German to take the O-level exam (the precursor of GCSE) and try to catch up with the rest of the class. After a few weeks I started to dream in German, but without understanding what the voices in my dreams were saying. Like the voices I used to hear in my childhood, they were patterns of sound and cadence rather than actual words, but this time the pattern was recognisably German and the frustration at not understanding them was more closely focused. Those dreams stopped after five or six weeks as my German improved, but I think my need to find out what those voices – both the original voices and the German ones – were saying was one of the impulses that led me, eventually, to translation. Certainly the translations we had to do each week from passages of German and French, usually extracts taken from literary works, were what I found most exciting about studying languages, and I continued to translate in my spare time. The fact that there was not just one way to translate what the other language was saying, so you had to interpret what you were reading, made the search for what felt like the best words utterly absorbing.

'Translators are people who read books for us,' writes the novelist and translator Tim Parks, reminding us that translation is, as I've said, first and foremost a kind of reading, and so also of interpretation. But it could be added that translation begins as a way of reading for oneself, both the translation into our native tongue of texts written in other languages and the everyday activity of relating what we read to our own experience: the word 'translation', after all, historically also could mean to express differently, or to transcribe or transplant, or even move something or somebody from one place to another. In her brilliant and fascinating book about being a translator, *This Little Art*, Kate Briggs describes translation, the impulse to translate, as 'a laborious way of making the work present to yourself, of finding it again for yourself, *for yourself*'.

My first serious forays into the practice of translation (excluding those school exercises) came when I was a university student trying to read poems by Rimbaud and Valéry and translating them to try to get closer to them; and in my early twenties when I was trying to get to grips with Jacques Lacan's psychoanalytical writings in French. Hardly anything by Lacan had been translated in 1971, and recognising that I didn't know enough about the psychoanalytic context of his work, I abandoned any attempt to translate whole essays, trying instead to work out a few pages here and there. There were too many loose possibilities floating around in my head as I read his prose: only by finding a way to express his thinking in English could I pin it down enough to think about it for myself.

It was the period when I was enthusiastically and deeply involved in far-left politics, trying to fit Marxism, psychoanalysis and poetry together into a coherent left-revolutionary aesthetic, something the French surrealists seemed to have been doing fifty years earlier. I started translating French surrealist poetry as a way of discovering what it was trying to do. I read André Breton with excitement and translated some of Paul Éluard's poems, but it was Tristan Tzara who really captured my attention, especially his long poem *L'Homme approximatif*, much of which I translated and fragments of which I incorporated into poems I was writing myself. (The title itself, which I translated as 'Roughly Speaking', became the title of a book of poems I published some years later.) I also tried translating some poems by Brecht, but couldn't find a way of making them work properly in English. I wasn't trying to write definitive translations; it was more a question of working through things, a process rather than an end in itself, seeing what worked in my own writing and what was inert, second-hand or merely decorative.

I was thinking a lot about translation then too, because so much of the political theory and history I was reading, from Marx onwards, was translated from other languages, and sometimes felt awkward or disjointed to the extent that I didn't know whether to trust what I read. Was it made awkward on purpose to remind me I was reading a translation, or was the awkwardness a product of carelessness or mistranslation? With the languages I knew, I could sometimes check the translated version against the original, but in other cases I wasn't competent to do that. Where I could, I started to retranslate essays or parts of essays I thought misrepresented the original, though I would be reluctant now to claim that I really knew what I was doing. It was all a bit scrappy.

Then, fortuitously enough, Michael Kidron of Pluto Press asked me out of the blue whether I'd be interested in translating a book for them. I thought it would be interesting and helpful to find out what it would be like to do a whole book, so I said yes. The book, as I mentioned earlier, was the abridgement by Daniel Guérin of his two-volume work on class struggle in the French First Republic. It was a daunting prospect, as I knew practically nothing about the subject, so I started by reading everything I could find, and collected a small library of books I could use for reference purposes. When I began the work of putting the text into English, I quickly became aware of the sort of problems that translators always face: how to translate names and technical terms and key words, and how far to explain the ones that are unfamiliar to anglophone readers. Because the existing translations of books on the subject didn't always use the same terms, I had to do a lot of cross-referencing in libraries and among my own books before I was confident which would be the best ones to use. The whole process was difficult and took somewhat longer than the publisher had anticipated, but it was hugely educational; I had also proved to myself that I could do it well, and that (for the most part) I'd enjoyed doing it.

What I liked best was the twofold task of translation and research. The academic books I went on to translate over the next decade and a half ranged across a variety of subjects, from social psychology and linguistics to economics, political theory and medieval history, and they all required a lot of background research. I took to working whenever I could in the university library so I could look up anything I needed on the spot. I soon discovered that French practices of quotation and referencing could be very approximate, and sometimes completely wrong, with quotations included in the text without acknowledgement, or the author's own paraphrase printed as a quotation. I had to spend hours checking footnotes and finding the actual quotations, which taught me a lot about editing and research as well as allowing me to discover all sorts of books I would never have encountered otherwise. (That, of course, is one of the great benefits of libraries that keep their books available on open shelves; you never know what you may find adjacent to the book you're looking for. Alberto Manguel quotes the great scholar and book collector Aby Warburg saying that the purpose of libraries with open stacks is to let you discover that what you really need to read is the book next to the one you've come to find.)

I also learnt that translation was very poorly paid and translators were generally undervalued (though that situation has improved somewhat in the decades since). I knew that that was the case, but the reality was still painful. That first translation can be excluded, though, because instead of being paid in money, I asked for my fee to be used to buy me a complete set of Freud's works, the Standard Edition, at the publisher's discount rate, which added an extra chunk of purchasing power to my payment. But for subsequent books I had to put up with the rates of pay the publishers were offering. As I was not bilingual – in fact, my only qualification was a B in French A level and a good ear – I didn't work very quickly, which made the rate of pay worse, and it was before word processors were available, so I would translate the book in longhand and revise the translation as I typed it out with two fingers. It was not a way to get rich. Eventually, when I was rung up one day by an editor at a well-known publishing house and asked if I would translate a new book by a French sociologist who had specifically named me as the translator he wanted, I said I would do it if they would pay me the rate recommended by the Translators Association, which was some 80 per cent more than they were offering. They declined, quite forcefully, and put the phone down. I didn't hear from them again. That was when I decided to stop doing that sort of work.

A little later, though, I was asked to contribute a translation to a series of texts in political thought published by Cambridge University Press. The text was *The Theory of the Four Movements*, by the utopian thinker Charles Fourier, with an introduction to be written by Gareth Stedman Jones. It's a weird book in many ways, but it played an important part in the development of socialism. In it, Fourier sets out his discovery that the world is still in the process of development, and what we call 'civilisation' is a late form of the Chaos period. The four movements of the title are kinds of attraction; he believed that Newton's discovery of the attractive power of gravity (labelled 'Material Movement' in Fourier's system) was only one of the four powers of attraction at work in the universe, the others being Social Movement, Animal Movement and Organic Movement; and that 'passionate attraction' was the source of all movement, 'the drive given by nature, prior to reflection and persistent despite the opposition of reason, duty, prejudice, etc.'. Only when the Chaos period ends will mankind see the Dawn of Happiness. There are complicated movements towards the Apogee of Happiness, which will eventually be followed by a slow period of decline until the animal and vegetable world finally ends. Much of the physical change that Fourier believes will accompany the progress out of Chaos is fanciful: the climate warms, the sea becomes a sort of lemonade, hostile creatures become tame and useful, and so on. But much is serious and important, like the full equality – indeed superiority – of women, the fulfilment of all sexual desires, and the improved organisation of industry and social life in harmonious accord with, and led by, the passions. Social life would be communal, associations of 1,620 men, women and children living in 'phalanxes'. Researching, editing and translating the book, with its bizarre and imaginative politics and its enviable self-confidence, was absorbingly complex and it reignited my interest in the problems of translation; I returned to translating poems from French and German, partly as aids to reading but also in order to experiment with different ways of doing it and, as ever, to deepen my reading of the originals.

It was a good thing I was becoming interested in translation again because the next thing that happened was that I was asked whether I'd be prepared to translate one of the volumes of Proust's *À la recherche du temps perdu*. Penguin was proposing a new translation, each volume to be translated by a different person – both to demonstrate the provisionality and variety of possibilities offered by Proust's text, and to avoid the inevitable delay inherent in commissioning a single person to do the whole thing. I was uncertain at first whether to take it on: I'd read most of it, but not for many years, and even then I had tended to skip the difficult or long-winded bits. Also it would be a more public task than any of the translations I'd done during the previous twenty years and I was nervous of the critical reaction to my work. But I remembered that Barthes somewhere asks whether anyone has ever read every word of Proust, Balzac or *War and Peace*, adding that one of the great pleasures of reading Proust is that you never skip the same bits twice, so I took courage from that and said yes, I would. The difficult thing was deciding which volume to choose. The opening sentence of the first volume is one of the best known of all literary sentences – '*Longtemps je me suis couché de bonne heure*' ('For a long time I went to bed early') – but it is famously difficult to translate into English without losing some of the nuance of the original. I didn't want to start by worrying about that, so I chose the final volume, in many ways the most interesting and the most satisfying of them all. And the second shortest. It was only some years later that a friend pointed out that it was also the volume that had the fewest sales, as readers' stamina often became exhausted before they reached the end.

Writing about her experience of translating Proust, Lydia Davis (who opted to translate that first volume) makes a distinction between accurate and exact translation: an exact translation being one that as well as providing an accurate account of the meaning tries wherever possible to retain elements of the source text, even those that are partly invisible; so that when she could, she would choose a word that shared the etymology of the word to be translated, and try to retain the dynamic of the sentence, its rhythm, structure and features like alliteration, staying 'as close as possible to the original without sacrificing natural or pleasing English'. The opposite approach, I suppose, would be a translation that reimagined or reinterpreted the original in an attempt to re-create the impressions it makes on the reader, even perhaps transposing the whole cultural sphere of reference that surrounds any work in another language and rewriting the book in English. This kind of wholesale reimagining of a work can be done, as in Philip Terry's reworking of Dante (of which more later), but Proust's world, different as it is from our own, is not so far removed that it would benefit from that sort of updating. Also, and more significantly, unlike Dante's *Divine Comedy*, it is neither a poem nor an allegory, two more reasons why that kind of treatment would be inappropriate. It seemed then and still seems to me that the best way to make Proust available to non-French-speaking readers is to render as clear and exact an equivalent as possible, using annotation where necessary to explain unfamiliar names or terms or references, and to avoid the weakness that Terence Kilmartin finds in Scott Moncrieff's translation when he says that 'a whiff of Gallicism clings to some of the longer periods, obscuring the sense and falsifying the tone', something akin to writing with a French accent. There is a big difference between that and allowing the reader to be aware that this is a French novel.

The task of translating Proust posed difficulties, of course, but they were often also pleasures and sometimes small triumphs. He is a witty writer, often funny, wryly depicting pomposity, self-importance or distinctions of class, and much of the comedy lies in his use of language. Near the start of the volume I was translating, for instance, Proust has his narrator include a long extract from the Goncourt Journal. The brothers Jules and Edmond de Goncourt kept very extensive gossipy, literary journals, which they composed together from 1851 until Jules' death in 1870; Edmond continued them alone until his own death in 1896.* The point about them is that they were written in a somewhat precious, overwrought style, which Proust pastiches in about eight pages of exaggerated prose purporting to come from an in fact non-existent volume. The challenge in translating this short section was to find a way of echoing both the Goncourts' style and Proust's pastiche of it without going over the top, keeping the balance right and remembering that it is this extract, which Gilberte lends him to read in bed on his last night in Tansonville, that gives Marcel the impetus to think back over his life in a series of revisionary retrospects.

Proust's sentences can be long and convoluted, but they are also musical, using sequences of sound, tonality, near anagrams and rhythm, making the work sometimes as hard to translate as a poem by the notoriously difficult French symbolist poet Stéphane Mallarmé (in fact Gide said he'd like to see Proust's sentences set out on the page like Mallarmé's poem 'Un coup de dés jamais n'abolira le hasard').† Sometimes a fraction of these effects can be achieved in

---

* The Goncourts were an extraordinary pair. In the twenty-two years from 1848 to 1870, they spent only two days apart. Jules was eight years younger than his brother, but it was as if they were identical twins. When they were writing the diary they dictated it to each other, corrected and revised each other's sentences so that it is impossible to identify any part as written by either brother.

† This poem (the title in English is 'One throw of the dice will never abolish chance') is set out on the page in diagonals and zigzags, in different-sized type, from very large capitals to smaller lower case, and with a lot of white space. If Proust's prose were set out in the same way it might provide readers with a diagram of the sentence structure and make clearer the relations between its different parts.

English, but most of them unfortunately have to remain a feature only of the original French because they just don't work in another language. It may have been partly a wish to compensate for the untranslatable elements that led other translators to lean too far, in my view, towards interpretation, elaborating on Proust's vocabulary or filling in missing detail. Proust usually just writes 'he said' or 'she said', rather than using words like retorted, replied, questioned, but most of his translators seem to have been allergic to plainness. Andreas Mayor's translation of *Le temps retrouvé*, which formed the basis for Terence Kilmartin's version and the later revision of it, contains scarcely any sentences that haven't been rewritten, with allusions spelt out and lexical neutrality abandoned. I wanted to keep as close to Proust's own formulations as I could.

The earlier translations have many virtues, though, and sometimes I would have been lost without one or another of them. Shortly after I'd finished translating the Goncourt pastiche, I encountered a second, rather different challenge when for a couple of days I'd been puzzling over a sentence that wouldn't come right. I could see what it meant, I could feel how it ought to go in English, but none of the versions I wrote down was any good. I went over and over it until I almost decided to break my rule of not consulting any of the earlier translations. Then suddenly it came to me, the perfect way to make the sentence work in English. I was so pleased with it that I did break my rule, wanting to see what inferior versions the other translators had come up with. As I thumbed through the pages, I discovered that each translator of the four I consulted had translated the sentence in exactly the same way as I had. My two days of frustration had been useful as a test case, but two days was a long time to be making no progress: I resolved that next time I was stuck I would turn to earlier versions to see how they'd resolved the difficulty.

One of the curious things about translating a writer as distinctive as Proust was that as I grew more and more familiar with his prose style, his syntax and his way of thinking, I started to live inside it, and my own style, even my thinking, adapted itself to the rhythms of his French. To use an obsolete sense of the word 'translate', I was, for a while and intermittently, 'translated' into Proust; and Proust regarded himself as a kind of translator, quite separately from his work translating Ruskin's *Sesame and Lilies* and *The Bible of Amiens*. In one of his meditations about the nature of writing, he describes how he 'slowly became aware that the essential book, the only true book, was not something the writer needs to invent, in the usual sense of the word, so much as to translate, because it already exists within each of us. The writer's task and duty are those of a translator.' Translating Proust's self-translation felt more deeply involving than just translating his language; and then, language being part of a culture, Proust's draws deeply on his deep reading of French literature. His prose is not only idiosyncratic, it is very literary, shaped by his own reading, particularly by Ruskin, Saint-Simon and Chateaubriand. I've hardly read any Chateaubriand or Saint-Simon but I do know and like Ruskin, and I can feel something of his sentence structure in Proust's.

The other thing is that everybody in Proust's novel reads; some are better at reading than others, which the narrator likes to point out and relate to their character, but reading, literature and life are all caught up with each other. At one point he makes the discovery that 'real life, life finally uncovered and clarified, the only life in consequence lived to the full, is literature'. And his novel would not be read for its truth to his own experience, as his readers weren't *his* readers 'so much as readers of their own selves, my book being merely one of those magnifying glasses of the sort the optician at Combray used to offer his customers; my book, but a book thanks to which I would be providing them with the means of reading within themselves'.

T.W. Adorno noted Proust's (Ruskinian) fondness for the gargoyles and ornaments in medieval cathedrals, hidden away in corners so high or invisible that their carvers knew nobody would ever see them, and argued that 'Proust should be read with the idea of those cathedrals in mind, dwelling on the concrete without grasping prematurely at something that yields itself not directly but only through its thousand facets.' He might also have mentioned Proust's fondness for the *Arabian Nights*, with its unpredictable shifts from one story to another, its subordinate narrators, its nested recollections and its reliance on the sheer power of narrative continuance. Both have parallels in the digressive, diagonally moving elements of his sentences, and both need to be borne in mind by the translator. As Malcolm Bowie writes in *Proust Among the Stars*, 'the novel is built from a multitude of different layers or levels, and the ready communication between layers that is encouraged by Proust's writing creates an astonishing sensation of semantic depth and resonance'. This is at work, too, in the sounds and music of the sentences, and in the temporalities of the syntax, its delays, shifts, recollections and revelations.

All the strands start to come together as the narrator waits, appropriately enough, in the Guermantes' library, and culminate first in the mismatch between interior time or memory and the exterior passage of time marked by ageing that he experiences in the subsequent party; and finally in his vision of time as a vastly extended spatial dimension, in which people are simultaneously in contact with different points in their lives. Time is central to Proust's novel, both in subject matter and in the way he writes, the way he structures experiences and memories and the way he uses tenses, so that grammar and rhetoric become a poetics of time and memory. The centrality of memory and the importance of reading in the novel have both taken on a new salience with the development of computer technology and AI. In his book about the effects of the internet, *The Shallows*, Nicholas Carr has shown how substituting Web memory for human memory is dangerous, as the electronic processing of information cannot replicate the organic nature of biological memory. 'What gives real memory its richness and its character, not to mention its mystery and fragility, is its contingency. It exists in time, changing as the body changes,' he says.[1] Proust would agree, and he would also emphasise, as he does so crucially in the *Recherche*, that there are two kinds of memory, voluntary and involuntary, and that the force of a sudden involuntary recollection, sparked by an apparently insignificant sound or taste, can reveal things about oneself that no amount of racking the brain's conscious memory will come up with. Involuntary memories and dreams are the only means we have of getting in touch with our unconscious. But the more we rely on phones and computers and the less work our own memories have to do, the weaker our memory grows, and the less capable of extended concentration or imagination it becomes, and the less capable of reading whole books. The more faith we put in the information at our fingertips, the less knowledge and understanding we have of the world, other people and ourselves.

Machine translation is improving all the time, and is very useful for uses of language where nuance or ambiguity aren't at stake. But let me give an example of a difficulty I encountered with Proust that I don't believe any computer could have coped with. Towards the end of his meditations in the Guermantes' library, the narrator is developing his thinking about the nature and primacy of involuntary memories, both sensory and figurative, realising that their 'primary character' was that he 'was not free to choose them, that they were given to [him] just as they were', and this was 'the mark of their authenticity'. He describes this, tellingly, as 'the inner book of unknown signs . . . for the reading of which nobody else could provide me with any rules'. The point about these confused impressions of a life is that they are the only kinds of knowledge that are unique to one person. Proust explains that 'anything we have not had to decipher, to bring to light by our own effort, anything which was already clearly visible, is not our own. The only things that come from ourselves are those we draw out of the obscurity within us, which can never be known by other people.'

This 'inner book of unknown signs' that the writer must translate has itself usually been translated as a book of unknown 'symbols', despite Proust's using the word '*signes*', but as Walter Benjamin pointed out many years ago, these signs are resemblances, as in Baudelaire's 'domain of the *correspondances*'.* Proust knew and loved Baudelaire's poems, and Benjamin's claim is that Proust was the only writer to reveal the part these correspondences play in our lives. The signs in the 'inner book', Benjamin goes on, are 'the work of the *mémoire involontaire*, the rejuvenating force which is a match for the inexorable process of ageing'. The meaning and associations of the word 'symbol' are wrong here (and anyway Proust didn't use the word '*symbole*'): the original impressions aroused by the various stimulants of taste and touch ('the sensation of the uneven flagstones, the stiffness of the napkin, the taste of the madeleine') are not stirred by symbols of themselves but by associative signs, metonymies. This is why the singularity, the detail, is so crucial.

It is also the detail that makes translation enjoyable. Writing with self-imposed constraints as you might do when writing poetry is one thing, but writing with the constraint of finding the best way of rendering another writer's words is both freeing and limiting, involving research, attentiveness, discernment, failures, frustrations, tact, thought, imagination, invention and, in the end, something like love. Love of whatever mind is embodied in the text you have come to know and to write so intimately, even if you don't like the text itself. Sometimes of course it's extremely hard to like the task, let alone love it, and heaven

* Baudelaire's 'correspondences' might be thought of as a poetic theory of subjective perception, involving synaesthesia, associative imagination and memory, and the capacity of objects in the world to stimulate thought through instances of similarity and connection. It is famously evoked in his sonnet 'Correspondances'.

knows it can seem endlessly frustrating and annoying, but there's always the promise of a kind of satisfaction, even with the dullest academic article. For a novel, especially a long and difficult one like Proust's, the rewards are much more substantial. Working on that scale, on both the physical scale of the novel and the breadth and scope of the author's vision, finding and matching the large rhythms as well as the small details, is not a minor pleasure. Finding ways to translate the malapropisms of Françoise, Marcel's family cook and housekeeper, or following the way the sound or the meaning or the shape of one word leads to or echoes or relates to another, occupies one part of the brain while another is storing a sense of the novel's changing themes or developing topics or recurrent characters. It's absorbing, but the absorption is balanced by the need to be critical, alert for the tone or style of a sentence.

Yet it's as well to bear in mind what Michael Wood says, that 'in a practical sense, the untranslatable does not exist. We can always translate badly, just as what we call the unthinkable has usually been thought, if not enacted, by many people.' Is a bad translation better than none at all? Probably. But I don't translate books any more. I decided when I completed *Finding Time Again* that it would be the last one I did. Several times since then I've been a judge for the Scott Moncrieff Prize, awarded each year by the Society of Authors for new translations from French; some of the translations I've read are brilliant, as are some of the books translated, some are less so, but the general standard is pretty high. Each time, despite the labour involved in reading everything in two languages, I wished there were more. The publishers that exist, at least in part, to promote translated work are excellent, but there still aren't enough of them; publishers like Fitzcarraldo Editions, And Other Stories, Les Fugitives, Pushkin Press, Europa Editions, Cassava Republic Press and Saqi Books (to name a few) do brilliant work, but they're mostly small, and it's hard to make a living as a literary translator unless you can manage to do a number of books each year. For myself I prefer translating poems. Poems are shorter, often denser, and have at their heart the premise that they can't be translated, because they exist by making their sense out of the language they're made in and made of. Their form, too, carries its own cultural history; different languages have different prosodies, different approaches to metre and rhyme, and so on.

Walter Benjamin, you will remember, argued that the translator's task was somehow to sense the original, ideal poem somewhere nebulously behind the poet's version of it, and then to (fail to) re-create it in the new form of her own language, remaking the first poem into a new poem that is as true to everything about the putative original poem as it can be, given that both versions fail to capture the ineffable ideal. This is a seductive notion, and one that valorises all kinds of translation – but I don't think it's right. First because it is rather too mystical for my materialist taste, and second because it doesn't tally with my experience of writing poems or, come to that, my experience of reading them. And when I translate poems, I either want to make a version that works perfectly in English and even feels as if it was written in English, or else to make something radically different that uses the source poem for my own purposes. So in the first case, I like to linger in the psychic mist between two languages, with etymologies, synonyms, alternative meanings, homophones and divergent interpretations zooming around like word-bees until I can write it in my language, out of my being, which includes my experience, my reading – my life and everything that has shaped me to understand things the way I do. All those things may come into play for the second way of treating the source text, but to quite different ends. So my understanding of Benjamin's claim is partly to do with interpretation, which means putting it into my own words or perhaps better putting my words into it. The constraint that makes this difficult is that I have to find a way to be true to the poet's own words at the same time. Which might mean reproducing the poem's form, metre, rhyme-scheme and so on, or might mean something vaguer, to do with the kind of words the poem uses or their history, or an atmosphere the poem creates in the reader's mind, or its emotional or intellectual contour.

This involves thinking about difficult questions. Why do some lines or phrases in a poem stick in your mind after you've read it? Is it just words and rhythm or is there more to it than that? Why do you feel some parts of the poem, or even some words, more deeply than others? What kind of contour does the poem have as you read it? Where are the moments of maximum intensity? How does the stress work? Does the nature of your attention fluctuate as you read it? What do you think of as you read? How do you contextualise your reading? Does the poem encourage you to read straight through it or does part of your mind, as you read, flicker back to earlier words or lines or ideas? Thinking about questions like this raises the larger question of what exactly it is you're reading and what it is therefore that you're translating.

Clearly it isn't just a matter of translating the sense of the words, if only because words can have more than one equivalent in another language – you have to choose *how* to translate words, how to interpret the way they are being used, even apparently simple and straightforward ones, though as a rule the more specific the word is ('trigonometry', say, or 'elbow'), the easier it is to translate. And choosing how to translate words, phrases, lines entails all sorts of choices even before you start to think about what happens in or through the syntax of those words, phrases and lines. You have to decide about rhythm, both verbal and affective or emotional: can you reproduce it? Should you? Can you do something equivalent but different? Or should you try to do something altogether different but that aims to capture something of the same pattern of feeling as the original. And that's just at the level of one line, or at most a very few. What about the poem as a whole? Will you decide to be constrained by the original work, or to translate more freely? If the former, what constraints will be productive?

Back in 1968, the *Sunday Times* ran a competition to translate the poem by Baudelaire that begins '*Je suis le roi d'un pays pluvieux*' ('I am the king of a rainy country'). Nicholas Moore, who in the 1940s had been one of the best-known and most productive young poets in the country, but who had published no poetry for almost twenty years and had fallen under the radar, contributed thirty-one different versions, all written in different voices, some satirical, some whimsical, all in varied idioms. They were submitted under anagrammatical or otherwise ridiculous pseudonyms, and posted from addresses all over the country. The competition was judged by George Steiner, who dismissed Moore's entries rather high-handedly, refusing to take them seriously. But when they were published a few years later by Barry MacSweeney and Anthony Rudolf in a limited edition, Moore wrote an introduction in which he argued a case for the impossibility of translation: 'A poem is the result of translating any subject-matter, seen or heard or read or felt, smelt or tasted, imagined or perceived, into poetic terms; but into the particular terms of the poet who writes it. That is why translation from one language to another in poetry is so impossible. The translation of the poems' materials into what they have become has already been done. It cannot be done again other than differently.' His variations on the Baudelaire poem were intended to bear out this contention. The two specimen translations chosen to illustrate the task set by the competition, by Roy Campbell and Robert Lowell, were not, Moore argued, 'Baudelaire speaking through a translator' but Campbell or Lowell speaking 'through or with the use of Baudelaire' and producing poems typical of their own work though 'somewhat below their best'.

The criterion Nicholas Moore sets for translation is indeed an impossible one: only Borges' Pierre Menard could meet it,* and even then the resulting poem would be in

* In the story 'Pierre Menard, author of the *Quixote*', Borges recounts the (imaginary) French writer Pierre Menard's 'impossible' self-appointed task of learning sixteenth-century Castilian Spanish and as it were becoming Cervantes in order to emulate him by writing (not copying) some of *Don Quixote*. He succeeded in writing 'the ninth and thirty-eighth chapters of Part I of Don Quixote and a fragment of Chapter XXII'.

Baudelaire's French. What Moore's versions demonstrate is that writing is inescapably personal; it comes from a body with a history, a habit of thought and breath, and is marked by its origin. I like translations that make a virtue of that. Some of the liveliest and most rewarding instances of the reimagining approach to translation are the ones that do take liberties with the original, change the settings or modernise the narrative so that they are in effect creating new works closely based on the source text but rewriting it for a contemporary readership. Or even just for the pleasure of it. One of the best examples I know is Philip Terry's version of Dante's *Inferno*, which relocates the entire book to the University of Essex and updates the identity of the figures he meets there as he is shown the circles of hell by his guide, no longer Virgil but the 'one-time Essex Visiting Professor of Poetry, and legendary presence on the New York poetry scene, Ted Berrigan'. In a later article, Terry explained why he chose the university to figure hell. 'One starting-point was architectural: the walled cities of the Italian city-states in the Middle Ages, typified by Montereggione with its fourteen high towers that stood on its perimeter like giant sentries, to which Dante makes allusion in Canto XXXI, and which underpin the iconography of the Inferno, also, by happy chance, underpin the architecture of Essex University, where a number of towers surround a central campus, divided up into squares modelled on Italian campi (the origin of our modern word "campus").' One result of this updating is to make Dante's project more accessible to a modern reader, Terry's version retaining loose three-line stanzas but abandoning Dante's interlocking *terza rima* rhyme scheme and any other form of rhyme or regularity;

another is to make it a good deal funnier and more scabrous. The opening lines, which Longfellow translated as 'Midway upon the journey of our life / I found myself within a forest dark / For the straightforward pathway had been lost', appear in Terry's version as: 'Halfway through a bad trip / I found myself in this stinking car park, / Underground, miles from Amarillo.' I suppose this kind of translation only works with poetry, not novels, though updated settings are commonplace in the theatre, and something similar has been a feature of painting for a long time.

Philip Terry, of course, is not the only poet translating like this, though his Dante may be the most striking recent example. Peter Hughes' versions of Petrarch, Cavalcanti and Leopardi operate with a comparable panache; just to take one example at random, his version of Petrarch's sonnet 44, which begins with references to Caesar and Pompey, ignores the classical figures, replacing them in the first quatrain with Mussolini, Michael Gove, George Bush and Pol Pot. In line with this more freewheeling approach, the tone is much less formal, wittier, more culturally inclusive, and the versification looser, or as Hughes puts it in another sonnet, 'bang up to date'. In fact the variety in approaches to translation is enormous, and although the traditional 'faithful' translation continues to be popular, there is an increasing focus on new theorisations and practices, from the reconstructive translations that Clive Scott has argued for, where the experience of reading a poem can be represented by spatial, typographic or pictorial means, to feminist and anti-colonial projects that aim to show the inequalities and incommensurabilities that translation can obscure or distort, a varied and thoughtful selection of which is to be found in Sophie Collins' important anthology *Currently & Emotion: Translations*, which has the stated aim of changing the way translations are regarded, from 'a kind of literary service that simply facilitates access to foreign and/or historical texts, to one that recognises an influential, political and manipulative act'.

What if, then, translation isn't just about letting monoglot readers, or those without knowledge of a particular foreign language, discover works written in that language? What if it is also to do with the whole experience of reading the text and making different kinds of sense out of it, or with the process of translation itself and the meditation it throws up on the relations between the languages in question, their cultural valences, their places in the world? The kind of literature that makes up what we loosely call 'the canon', however subversive or revolutionary it may have been at the time it was written, has long been absorbed into the culture and lost most of its ability to anger or upset; and as novels and poems from non-Western countries, particularly former colonies, are translated into English, the imbalance between cultures often tends to be erased, and with it the specific qualities of voices of resistance. Can translation retain this necessary difference, or must all translations bring these Others into the same current English fold? It's a problem, and one that is requiring experimental approaches as well as commitment to carrying across the values of the source texts, maybe disrupting expectations of conventional reading along the way. It's a problematic that is changing the way poetry and prose are being written and read, too, not just translations, as the world begins to adjust to a more global way of thinking and the West is forced to come to terms with the consequences of its colonial and imperial rapacity.

All translation is more constraining than writing your own work, but poetry is usually more constraining than prose. If the task of the literary translator is to make a text available to readers who can't understand the original language, and at the same time to show something of how it works structurally, syntactically, phonically, rhythmically and so on, then the constraints are huge. It is clearly impossible to reproduce all the semantic and paralinguistic features of a French or Chinese or Russian or Arabic or Italian poem in an English translation. Each language has its own history of writing, sometimes also absorbing influences from other cultures, sometimes sticking more closely to its own traditions and conventions. It's not just a matter of language, either. It's political. Questions are constantly making themselves felt about this process, about how best to make the literature of another culture, particularly one from the developing world with a history of colonialism, available to Western readers without taking it over, appropriating it. For instance, I am struck by the care with which Tilted Axis Press describe themselves on their website as 'an independent publisher of contemporary literature by the Global Majority, translated into or written in a variety of Englishes'. That last phrase, 'a variety of Englishes', poses an exciting challenge to the staider assumptions and conventions of the publishing world.

The more translations we can read, the better we shall understand the past and present of the peoples of the world, or so I hope. We are well served in English for translations of the Latin and Greek classics, with any number of translations of Homer, Plato, Aristotle and the tragedians, and of Horace, Ovid, Catullus, Virgil and the rest. Any library should have some, along with works by Boccaccio and Dante, Cervantes' *Don Quixote*, Goethe, Heine, Pushkin . . . and there are hundreds more. Think of the more recent work of Rilke, Proust, Musil, García Márquez, Sebald, Calvino, Camus and Beckett.

Think of Fitzcarraldo's translated Nobel laureates, Annie Ernaux, Svetlana Alexievich, Olga Tokarczuk and Jon Fosse. But these are all European – what about Asian writing, Han Kang from South Korea for instance, now so well translated by Deborah Smith? What about Chinese, Japanese, Vietnamese, Indian, Iranian, Afghan, Armenian? What about writing from the African and South American continents? We have a lot to read yet, and a lot to learn. It's a good thing there are so many good young independent publishers now taking translation seriously. If it's true as Jacques Derrida claims that translators are 'the only ones who know how to read and write', then we have a responsibility to listen to them, encourage their work, fund it well and buy and read the books they translate.

I wondered whether the process of transforming the coach house into a library, working within the constraints set by its being Grade II listed, was similar to translation. Could it perhaps be called that? It would, in fact, be closer to its original form than it had been when it was extended to be a garage. So perhaps a retranslation, more faithful than the previous one. After the delays caused by all the rain in the spring, it was now really taking shape, every day another detail done. All the insulation was in place, including the new ceiling, so except for the places where there were going to be plugs or lights or other fixtures the wiring was now hidden. The oak floor was laid, and now the glazed doors were hung, I could finally feel the kind of space it was going to be. But it would still be a couple of months at least before I could take possession and reclaim my books from storage. The bookcases had to be made and painted and installed, and the lights and radiators, and the old stable needed to be cleaned up, the wood and the brasswork polished. There would be room there for an armchair and filing cabinets, a CD player, record player and speakers. In my mind I was beginning to plan the arrangement of the books, the first room almost entirely poetry after 1900 and poetry in other languages and in translation; the inner room earlier poetry, my collection of twentieth-century poetry journals and poetry magazines (there wouldn't be room for them in the main room), philosophy, history, psychoanalysis, literary criticism and theory – all greatly reduced in number from the days when they sprawled along the shelves of my rooms in college.

7
Tradition and Innovation

> Many people like books because they're suspenseful or scary or touching or inspirational or because one admires the characters as if they were real people. Maybe it's only writers who like the writing.
>
> Edmund White, *The Unpunished Vice*

The early twentieth century was the great age of avant-garde artistic movements and manifestos – naturalism, expressionism, acmeism, post-impressionism, futurism, Vorticism, imagism, Dadaism, surrealism, Négritude, socialist realism and dozens more. Modernism, a catch-all term that might embrace any or all of the above, was not a movement. Nor was it a period, though it is sometimes used to refer to the cultural products of the years between 1912 and (say) 1940, a time of revolution and war, and of rapid change, both technological and social. When it first became current in academic circles it referred in general terms to the writers and artists whose work illustrated crises in the practice of representation during those years, a disagreement with traditional modes of picturing the objective world such as can be seen in cubist painting, in Virginia Woolf's novels, in T.S. Eliot's poems or in the music of Stravinsky or Schoenberg, a restructuring of subjective perception and its expression in new forms and new subject matters. The rebellion in these works, explicit or implicit, was against the realist artistic conventions of older generations, which no longer seemed to fit a changing world, which is why they appealed to me in my teens and twenties and beyond. They had an energy and a commitment to innovation that caught my imagination and made the mainstream cultural output of the fifties and early sixties in Britain look dull and unambitious by comparison.

As time went by, their novelty and their hostility to mass culture or bourgeois ideas or other artistic creeds seemed less necessary as their claims and innovations were adopted or rejected or noted, lost their edge of strangeness or incomprehensibility and were welcomed into readability, although some others, like Gertrude Stein's poems or James Joyce's *Finnegans Wake* remained on the edges, still regarded as 'difficult' or even unreadable. When Stravinsky's *Rite of Spring* was first played, in Paris in 1913, it was received by many in the audience as barbaric and insulting, and rioting disrupted the performance. *Ulysses* was denounced as pornographic and offensive and banned in Britain and the USA. And abstract art was often derided or dismissed by people asking 'What's it meant to be?' and saying a child could have done better.

But there are always political or cultural reasons for changes in literary fashion and artistic approaches. In the UK in the twentieth century, the increased polarisation of political attitudes that culminated in the Second World War brought with it in some quarters an increased directness of style and a deepening focus on Englishness. After the war, and with the onset of the Cold War, there was an influential school of thought that associated modernist art and writing with extremist fascist or communist politics and flourished under the conservative social-democratic regimes of the 1950s and '60s. The staidness and conventionality of post-war British life in the period encouraged an islanded and unadventurous mentality in poetry and film and to some extent in fiction, a reaction against the achievements of modernism, especially when they were foreign (and therefore un-English). You can see this exemplified in poetry by the 'Movement' poets like Philip Larkin, Robert Conquest, Elizabeth Jennings and Kingsley Amis, who wrote formally conventional poems with a fairly restricted subject matter. At the same time, there was the new realism of the 'kitchen sink' drama of John Osborne and Arnold Wesker, and novels of working-class life by Alan Sillitoe, John Braine and David Storey. Modernism and its explorations of new forms of art looked to many, though not all, as if it had been a dead end. The same could not be said about the visual arts or architecture or music, but poetry and novels, for the most part, turned their back on experiment. Broadly speaking, there was a return to the idea that the relation between the world and its representation was straightforward and unproblematic; that as George Orwell said, good prose should be like a windowpane, clear and unnoticeable.

Yet not everybody was persuaded. Lines of continuity run through versions of surrealism, poets of the New Apocalypse movement and those associated with them; and writers like Henry Green, Elizabeth Bowen, Samuel Beckett and many others were working with a consciousness of the oddness of the mind and of perception, allowing that to show in their practice of representation, changing the way representation or style were thought about. If the common-sense view of the connection between language and the world was inadequate, then the question of how to write, or even of what to write, continued to require new answers. It was not so much that the artistic projects of modernism continued or survived as that the questions raised by the rapidly changing world could not be seriously resisted or ignored for long.

Some writers, though, did try to ignore them, or at least to believe that the old ways were adequate for a new world. A few years ago, one poet was reported as saying that he'd read no poetry written between 1910 and 1980 in order to make sure he avoided 'the aridity and intellectualism' of modernist writers. Sneering at the intellect is just silly; writers need intelligence and thinking, and if their writing is not animated by intellect as well as feeling, it won't get us very far. Throughout the second half of the twentieth century a form of neo-realism took on the guise of anti-modernism as a form of defence for what were frequently narrow provincial attitudes, a wish to be separate and untouched by foreign ways of thought, and a conservatism that was instinctively pragmatic, hostile to innovation and to new ideas. First Evelyn Waugh and Philip Larkin, then Brexit, as you might say.

Trying to discern patterns and movements in literary culture across time is an entertaining critical game, but it simplifies an almost infinitely complex field. Writers can be praised or denigrated for pretty much anything, but only a very few have the capacity to influence currents of thought by being both highly regarded and widely read, though it often turns out that their popularity doesn't last because they were too good at incorporating the more superficial attitudes of the time in which they were writing. Think of the bestselling writers of the 1930s, like A.J. Cronin, Hugh Walpole, St John Ervine, Marjorie Bowen or Mary Webb, now hardly read at all. They have stopped being readable because they've become dated in a way that some of their contemporaries haven't. Reading them you feel too much the presence of stale modes of thought and uncomfortable ideologies. Others, though, such as Eric Ambler, Elizabeth Bowen, Graham Greene, Patrick Hamilton, Aldous Huxley, George Orwell, Jean Rhys, Sylvia Townsend Warner, Rebecca West and Virginia Woolf are all not only readable but much read and in print, not because they aren't visibly products of their period but because they do more than just articulate the discursive froth of the age; their writing has a depth of feeling and thinking that understands and investigates their place in time.

Recent research has shown that the mind can take in a whole sentence in one split-second glimpse, so long as the sentence is very short and composed of a familiar grammatical structure. (It had previously been thought that all reading happened sequentially, word by word.) I was interested in this because it suggests to me two things that are already well known: first, that the more familiar we are with things, the easier it is to take them in; and second, that simple recognition of sentences is not the same as reading in its fullest sense, which calls on related activities of the mind like thinking, questioning and imagination. It also points up the difference, at least by implication, between the short-term pleasure of consuming a book and the more lasting and complex pleasure of its writing and the thinking it gives rise to.

Of course both always exist, sometimes in the same book, but complexity is too often equated with elitism or difficulty, just as difficulty is often regarded as a legacy of modernism, to be avoided wherever possible. This takes us back to Orwell's 1946 essay 'Why I Write', which is where he said that 'one can write nothing readable unless one constantly struggles to efface one's own personality. Good prose is like a windowpane.' The personality he wants to efface here is not much like the personality Eliot famously thought poets should escape; Eliot argued that the poet's mind should be a 'medium' that incorporated a 'consciousness of the past', knowledge of history and especially literary history – though not, he makes clear, the sort of knowledge that 'can be put into a useful shape for examinations, drawing-rooms, or the still more pretentious modes of publicity'. Poets, he thought, should sacrifice their own personality in the process of writing and allow the right catalyst when it occurs to fuse 'significant emotion' into the words of the poem. The 'emotion' should be in the 'impersonal' poem, not in the poet.

Orwell, though, was talking about prose, especially non-fiction prose, and is not concerned with art. We can agree that no writing should be muddled or contradictory without getting cross about Orwell's example, in another essay, of muddled metaphoric thinking of the sort exemplified by expressions like 'the fascist octopus has sung its swansong', which I quite like. Its meaning is clear enough, and figures of speech don't require perfect internal consistency. It's worth saying here, too, that there is more than one kind of clarity: Orwell's epistemology assumes an unproblematic relation between language and the world, whereas two of the most important discoveries of modernism were that language itself, in all its arbitrariness, constructs our perception of the world, and that we are all motivated by unconscious desires. Julia Kristeva, as we saw earlier, has described the clarity that comes from what she calls 'exile', an ability to step out of your normal self and your social role and look at the world as if you're seeing it as a stranger, seeing it for the first time. Rimbaud famously said that '"I" is another person.' Clarity is complex; we are always split beings, and the stylistic idiosyncrasy of Stein or Joyce as well as the apparent clarity of Orwell or Hemingway are choices made in pursuit of truthful representation.

Stein and Joyce are extreme examples, although their work emphasises an often overlooked element in good writing, namely pleasure in play – play on words, play with the sound of words, play with syntactical repetition; in short, play with language: but others like Virginia Woolf, John Dos Passos, Wyndham Lewis, Dorothy Richardson and Jean Toomer all experimented with new ways of writing, as some writers at least of every generation must, and their innovations were taken up to a greater or lesser degree by many of the writers who followed. And yet it became almost a commonplace in the late twentieth century to dismiss modernism as a cul-de-sac, a dead end, and to call for the novel to reclaim the realist tradition. Even when the younger novelists of the 1970s proclaimed their allegiance to the new American novel, it was the expanded subject matter they responded to, not anything new or particularly interesting in the ideas or the writing itself. But 'It ain't what you do, it's the way that you do it',[1] as the song says.

If you look at a list of the bestselling novels of the last twenty-five years, you find, predictably enough, plenty of J.K. Rowling, some Dan Brown, the *Twilight* saga, *Hunger Games*, Stieg Larsson, Mark Haddon, Neil Gaiman; and representing literary fiction Yann Martel, Kazuo Ishiguro, Anne Tyler and Ian McEwan. All obviously very readable, even captivating, mostly very visual and easily transferred to the screen, often simplistic and sometimes composed in ways that lend themselves to being studied in schools. But hardly any of them are interesting for the quality of their writing, apart from their narrative ability, nor for serious intellectual or philosophical thought. 'If we are to have a literary culture,' wrote Brigid Brophy once, 'we need bad books as well as good books. This is partly because everyone *begins* on bad books . . . but it is mainly because that is the way art works.' All writers, not only the good ones, emerge from the great miscellaneous mass of published books, and just as most readers continue to read at least some 'bad' books however highbrow their tastes, so hardly anybody's writing career starts off with their best book.

Here I want to look at some writers in more detail, using them unfairly as representative of different strands in 'literary culture'. First, Ian McEwan, well established (though now beginning to look a bit passé) as one of the most read and most studied of contemporary English writers, one of the exemplars of 'the novel' that school students come across and that shapes their taste. McEwan too is on record as saying that modernism was a dead end, an attitude that ignores a whole swathe of the most interesting writing of the twentieth century and loses the chance to explore a whole range of potential pleasures for readers. As a writer, he has always been interested in crises and disasters and the ethical problems that ensue, and in human fears and desires, especially when they don't follow expected paths, but he doesn't seem to give much thought to what fears and desires are really about, generally preferring to show them at work from the outside, focusing on their consequences; for him, as he wrote in a *Guardian* article in 2013, 'fiction's generous knack of annotating the microscopic lattice-work of consciousness, the small print of subjectivity' stops short before it reaches the unconscious; he prefers to investigate the more evidently knowable realms of being, and to use realism to think about reality.

This realism – the sense that his fiction reproduces and analyses actual contemporary life, with all its pressing issues and conflicts – is a large part of why McEwan's novels have come to occupy the place they do in the cultural life of the UK. Scarcely any A-level or university literature student in the last twenty years will have escaped studying them – *The Child in Time* first became a set text for A level in 1995 – and commentary on them, particularly on *Enduring Love* and *Atonement*, has become an academic industry. He is agreed to be an Important Writer, readable but amenable to close reading and easily available to critical analysis; and as if in answer to his position in the pantheon, his novels since 2001's *Atonement* seem increasingly to have been designed to satisfy just such efficient unpacking.

McEwan has spoken frequently in interviews about his dislike of the sort of novels that were around when he was approaching maturity and casting about for models, novels about marriages slowly collapsing near Hampstead. From Iris Murdoch and Angus Wilson to Alan Sillitoe and David Storey, he found the dominant presence of social class off-putting. When he discovered American writers like Updike, Mailer, Roth and Bellow, they seemed to offer ways to explore life without the social, sexual and stylistic hang-ups of English prose fiction, or the legacies of modernism. In an interview with David Lynn in 2006, McEwan claimed that 'although . . . in the United States, literature, fiction, largely bypassed all the problems posed for it by modernism, in continental Europe there was a long fading off through the fifties, sixties and seventies of authors still writing novels that never really engaged the world in the way that, say, Saul Bellow could'.

The notion that writing needs to 'engage the world' has led McEwan to write increasingly wooden dramatisations of contemporary moral problems. Believability is never a requirement in a McEwan novel, but he likes to ground even the most far-fetched fantasy – like the foetal narrator of *Nutshell* – in an everyday world, usually a tastefully middle-class one. At points, the novels feel more like essays pinned onto a fictional character's thought, rather than intrinsic to them. In *Saturday*, published in 2005 and set in 2003, the neurosurgeon protagonist has firm views on terrorism, religion and the fanaticism of anti-war protesters. In *Nutshell*, the precocious foetus holds forth in an overheated and underdetermined way about everything under the sun: climate change, the Middle East, the US, China, art, identity politics and the decline of the university. The book tries to hedge authorial attitudes by surrounding them with narrative irony, but by trying so visibly it ends up inadvertently exposing the author to view, like watching a Punch and Judy show from behind the tent.

McEwan has made quite a study of intractable ethical issues in his novels, but in recent years they have tended to lie inert at the heart of them, refusing his best efforts to give them real intellectual and emotional life. This is a pity because he is a writer of great skill. His narratives usually have enough force to engage the reader's curiosity, and enough complexity to distract from the relatively undistinguished nature of their thinking; he has studied the elements of fiction and experimented with unreliable narration, varying point of view, authorial tone, genre and all sorts of ways of creating tension. And yet the two elements just don't come together. It makes the novels easy for school students to write essays about, especially in a world where poems, paintings and novels are judged more by their depiction of subject matter than by the art with which they are made, but leaves them open to dismissal as confected propaganda vehicles.

A powerful advocate for freedom of expression, McEwan has often been called upon to give his views on world events as a pundit from the centre left, but as a writer occupying such an elevated cultural position, as Ryan Ruby pointed out in a review of his novel *Lessons* in 2022, 'he has a special responsibility to freedom of expression that goes above and beyond that of the pundits who argue in its defence in op-eds . . . It is this: to create a work of literature whose aesthetic power justifies the privilege in the first place . . . Just as people living behind the Iron Curtain had no shortage of reading material as mediocre as *Lessons*, the market is currently condemning far better books than it to smaller print runs than a samizdat.'

What does McEwan want his novels to do? He said in an interview with Daniel Zalewski that he found 'most novels *incredibly* boring . . . Not being boring is quite a challenge', and is on record as saying that one of his aims is 'to incite a naked hunger in readers'. 'Narrative tension,' he explains, 'is primarily about withholding information', which might suggest something closer to a conventional detective story rather than the literary heights. I'm in favour of the merging of genres, of letting the writing decide what's required, as long as the writing is the point. I can't help feeling when I read McEwan or the numerous other writers I'm using him as a punchbag for that the actual writing, the language, is just how they get from one scene to the next, with occasional pauses for a bit of 'fine writing'. When McEwan talks about style, he is more often than not talking about perfectly turned phrases, surprising words, apt metaphors that create a 'precise insight into a human moment', a view in which 'literary language' is 'poetic' but where 'poetic' implies a focus on the right words with which to communicate tone and feeling. It's a view rooted in a version of realism and a strong sense of the aesthetic as ornamental rather than constitutive or epistemologically independent, and it is still propagated in schools and universities and has until recently dominated publishing and reviewing.

When I finished reading McEwan's first novel, *The Cement Garden*, back in 1980, I felt queasy, unsatisfied and vaguely cheated. In some ways it was pallid compared with other writers on the family such as Freud or Ivy Compton-Burnett, or compared with writers who challenged the limits of expectation, like Kafka, J.G. Ballard or Philip K. Dick. Reading it again ten years ago, I felt a powerful tension between partly conscious authorial phantasy destabilising the ostensibly measured narrative voice and the physical details of its setting, which are simultaneously hyper-real, somewhat allegorical, and not fully believable. Like allegory, the novel floats above its place in time and space, but in this it becomes vulnerable to its author's dream. The critic James Wood long ago pointed out that the narrative is 'highly secretive'. He goes on to explain that 'McEwan is addicted to the withholding of narrative information, the hoarding of surprises, the deferral of revelations; this manipulation of secrecy, apart from its obvious desire to keep the reader reading, seems to incarnate a desire to repeat the texture of the originating trauma, and in so doing to master and contain it.' In this case, though, I think it undermines his attempt at control and leaves the reader, as I was, queasy and unsatisfied.

This manufactured suspense also complicates and upsets what has now long been another of McEwan's purposes, and indeed the novel's: namely to show the drama or trauma of individual lives in relation to the time they're happening in. At one level this is very skilfully done: the slightly pastiche style of the first section of *Atonement*, later revealed to have been written by the character of Bryony, is a good example. Colm Tóibín, describing the deliberately stilted style of *On Chesil Beach*, wrote that 'the style of the book may seem plain: there is no recourse to the use of cadence for effect, and there are no elaborate sentences or pyrotechnics of any sort. We are, after all, in England, where words mean what they say.' His irony here seems to echo McEwan's, but at some level McEwan thinks words do actually mean what they say, rather than never being quite under our control. The historical details he puts into all his books except the earliest ones works well to introduce sharp wafts of the period, but their rather studied presence means they never quite connect with the characters. This is perhaps most pronounced in *Saturday*, but it is a recurrent problem, as it is in the work of plenty of other writers. The relation between individuals and their cultures and ideologies, let alone the memorable events of the time, is endlessly varied and complicated, and needs to be explored through the writing rather than, however obliquely, by a historically informed narrative voice.

The historical novel has been a popular genre since the development of a modern sense of history in the eighteenth century; its descendants proliferated and in the interwar years of the last century became a significant way of thinking about the social and political crises of the time, deflected into recent or distant pasts or, in the case of Virginia Woolf's *Orlando*, both: Sylvia Townsend Warner's *Summer Will Show* and *The Corner that Held Them*, Naomi Mitchison's *The Corn King and the Spring Queen*, Jack Lindsay's *Last Days with Cleopatra* and *1649: A Novel of a Year*, Geoffrey Trease's children's books like *Comrades for the Charter*, Mary Butts' *Scenes from the Life of Cleopatra* and *The Macedonian*, John Cowper Powys' *Owen Glendower*, James Barke's *Land of the Leal*, Robert Graves' *I Claudius* – these are just a few relevant examples from the UK, but it was an international phenomenon. More recently still, the popularity of historical novels has seen a kind of postmodern genre-melding as the flexibility of time inaugurated by the example of magical realism has led to counterfactual histories (and their mirror image in novels of dystopian futures), semi-histories, anachronistic histories and historicised attempts to analyse the connection between time, the times, society and individuals. McEwan's explorations, including the counterfactual *Machines Like Us*, are set in recent pasts which is one of the reasons their history lessons come across as rather earnest. Like those of his friends and contemporaries, his novels display a confidence in the world as found, as well as in its relation to a mostly second-hand use of language. But words don't always mean only what they say, let alone what you think they say.

But I'm only using Ian McEwan's novels to stand for one relatively incurious and ultimately reassuring kind of writing. The novel is multiform and various and too many are published each year for generalisations to have much truth to them. It will be clear by now that I'm not entirely keen on realism, but I don't want to proscribe it. In fact, I don't want to proscribe anything except writing without consciousness of the impossibility of always making words mean what you think they mean. History involves memory and writing, neither of which behave in the ways we believe they do. The writers I admire know this. And while most of the novels published today are realist or, as Zadie Smith says, written with 'lyrical realism', there are plenty that aren't.

These are, for the most part, novels that bring something new to the novel form and make the reader question things. One of the original meanings of 'novel' or 'novels' was 'news', and since its inception the novel has been the art form that most obviously needed to keep up with a changing world and a changing society. With the modernism of the last century came a new awareness of the pervasiveness of contingency, the avant-garde additionally committed to breaking with the past. After the Second World War, as we've seen, a new wave of modernism sometimes influenced by William Burroughs and the Beats in America, or by European writers like Samuel Beckett and Alain Robbe-Grillet, appeared in writings by Brigid Brophy, Sam Selvon, Ann Quin, Alan Burns, B.S. Johnson, Christine Brooke-Rose, Eva Figes, Nicholas Mosley, Eva Tucker, Gabriel Josipovici and many others, including Iris Murdoch. Some of these writers wanted radical change in the form and nature of the novel, most wanted more, and more serious, questioning of accepted realities, some were more interested in milder kinds of originality, but like the dramatists who wanted to get away from the kind of plays where young men pop in through the French windows waving a racket and asking 'Anyone for tennis?', they all wanted a change from the standard inoffensive fare.

In 1964, I was fifteen and had just discovered commitment. It took the form of a black polo-neck jersey, French cigarettes and a copy of Camus' *L'homme révolté* (*The Rebel*), which I found very hard to read. *Peace News* was easier but less intellectually exciting, and whatever else commitment was, it was certainly intellectually exciting. The word 'intellectual' itself was exciting, maybe even the most exciting thing. It was probably the word I wanted to identify myself with. A commitment to words was what being an intellectual meant, committing things to words, writing yourself as a poet. Looking back now, it's hard to disentangle the pose from the poesy, but at the time it was completely absorbing.

Then when I was sixteen, I bought a copy of *Watt* by Samuel Beckett in Charing Cross Road, probably at Poole's or Better Books; I have a very vivid memory of reading it one afternoon at school while I was playing cricket (or meant to be), standing on the boundary hoping nobody would hit the ball in my direction (Beckett, a very accomplished cricketer, would not have approved), mesmerised by the strangeness of the writing and by the book's lack of incident. I was drawn in by the first sentence: 'Mr Hackett turned the corner and saw, in the failing light, at some little distance, his seat.' It was the banality of the subject matter and the precarious balance of the unexpected syntax that really struck me. The writing was unlike anything I'd read before, and it showed me that novels didn't have to follow the same sort of pattern all the time. Writers could make up their own rules. That was the beginning of my fondness for Beckett and for the kind of writing sometimes referred to as 'experimental'; after I finished *Watt*, I read *Molloy* and was hooked. Some times are more favourable to experiment than others, and from that point of view the sixties was a good decade to be growing up in.

Beckett's novel was published by John Calder, and I soon came to recognise other Calder books in the same format, hoping they would appeal in the same sort of way. Many of them were in translation; almost all the writers were names I was coming across for the first time, Eugène Ionesco, Marguerite Duras, Jorge Luis Borges, Michel Butor, Nathalie Sarraute, Alexander Trocchi, Wyndham Lewis . . . I would open one after another in the Charing Cross Road bookshops, reading pages at random until I found something I liked. The book I read after *Watt* and

Molloy was probably *Berg* by Ann Quin, another writer published by Calder, and another writer who attracted me by the ways she departed from conventional realism. All this would have been in about 1964 and '65, when I was discovering numbers of other writers, as well as left-wing politics, ideas, literary and intellectual history, poetry, music, everything. It was exciting and it all came in a consuming rush of cultural enthusiasm. And mostly, of course, it came in the form of books. It was haphazard and I didn't like everything I tried: I wanted to read everything, and did my best to, but there were books to come to terms with in English lessons at school as well as my undisciplined reading and book buying, and I was finding some of the works we were reading there deeply interesting; Blake's poems, Shakespeare's history plays, Chaucer, the poems of Donne, Wordsworth, Yeats all opened my eyes, my heart and my mind to new experiences and new thinking. In the same way and at the same time, John Coltrane and Thelonius Monk, Bach, Schoenberg and Poulenc were stretching my sense of what music could be, alongside my enthusiasm for the rhythm and blues of Sonny Boy Williamson, Brownie McGhee and Sonny Terry, Muddy Waters, Sister Rosetta Tharpe and Blind Gary Davis, and of course the Rolling Stones, the Kinks, Bob Dylan and Joan Baez. Sometimes I felt like Worzel Gummidge, with a different head for each set of enthusiasms.

Experiment of one sort or another, I was discovering, was endemic in literature. Poets, playwrights and novelists have to find new ways of writing if their work is not to repeat what already exists, and to find a way to account for the world they're responding to and to express something inexpressible about it. For many, this just means incorporating a more up-to-date world or more up-to-date attitudes in their work, but there will always be some who take a more radical approach to writing and form (and in the process upset many traditionally minded readers). My own taste is for plotless narrative, or at least narrative where plot is not dependent on moral causality but is open to pointlessness, randomness, the accidental; and most of all, for writing that finds ways for the reader to break through the numbing habits of consumer culture and literary convention. There are two things here: one is habit, which Beckett characterises very well in his essay on Proust. 'Habit is . . . the guarantee of a dull inviolability . . . Breathing is habit. Life is habit. Or rather life is a succession of habits, since the individual is a succession of individuals; the world being a projection of the individual's consciousness . . . the pact must be continually renewed . . . the creation of the world . . . takes place every day.' The other is the particular form of alienation that afflicts everybody in advanced capitalist societies, the 'spectacle' as Guy Debord named it, in which we all have our place and dance to the tune we are made to hear.

Unless art can break the spell. Which in the end is not possible, but it is the aim, or it ought to be. Since at least the late eighteenth century, fiction and poetry have tried to revolutionise writing to engage the power of the imagination to think things differently. Blake, Wordsworth, Rimbaud, Oscar Wilde, Gertrude Stein, Ezra Pound, Virginia Woolf, Anna Kavan, Samuel Beckett all have their place on that shelf. And as I have said, I discovered this as a living tradition through reading first Beckett and then Ann Quin, who published four extraordinary novels between 1964 and 1972, after which she walked into the sea in Brighton and ended her life at the age of thirty-seven. After her death, her books were almost forgotten, although there were enough short-lived revivals of interest for her to keep a cult reputation among writers. But recently she's reappeared as a tutelary figure for a new enthusiasm for 'experimental fiction'. Writers such as Ali Smith, M. John Harrison, Diane Williams, Deborah Levy, Jenny Diski, Adam Mars-Jones, Lydia Davis, Leanne Shapton, Lara Pawson, Kevin Davey, Isabel Waidner, Rachel Cusk, Lee Rourke, Tom McCarthy, Eimear McBride, Lucy Ellmann, Mark Bowles, Claire-Louise Bennett and Eley Williams, many published by independent presses, started to attract more attention, and there has been a flurry of excitement about writing that departs in one way or another from the conventions of realism.

Ann Quin has all the biographical qualifications for the job of precursor, as well as being famously and gratifyingly unpredictable, or reluctant to do what was expected of her. She was born to a single mother in Brighton in 1936. A wartime childhood and a convent education gave her a strong desire to explore 'the whole sinful world that lay before me' when she left school. Her first enthusiasm was for the theatre. At the age of seventeen, she worked in a repertory company as an assistant stage manager, then went for an audition at drama school but 'was struck dumb, and rushed out, silently screaming down Gower Street'. It was a decisive moment. Instead of acting, she wrote later, 'I would be a writer. A poet. Where what I had to express, say, would be my own interpretation, my own vision and be accepted by an unseen audience.' She took a secretarial course and worked in a newspaper office until the editor hanged himself in a cupboard, after which she returned to Brighton for two years, started painting as well as writing, returned to London, worked for a publisher, rented a room in Soho, wrote a novel, had it rejected, started another one, worked in a Cornish hotel, had a breakdown, escaped to Paris, came back, worked part-time as a secretary at the Royal College of Art, finished a second novel, had it rejected, wrote a third novel, *Berg*, and this time had it accepted. It was published by Calder in 1964. 'Reading what I had written,' she wrote, 'seemed like someone else's dream. A kind of involuntary commitment.' 'Commitment' is an interesting word to use about the process of writing, with its associations of delegation and entrusting, consignment and detention, as well as committing a crime, or committing to memory or (as here) to paper. Then there's the existentialist sense of engagement with the world or to a course of action. And the primary sense of an obligation and a dedication. All of these resonate with *Berg*, which is a strange piece of work, recursive and mythic as the much-quoted epigraph suggests: 'A man called Berg, who changed his name to Greb, came to a seaside town intending to kill his father' – though in the end he only succeeded in killing his father's ventriloquist's dummy.

A mixture of the surreal, the whimsical and the macabre, with touches of the English music-hall tradition, the novel's overdetermined atmosphere of seedy blowsiness is vaguely reminiscent of Archie Rice in Tony Richardson's film of *The Entertainer*, as well as early Graham Greene. The style is distinctive in the way it wanders in and out of interiority, with private thought and public speech undifferentiated by punctuation or *mise-en-page*. The central character, the focalising consciousness of the novel, is the eponymous young man, but the overwhelming sense is of a slipperiness, a difficulty in finding your bearings or keeping your footing in the story. It circles repetitively around its receding purpose, as much Hamlet as Oedipus, but it's even less hopeful than either and much more absurd than both. It is funny and profound, intensely of its time but not in the least dated.

The late 1960s and early 1970s were a time when innovation and a commitment to change were genuinely widespread, to the extent of requiring the term 'counterculture' to account for them, and Quin's writing participates in a more generally shared experimentalism. Discovering the scope and ambition of modernist artists from Europe and America was an important task in her cultural world. There is another implication of the word 'experimental', namely that the writing is hard to read, or at least less than straightforwardly pleasurable. And it's true that Quin's novels don't make concessions to her readers. In this she is following a tradition that runs from Djuna Barnes and Joyce, say, through Henry Green and Beckett and Robbe-Grillet to William Burroughs and Christine Brooke-Rose. According to the novelist, biographer and art critic Paddy Kitchen, Quin 'was not one of those authors who self-consciously strove to be an innovator, rather she had to seek a different form for each theme which occupied her mind'. The same is probably true of most innovators.

When I was first reading her novels, the people I knew who liked that kind of thing were mostly poets. The most interesting sorts of poetry being written then, as now, were broadly speaking modernist, with a vision of poetry that was opposed to the limited horizons of the Movement, poets like Larkin and Amis and their followers, open to the influence of Europeans, especially the surrealists and the French poet and translator Paul Celan, and to the work of Americans such as Charles Olson, Ed Dorn, Jack Spicer, Frank O'Hara and the New York poets. When I look back on it now, it's clear that Quin's writing sits more easily alongside this internationalist milieu. She was always critical of English narrowness and its 'safe comfortable rituals, the monotony that keeps the fantasies moving', things she explored, anatomised and dramatised in her first two novels. You can feel that hatred of monotony throughout her work, a restlessness, an unsatisfied feeling, both in the characters and in the work itself.

Impulsive and impatient, unable to settle anywhere, she seems to have had an affinity with the movement of the sea, the presence of which is variously but intensely felt in her first three novels, and in some of her short stories. It can be menacing or welcoming but it's never inert, always inhabited by something, whether by crabs or a dead seagull, a starfish, seaweed or fishes. But there is also an emptiness in her work; she gives her characters an almost tangible evasion of choice as they drift through a world of unexplained contingencies. Or if they ever do seem to make a decisive choice – by committing suicide, say, as in her second novel, *Three* – there is no conclusive evidence that this is what has actually happened.

Both *Three* and her third novel, *Passages*, assemble their narrative from different points of view, which intensifies the uncertainty. *Three* uses diaries and tape recordings (as well as glimpses of home cine film) to complicate the texture of the events described or reconstructed in the novel and to cast doubt on any authoritative account. In *Passages*, the diary extracts are annotated with marginal references to their stimulus or parallels in Greek myth or artefacts. But the most striking departure from conventional fiction writing is Quin's use of quotation, which becomes a major, if invisible strand in *Tripticks* but appears first in *Three* when S writes, 'All afternoon surrounded, exchanging newspapers. I came across the following . . .' and follows it with two pages of almost verbatim quotation from a 1966 article about the Auschwitz trials by Sybille Bedford. The character makes no comment on the extract, but the pattern of emotional disengagement Bedford reports has clear resonances within the novel, which is built round the need for the young convalescent character S to mean something to her hosts, an older married couple.

Tripticks, Quin's fourth novel, marked a departure in her writing. She had spent some years in the United States on scholarships, living for a while with Robert Creeley, later with another poet, Robert Sward, associating with poets, attending the famous 1965 Berkeley Poetry Conference, where she would have heard Charles Olson, Ed Dorn, Robert Duncan and Allen Ginsberg, among many others. She thought of herself, I think, as a poet almost as much as a novelist. When she came to use the landscape and culture of the US in *Tripticks*, she drew on her own experiences and the techniques of the poets and of writers like Burroughs to create a fast-moving, jump-cutting, semi-absurd, road-trip quest narrative in which text from newspapers and magazine advertisements is folded in throughout. Current events, Superman comics and ads for erotic underwear appear alongside the words of Richard Nixon or Lyndon Johnson, sometimes on their own terms, sometimes as words spoken by characters. But, always restless, she seems to have been dissatisfied with this collage-like way of writing. The unfinished novel left behind on her death is forceful, direct and straightforward in style, and depicts a woman in a psychiatric ward in conflict with her doctor, nurses and herself. Although she uses elements of detective stories and thrillers in her earlier novels, Quin is not interested in narrative for its own sake; indeed she delights in failing to supply the kind of closure such genres conventionally require. What she likes is the scope they provide for a continually unanswered questioning and self-questioning. 'They couldn't bear it a minute longer. They knew they were being followed'; 'She feels we are being watched.' Paranoid states of mind are present to some extent in all her books, but in this last one she is beginning to address the matter directly, perhaps to come to terms with it, perhaps to be carried away by it. She was seriously knowledgeable about psychoanalysis: *Berg* and *Passages* are attempts to rethink the myths of psychoanalysis and the psychoanalysis of myths through the figures of Oedipus and Antigone, giving the interpersonal a social and political resonance, and it may be that the contemporary relevance of that project accounts in part for Quin's new readership.

It is good that new generations of writers and readers discover their literary ancestors so long as it serves the demands of the present rather than answering to a nostalgia for a future that belongs to the past. Writing like Quin's is part of the modernist tradition, a continuing dialogue and development, a way of creating art that needs to be constantly remade, a springboard, more than just something to be reclaimed. The writers I've mentioned so far have mostly been British, but there are plenty of US and Canadian writers who might be grouped with them. Poets like Clark Coolidge, Lisa Robertson, Joshua Clover, John Wieners, Susan Howe, Rae Armantrout or John Ashbery, writers like John Cage, Kathy Acker, Gilbert Sorrentino, Dodie Bellamy, David Wojnarowicz. And sometimes things that look radical aren't. Leanne Shapton's sort-of-novel *Important Artifacts and Personal Property from the Collection of Lenore Doolan and Harold Morris, including Books, Street Fashion and Jewelry*, as its title suggests, is cast in the form of an auction catalogue, with photos of confected lots. A radical form and method, but in the end a predictable story of failed love, more reliant than you'd hope on all the notes, postcards, letters and diary entries listed and transcribed in the catalogue.

There's a sense in which every piece of writing is an experiment, a process of finding how to translate thought, observation, memory or experience into words, and then improve the words, put them into the right order and order them into the right kind of form. But properly experimental writing is writing that makes some demands on the reader, pushing boundaries, breaking rules if necessary, challenging the resources of the language and the reader's assumptions. That may not always make for relaxing or comfortable reading, but it can provide something better than comfortableness: it can be difficult, challenging, transporting, revivifying, exciting, upsetting. It can make you feel alive, intellectually and physically.

Our culture tends to pay lip service to the experiments of the past but marginalise the experiments of more recent times, partly because experiments result in ways of writing that others take up, copy, duplicate or adapt for their own purposes so they become familiar, part of the fabric of the present. But there continues to be a degree of hostility to radical experiment, the anti-modernism I've outlined. It may be that there is something peculiarly British, or more likely peculiarly English, about this, politically conservative, suspicious of difference, nostalgic for a fictional past composed of reassuring images and largely created by advertising. There is something inherently conservative about English reading habits, fed by the relative conservatism of the major publishers. Where there's a chance of success, marked by literary prizes and sales, books that look radical, new and challenging may find mainstream publishers, but much of the most interesting writing, by which I suppose I mean authentic writing, especially poetry, is still to be found, alive and well, on the margins, supported by small presses and independent publishers. Not all, by any means, but a great deal of it. Some of the best are published by the well-known publishing houses: no library should be without books by Ali Smith, especially *How to be both* and the *Seasonal Quartet: Autumn, Winter, Spring and Summer*, Deborah Levy, especially *Swimming Home*, short stories by Diane Williams and Lydia Davis, and something by Lucy Ellmann. In fact, all the writers I've mentioned in this chapter are worth investigating.

I've written about genre fiction in an earlier chapter, but I need to add a qualifying coda here, because one of the interesting features of fiction over the last few decades has been what one might call the supersession of genre. One could trace this back at least as far as Raymond Chandler, but in recent years we have seen genre used against itself, or despite itself, in fiction of a more broadly ambitious kind. In some recent novels by M. John Harrison, for instance, we find elements of science fiction but used for a more existential teleology, with strange things sensed, an air of uneasiness, a lostness, as well as what Harrison himself has summed up as 'the psychic structures & contemporary repressed tragedies of alienation, dissociation, loneliness & paranoia under contemporary politics'. When I read his work, I feel something of the same glimpsed mystery as I do when I look at Henry Moore's mysterious 1942 pen-and-ink drawing 'Crowd Looking at a Tied-up Object'. Huge and unknowable, the object stands in a bleak landscape, wrapped in some sort of shroud-like cloth, secured with ropes; it dwarfs the tightly regimented crowd of expectant onlookers, the sky behind them sullen, cold and uninviting. The object could be thought of as reclaiming reality from surrealism, just that things are weird, and the future is still entirely wrapped up and unfathomable. The drawing catches the moment in which a person might be about to suggest unwrapping the object to see what it is, while others disagree. It is a haunting vision of the probability of lost possibility, and of the way we know something but don't know what it is we know. Rather like good artworks.

In his blog, Harrison talks about the merging of genre and other kinds of writing, in the context of abandoning story. 'In genre,' he writes, 'story is a non-negotiable assumption, baked in before the beginner-writer even begins to write. It's one of the assumptions no one can argue with.

But there are ways of destorifying fiction, and they are easily imported from other writerly regimes, other sets of unbreakable founding assumptions. Thus the sudden contemporary appearance (or reappearance) of hybrid writing.' Much of our understanding of our lives, including our sense of ourselves, is based on stories, and too often the stories are not really our own. Like any editor we excerpt, cut, rewrite and reshape the story to create a coherent, continuous person, ignoring or repressing the uncomfortable parts, happy to believe we are what we tell ourselves we are. To escape from the stories we've introjected over the years is painful and not easily done: almost every aspect of our culture, from politics and advertising to work and family, is constantly being modelled for us in the way we interact with society, and escaping from it can be almost impossible. But writing that shows the cracks, offers glimpses of an alternative, hints at things repressed – that can help make us conscious of the fantasies we live in and live through.

It's not just a matter of awareness of repressed material. The unconscious deals with things that happened in the past. It's not utopian to think about the future, however little we can know about it; we can certainly recognise that there is something unfulfilled in us. In Ernst Bloch's notion of the 'not-yet-conscious', rooted in the workings of daydream and the imagination, we can find a way of figuring the future coming towards us, manifesting as moments of surprise or coincidence, the new and the unexpected, each time opening a crack in the shiny surface of our days. Bloch coined another useful term, *Ungleichzeitigkeit*, or non-contemporaneity, for the way different temporalities can co-exist at the same time, old ideas can still hold sway in some minds or some movements or some places, the past present in the present. Some writers still write in what can be regarded as old ways, and do it well. Radical young (or not so young) writers share space on the shelves with more conventional figures, all trying in their different ways to find a true representation of what they take to be significant reality. They all have a place in the library.

My library was almost finished, the old stable cleaned and polished, brasswork gleaming. The radiators were in place, the lights worked, the walls and woodwork were painted, and best of all the bookcases had been made, painted and installed. The doors all had locks, the whole place was fresh, immaculate and new.

8
The Library

> I always look at my library with a sort of befuddled amazement: every book, every oeuvre, does something crazy and miraculous . . . Beckett, Faulkner, Sarraute, Sebald, Kertész, Ernaux, Michaux, Kafka, Roubaud, Aïgui, Chekhov . . . I mumble some names; it's absurd – I would have to say every one in the entire library.
>
> Nathalie Léger, interview with Amanda DeMarco

It was June when the library was finished, a sunny day. The garden was looking wonderful. I opened the library doors and breathed the smell of paint and newness. Sitting at my table there, I looked out over the new pond and the replanted garden to the wall, and beyond that, the church spire and a few white clouds. But another task was waiting. All the boxes were out of storage and sitting in John-next-door's garage. It was time to get on with the final stage of fitting the shelves and getting the books out and in place. I knew roughly where they'd all go, but the boxes weren't labelled so there was a fair degree of chaos to begin with. Also unpacking one's library can be a slow job as you pause over books, remembering their history or their contents, thinking about their place in one's life. I told myself there would be plenty of time for that later, and tried to concentrate on getting the shelves in the right place (they were all adjustable, and needed to be readjusted every time I found another book that belonged but was too tall to fit).

Categorisation of books is never as easy as you'd think, as any librarian will tell you. Alphabetical order within subjects was my plan, but there was a lot of plonking books down in roughly the right area and leaving the fine detail till later. It all took days and days, and in the end there were well over a hundred flattened empty boxes to go to the recycling centre. And thirty boxes, mostly modern fiction, to get rid of as there was no room for them in the library or in the house. Not for the last time, I wished the library could have been twice its size. Or three times, with all the books I'd sold when I left my college rooms. Or bigger still, with all the books I'd ever owned magically restored to my shelves. But it wasn't, so I had to be grateful for what I had, which was, it must be said, entirely wonderful. When I'd added an armchair and a record player and CD player in the stable, it was perfect. And there was no Wi-Fi to distract me from the books.

It's not just books. There's also a large collection of almost a hundred complete runs of twentieth-century literary periodicals, many of them ephemeral poetry magazines but also more substantial magazines such as T.S. Eliot's journal *The Criterion*, as well as *The Tramp*, *Left Review*, *New Writing*, *Horizon*, *Fact* and *Life and Letters Today*. Reading writers and poets in the places they were first published reveals a whole ecology of intersecting works and helps to build up a sense of the cultural currents at play at the time. They are great, but they take up a lot of room, more than I'd calculated. Walter Benjamin says 'periodicals can form the prismatic fringes of a library': mine are more central than that. Just as detective fiction can tell us more about the detail of the past than most history books (indeed, Gertrude Stein says that the main element in all English literature is the description of daily life), so periodicals can conjure up the period by their design, their adverts, their editorial comments and so forth, all of which can form a commentary on the poems or stories themselves. It's a more obvious kind of history than book history, but it's just as useful.

Gradually the poetry, the core of the library, got shelved, ordered and organised. British poetry after 1960 occupies one side of the middle stack; between 1900 and 1960 (all the dates are approximate) is on the far wall, by the French windows. On either side of the door, American poetry, and in the furthest bay, books, mainly poetry, in French. There's a wall of anthologies, translations, poetry in other languages, anthologies and books about poetry, and my notebooks. On the far side of the central stack are biographies, autobiographies, memoirs and diaries. The shelves, fortunately, are deep enough to have a second lot of books piled up in front of the ones that have already been shelved. All the rest of the poetry, the periodicals, psychoanalysis, philosophy and the remainder of my non-fiction is in the other room. It's taken a long time to get everything sorted out, a lot of dipping into books, losing track of time, recollecting past events, finding forgotten items, finding envelopes, notes, letters and other ephemera among the pages. Even in its depleted state, even after disposing of so many books over the years, I am aware that this is a sort of autobiography as well as a poetry resource.

You don't need to build your own library to have books around you; all you need is some shelves. Or enough space to pile them up or line them along the wall. The important part is the books. And reading them, too. I'm not talking about books as an investment; I want everybody to be holding the books and reading them. They may not change your life, or not straight away, but they'll make it better. There is so much to discover, so many writers still unread. The older I get, the more I realise I'll never read everything I'd like to read, let alone reread the books I'd like to go back to again. But that doesn't matter. I've got plenty to be getting on with. Meanwhile, I want the public libraries that have been closed because of Tory austerity to reopen, I want books to be available to everybody, in schools, in prisons, in hospitals and care homes. I want them to help counter the organised mendacity boosted by social media. Almost a hundred years ago, in 1938, George Orwell sounded off about the press, left and right, and the lack of what we now call 'transparency' in politics and society. He wrote in a letter that 'It gives one the feeling that our civilisation is going down into a sort of mist of lies where it will be impossible ever to find out the truth about anything.' Now, with AI and the sort of disregard for truth shown by Trump and his followers and by the extreme right everywhere, the threat Orwell described is even more pervasive.

The polarised, binary thinking (or mindless mindset) encouraged by the mechanisation of education needs to be countered by free reading. William Davies put it very well in the article in the *London Review of Books* that I cited earlier when he said: 'If young people today worry about using the "wrong" words, it isn't because of the persistence of the leftist cultural power of forty years ago, but – on the contrary – because of the barrage of initiatives and technologies dedicated to reversing that power. The ideology of measurable literacy, combined with a digital net that has captured social and educational life, leaves young people ill at ease with the language they use and fearful of what might happen should they trip up.' We need to own our own language, not worry about whether something is the right or wrong word. Reading and discussing and writing helps people find their own voice, work out for themselves what they think, on the basis of actual evidence, and gives them the confidence to articulate it. It's what books are for, and why they are powerful. And why autocrats, despots, ideologically driven states and tyrannical governments employ censorship, burn books, outlaw free thought and jail free thinkers.

In April 1798 in 'Fears in Solitude', the poet Samuel Taylor Coleridge records a day he spent in 'A green and silent spot, amid the hills' of the Quantocks in Somerset.[1] There were rumours at the time that the French, under their new leader, Napoleon, might invade Britain, and in his poem Coleridge ponders his fear of this and all its implications. On the one hand, here he is in a 'small and silent dell', dreaming of better worlds, listening to the larks singing above him, while at the same time he feels cast down by the knowledge that the British have been 'very tyrannous', have 'gone forth / And borne to distant tribes slavery and pangs'. He accuses his countrymen of corruption, 'bartering freedom and the poor man's life / For gold', of war-mongering, war-profiteering and delight in reading about war, 'The best amusement for our morning-meal'. He wonders if retribution is about to come, to 'make us know / The meaning of our words', and imagines scenes of terror at the hands of atheistical French soldiers. The only hope is for Britons to repent their vices. 'We have been too long / Dupes of a deep delusion!' (what a great phrase that is, and how pertinent still today): it's no good relying on the government or demagogues, he says, people themselves need to change. Finally, he leaves the dell as the dew begins to fall, walking home and noticing how the suddenly visible landscape with its 'huge amphitheatre of rich / And elmy Fields, seems like society— / Conversing with the mind', as a result of which he feels refreshed and, after his day of solitude, calm enough to think positively again about 'human kind'.

After a while, he thought the poem was not good enough, too preachy and too prosy. He was worried he hadn't found a way of bringing the reality of his perturbation and the urgency of the political crisis into the poem without dulling them with the weight of his prescription for improvement. Yet he still hoped that the poem could vivify a combination of thoughts and feelings in the reader. It's a problem that is always central to literary practice, the struggle to find the right words and the right form to make the poem or the story or the play or the novel work as the writer wants it to. But the struggle is what gives life and meaning to the work, and provides stimulus and new thinking and feeling for the reader. The section of the poem Coleridge was least happy with were the lines that began with the exclamation

I quoted above, 'We have been too long / Dupes of a deep delusion!' But his first thoughts were better; the poem needs those lines, and it needs them now at least as much as it needed them in 1798. It's another work that should be in everyone's library, a reminder to think and read and not be duped by the deep delusions our culture has become so adept at providing and accepting.

Notes

Introduction

1 Julia Bell, *Radical Attention*, Peninsula Press, 2020, p.74.

1. The Library *or* 'I could not live without them'

1 Walter Benjamin, 'Unpacking My Library', *Selected Writings*, Michael W. Jennings, Howard Eiland and Gary Smith (eds), Vol. 2 1927–1934, The Belknap Press of Harvard University Press, 2005.
2 Sir Thomas Browne, *Religio Medici* I, 24.

2. Pleasures of the Imagination

1 Interview with Amanda DeMarco in *BOMB*, Fall 2020.

4. Forgotten Writers, Rare Books and Books to Change the World

1 W.G. Sebald, *Austerlitz*, Hamish Hamilton, 2001, pp. 30–1.

5. What Poems Know

1 Peter Larkin, 'If Flowers of Language Will (Have) Been a Language of Flowers: Trials of Florescence in the Poems of J. H. Prynne', in *For the Future: Poems & Essays in Honour of J.H. Prynne on the Occasion of His 80th Birthday*, ed. Ian Brinton, Shearsman Books, 2016, pp. 99–113.
2 James Russell, 'Souvenir from a Dream', in *The Griffin Brain and Other Stories*, Grand Iota, 2023.
3 Christopher Middleton, 'Notes on a Viking Prow', *PN Review* 10, Vol. 6, No. 2, Nov–Dec 1979.

4 Denise Riley, 'Introduction', *Poets on Writing: England 1970-1991*, Macmillan, 1992; 'How Do You Do It?' by Gerry and the Pacemakers (EMI/Columbia). Lyrics by Mitch Murray © 1963, Universal Music Publishing Group.
5 John Milton, 'The Verse' [note added to the second edition of *Paradise Lost*, 1674], in *Paradise Lost*, ed. Barbara K. Lewalski, Blackwell, 2007.
6 See Raymond Roussel, *How I Wrote Certain of My Books*, trans. Trevor Winkfield, Sun, 1977.
7 For more on Oulipo, see *The Penguin Book of Oulipo*, ed. Philip Terry (Penguin, 2020).
8 Luke Roberts, 'Making Games', *NLR Sidecar*, 5 February 2025.
9 Some relevant anthologies are: *A Various Art*, ed. Andrew Crozier and Tim Longville, Carcanet, 1987; *Conductors of Chaos: A Poetry Anthology*, ed. Iain Sinclair, Picador, 1996; *Dear World & Everyone In It: New Poetry in the UK*, ed. Nathan Hamilton, Bloodaxe, 2013; and *Arcadian Rustbelt: The Second Generation of British Underground Poetry*, ed. Andrew Duncan and John Goodby, Waterloo Press, 2024.
10 W.S. Graham, 'The Constructed Space', *New Collected Poems*, ed. Matthew Francis, Faber, 2004.

6. Reversing Babel: The Invisible Arts of Translation

1 Nicholas Carr, *The Shallows: How the Internet is Changing the Way We Think, Read and Remember*, Atlantic Books, 2020.

7. Tradition and Innovation

1 'It Ain't What You Do (It's the Way That You Do It)' by Fun Boy Three and Bananarama (Chrysalis). Lyrics by Melvin 'Sy' Oliver and James 'Trummy' Young © 1939, Universal Music Publishing Group.

8. The Library

1 S.T. Coleridge, 'Fears in Solitude: Written in April 1798, During the Alarm of an Invasion', *Collected Works of Samuel Taylor Coleridge: Poetical Works I: Poems (Reading Text) Part I*, ed. J.C.C. Mays, Princeton University Press, 2001.

Bibliography

Adorno, T.W., 'Short Commentaries on Proust', *Notes to Literature*, Vol. 1, Columbia University Press, 1991

———, 'Bibliographical Musings', *Notes to Literature*, Vol. 2, Columbia University Press, 1992

Ascherson, Neil, 'A society that falls back on miming the creation of its wealth is sick', *The Independent on Sunday*, 19 February 1995

Attridge, Derek, *Poetic Rhythm: An Introduction*, Cambridge University Press, 1995

———, and Henry Staten, *The Craft of Poetry: Dialogues on Minimal Interpretation*, Routledge, 2015

Atwood, Margaret, *On Writers and Writing*, Virago Press, 2015

Barnes, Julian, *A Life with Books*, Jonathan Cape, 2012

Beckett, Samuel, *Proust*, Chatto & Windus, 1931

Bell, Julia, *Radical Attention*, Peninsula Press, 2020

Benjamin, Walter, 'The Task of the Translator', *Selected Writings*, Michael W. Jennings, Howard Eiland and Gary Smith (eds), Vol. 1, 1913–1926/1927–1934, The Belknap Press of Harvard University Press, 1999

———, 'Unpacking My Library: A Talk about Collecting', *Selected Writings*, Michael W. Jennings, Howard Eiland and Gary Smith (eds), Vol. 2, 1927–34, The Belknap Press of Harvard University Press, 2005

———, 'On the Image of Proust', *Selected Writings*, Michael W. Jennings, Howard Eiland and Gary Smith (eds), Vol. 2, 1927–34, The Belknap Press of Harvard University Press, 2005

Bennett, Arnold, *Literary Taste: How to Form It, with Detailed Instructions for Collecting a Complete Library of English Literature* [1909], ed. with additional lists by Frank Swinnerton, Penguin, 1938

Berman, Antoine, *The Age of Translation: A Commentary on Walter Benjamin's 'The Task of the Translator'*, trans. Chantal Wright, Routledge, 2018

Bion, Wilfred R., *Attention and Interruption*, Karnac, 1993

Blake, William, 'London', *Songs of Innocence and Experience*, William Blake, 1794

Blatchford, Robert, *My Favourite Books*, Walter Scott Ltd, 1900

Bloch, Ernst, *The Principle of Hope*, 3 vols, trans. Neville Plaice, Stephen Plaice and Paul Knight, Blackwell, 1986

Bolzoni, Lina, *A Marvelous Solitude: The Art of Reading in Early Modern Europe*, Harvard University Press, 2023

Borges, Jorge Luis, *Collected Fictions*, trans. Andrew Hurley, Allen Lane, 1999

Bowen, Elizabeth, 'Out of a Book', *Collected Impressions*, Longman Green, 1950

Bowie, Malcolm, *Proust Among the Stars*, Harper Collins, 1998

Boxall, Peter, *The Value of the Novel*, Cambridge University Press, 2015

Briggs, Kate, *This Little Art*, Fitzcarraldo Editions, 2017

Brooke-Rose, Christine, *Remake*, Carcanet, 1996

Brophy, Brigid, 'The Librarian and the Novel: a Writer's View', in Richard Canning and Gerri Kimber (eds), *Brigid Brophy: Avant-Garde Writer, Critic, Activist,*

Edinburgh University Press, 2020
Bryher, *Two Novels*, ed. Joanne Winning, University of Wisconsin Press, 2000
Bucknell, Clare, *The Treasuries: Poetry Anthologies and the Making of British Culture*, Head of Zeus, 2023
Byers, Reid, *The Private Library*, Oak Knoll Press, 2021
Cain, Amina, *A Horse at Night: On Writing*, Daunt Books, 2022
Calvino, Italo, *The Written World and the Unwritten World*, Penguin, 2022
Canetti, Elias, *Auto da Fé*, trans. C.V. Wedgwood [1935, trans. 1946], Penguin, 1965
Cannan, Gilbert, *Sembal*, Thomas Seltzer, 1924
Carr, Nicholas, *The Shallows: How the Internet is Changing the Way We Think, Read and Remember*, Atlantic Books, 2020
Carson, Anne, *Nay, Rather*, Sylph Editions, 2013
Castillo, Elaine, *How to Read Now: Essays*, Atlantic Books, 2022
Chartier, Roger, and Peter Stallybrass, 'What is a Book?', in Neil Fraistat and Julia Flanders (eds), *The Cambridge Companion to Textual Scholarship*, Cambridge University Press, 2013
Coleridge, Samuel Taylor, 'Fears in Solitude: Written in April 1798, During the Alarm of an Invasion', *Collected Works of Samuel Taylor Coleridge: Poetical Works I: Poems (Reading Text) Part I*, ed. J.C.C. Mays, Princeton University Press, 2001
Collins, Sophie (ed.), *Currently & Emotion: Translations*, Test Centre, 2016
Cooper, Jilly, 'Jilly Cooper Talks to Margaret Thatcher', *The Sunday Times*, 1976
———, *Harriet*, Arlington Books, 1976

———, *Riders*, Arlington Books, 1985
———, *Rivals*, Bantam, 1988
———, *Score!*, Transworld, 1999
———, *Jump!*, Transworld, 2010
———, *Mount!*, Transworld, 2016
Crozier, Andrew, and Tim Longville (eds), *A Various Art*, Carcanet, 1987
Cummings, Brian, *Bibliophobia: The End and the Beginning of the Book*, Oxford University Press, 2022
Currie, Mark, *The Unexpected: Narrative Temporality and the Philosophy of Surprise*, Edinburgh University Press, 2013
Darnton, Robert, *The Case for Books*, PublicAffairs, 2009
Davies, William, 'How many words does it take to make a mistake?', *London Review of Books*, Vol. 44, No. 4, 24 February 2022. Available at: https://www.lrb.co.uk/the-paper/v44/n04/william-davies/how-many-words-does-it-take-to-make-a-mistake [accessed 16 June 2025]
Davis, Lydia, 'An Alphabet (in Progress)', *Essays Two*, Hamish Hamilton, 2021
———, 'Twenty-One Pleasures of Translation (and a Silver Lining)', *Essays Two*, Hamish Hamilton, 2021
De Bolla, Peter, *Art Matters*, Harvard University Press, 2001
De Quincey, Thomas, *Suspiria de Profundis: The Works of Thomas De Quincey*, fourth edition, Vol. XVI (Supplementary), Adam and Charles Black, [1871] repr. 1884
Derrida, Jacques, *Archive Fever: A Freudian Impression*, trans. Eric Prenowitz, University of Chicago Press, 1996
———, 'What Is a "Relevant" Translation?', *Critical Inquiry*, Vol. 27, Winter 2001, trans. Lawrence Venuti: https://www.sas.upenn.edu/~cavitch/pdf-library/

Derrida_Relevant.pdf [accessed 16 June 2025]

Dibdin, Thomas Frognall, *Bibliomania, or Book Madness* [1811], Cambridge University Press, 2010

———, *Bibliophobia* [1832], Cambridge University Press, 2010

Dirda, Michael, *Browsings: A Year of Reading, Collecting, and Living with Books*, Pegasus Books, 2015

Donoghue, Denis, *The Practice of Reading*, Yale University Press, 1998

Duncan, Andrew, and John Goodby (eds), *Arcadian Rustbelt: The Second Generation of British Underground Poetry*, Waterloo Press, 2024

Duncan, Dennis, and Adam Smyth (eds), *Book Parts*, Oxford University Press, 2019

Eaglestone, Robert, 'Contemporary Fiction in the Academy: towards a manifesto', *Textual Practice*, 27.1, 2013

Eco, Umberto, *The Name of the Rose*, Secker & Warburg, 1983

———, *Mouse or Rat? Translation as Negotiation*, Weidenfeld & Nicolson, 2003

———, and Jean-Claude Carrière, *This is Not the End of the Book*, Harvill Secker, 2011

Empson, William, *Seven Types of Ambiguity* [1930], Peregrine Books, 1965

Fadiman, Anne, *Ex Libris: Confessions of a Common Reader*, Penguin, 1999

Febvre, Lucien, and Henri-Jean Martin, *The Coming of the Book: The Impact of Printing 1450–1800*, trans. David Gerard, NLB, 1976

Fischer, Steven Roger, *A History of Reading*, Reaktion Books, 2019

Ford, Mark, *Woman Much Missed: Thomas Hardy, Emma Hardy, and Poetry*, Oxford University Press, 2023

Foschini, Lorenza, *Proust's Overcoat: The True Story of One Man's Passion for All Things Proust*, trans. Eric Karpeles, Portobello Books, 2010

Fourier, Charles, *The Theory of the Four Movements*, Gareth Stedman Jones and Ian Patterson (eds), Cambridge University Press, 1996

Fowler, Christopher, *The Book of Forgotten Authors*, Riverrun, 2017

Fraser, Antonia (ed.), *The Pleasure of Reading*, Bloomsbury, 1992

Graham, W.S., *New Collected Poems*, ed. Matthew Francis, Faber, 2004

Graves, Robert, and Laura Riding, *A Survey of Modernist Poetry*, Heinemann, 1927

Greer, Germaine, in Antonia Fraser (ed.), *The Pleasure of Reading*, Bloomsbury, 1992

Greywoode, Josephine (ed.), *Why We Read: 70 Writers on Non-Fiction*, Penguin, 2022

Grossman, Edith, *Why Translation Matters*, Yale University Press, 2010

Hamilton, Nathan (ed.), *Dear World & Everyone In It: New Poetry in the UK*, Bloodaxe, 2013

Hardy, Thomas, 'The Voice', *Satires of Circumstance*, Macmillan and Co. Limited, 1914

Harrison, M. John, *Wish I Was Here: An Anti-Memoir*, Serpent's Tail, 2023

Hill, Rosemary, 'Snob Cuts', *London Review of Books*, Vol. 38, No. 21, 3 November 2016: https://www.lrb.co.uk/the-paper/v38/n21/rosemary-hill/snob-cuts [accessed 16 June 2025]

Jackson, Holbrook, *The Anatomy of Bibliomania* [1930], Faber, 1950

Jacobus, Mary, *Psychoanalysis and the Scene of Reading*, Oxford University Press, 1999

James, P.D., *Talking about Detective Fiction*, Faber, 2010

Jameson, Fredric, *Raymond Chandler: The Detections of Totality*, Verso, 2016

Johnson, Samuel, *The Rambler*, No. 106 (23 March 1751)

Keats, John, *The Letters of John Keats*, 2 vols, ed. Maurice Buxton Forman, Oxford University Press, 1942

Kociejowski, Marius, *A Factotum in the Book Trade*, Biblioasis, 2022

Lahiri, Jhumpa, *In Other Words*, Bloomsbury, 2016

Lamb, Charles, 'Detached Thoughts on Books and Reading', *The Works of Charles Lamb*, Vol. 1, Oxford University Press, 1924

Lanchester, John, 'The Case of Agatha Christie', *London Review of Books*, Vol. 40, No. 24, 20 December 2018: https://www.lrb.co.uk/the-paper/v40/n24/john-lanchester/the-case-of-agatha-christie [accessed 27 June 2025]

Larkin, Peter, 'If Flowers of Language Will (Have) Been a Language of Flowers: Trials of Florescence in the Poems of J.H. Prynne', in *For the Future: Poems & Essays in Honour of J.H. Prynne on the Occasion of His 80th Birthday*, ed. Ian Brinton, Shearsman Books, 2016

Lau, Beth, 'Analyzing Keats's Library by Genre', *Keats-Shelley Journal*, Vol. 65 (2016)

Lee, Hermione, *Reading in Bed: An Inaugural Lecture delivered before the University of Oxford on 21 October 1999*, Oxford University Press, 2000

Léger, Nathalie, interview with Amanda DeMarco in *BOMB* magazine, Fall 2020: https://bombmagazine.org/articles/2020/09/11/nathalie-léger/ [accessed 16 June 2025]

Light, Alison, *Forever England: Literature, Femininity and Conservatism between the Wars*, Routledge, 1991
Lupton, Christina, *Reading and the Making of Time in the Eighteenth Century*, Johns Hopkins University Press, 2018
Manguel, Alberto, *A History of Reading*, Knopf, 1996
———, *A Reader on Reading*, Yale University Press, 2010
———, *Packing My Library: An Elegy and Ten Digressions*, Yale University Press, 2018
Mathews, Timothy, 'A Translator's Note: On the Voices of Love, or Why Translate Roland Barthes Again?', *CounterText* 9.1, 2023
Maugham, W. Somerset, 'The Decline and Fall of the Detective Story', in *The Vagrant Mood* [1952], Vintage, 2001
Mead, Rebecca, *The Road to Middlemarch: My Life with George Eliot*, Granta, 2014
Middleton, Christopher, 'Notes on a Viking Prow', *PN Review* 10, Vol. 6, No. 2, November–December 1979
Miller, Andy, *The Year of Reading Dangerously*, Fourth Estate, 2014
Milton, John, *Paradise Lost*, ed. Barbara K. Lewalski, Blackwell, 2007
Morrison, Toni, *Playing in the Dark: Whiteness and the Literary Imagination*, Vintage Books, 1993
Muhlstein, Anka, *Monsieur Proust's Library*, Other Press, 2012
Orgel, Stephen, *The Reader in the Book*, Oxford University Press, 2015
Orwell, George, 'Bookshop Memories', *Complete Works*, ed. Peter Davison et al., Vol. X, *A Kind of Compulsion: 1903–1936*, Secker & Warburg, 2001

———, 'Books v. Cigarettes', Complete Works, Vol. XVIII, *Smothered Under Journalism: 1946*

Ovenden, Richard, *Burning the Books: A History of Knowledge Under Attack*, John Murray, 2020

Page, Benedicte, 'Jilly Cooper and the shagsaga', *Bookseller*, 2006

Parks, Tim, *Pen in Hand: Reading, Rereading and Other Mysteries*, Alma Books, 2019

Pettegree, Andrew and Arthur der Weduwen, *The Library: A Fragile History*, Profile Books, 2021

Prendergast, Christopher, *Living and Dying with Marcel Proust*, Europa Compass, 2022

Price, Leah, *What We Talk about When We Talk about Books: The History and Future of Reading*, Basic Books, 2019

———(ed.), *Unpacking My Library: Writers and Their Books*, Yale University Press, 2011

———, and Matthew Rubery (eds), *Further Reading*, Oxford University Press, 2020

Proust, Marcel, *In Search of Lost Time*, ed. Christopher Prendergast, Allen Lane, 2002

———, *Finding Time Again*, trans. Ian Patterson, Allen Lane, 2003

———, *Days of Reading*, trans. John Sturrock, Penguin, 2008

Prynne, J.H., 'Mental Ears', *Chicago Review*, Vol. 55 (1), 2010

———, *Passing Grass Parnassus*, Face Press, 2020

Rabelais, François, *The Works of Rablais*, trans. Thomas Urquhart, 1653

Raven, James, *What is the History of the Book?*, Polity, 2018

———, Helen Small et al. (eds), *The Practice and*

Representation of Reading in England, Cambridge University Press, 1996

Rhys, Ernest, *Everyman Remembers*, J.M. Dent, 1931

Richards, I.A., *Practical Criticism*, Routledge & Kegan Paul, 1924

Ricoeur, Paul, *On Translation*, Routledge, 2006

Riley, Denise (ed.), *Poets on Writing: Britain 1970–1991*, Macmillan, 1992

Roberts, Luke, 'Raspberries', *NLR Sidecar*, 31 May 2024: https://newleftreview.org/sidecar/posts/raspberries [accessed 16 June 2025]

———, 'Making Games', *NLR Sidecar*, 5 February 2025: https://newleftreview.org/sidecar/posts/making-games?pc=1655 [accessed 16 June 2025]

———, 'By Law In Sound: J. H. Prynne's Recent Poetry', *Chicago Review*, 2020: https://www.chicagoreview.org/by-law-in-sound-j-h-prynnes-recent-poetry/ [accessed 16 June 2025]

Roberts, Michèle, *Paper Houses: A Memoir of the '70s and Beyond*, Virago Press, 2007

Roberts, Ryan, *Conversations with Ian McEwan*, University Press of Mississippi, 2010

Robertson, Lisa, *The Baudelaire Fractal*, Peninsula Press, 2023

Rose, Phyllis, *The Shelf: Adventures in Extreme Reading*, Farrar, Straus and Giroux, 2014

———, *The Year of Reading Proust: A Memoir in Real Time*, Vintage, 1998

Roussel, Raymond, *How I Wrote Certain of My Books*, trans. Trevor Winkfield, with two essays on Roussel by John Ashbery, and a translation of Canto III of *Nouvelles*

Impressions d'Afrique by Kenneth Koch, Sun, 1977
Royal, Nicholas, *White Spines: Confessions of a Book Collector*, Salt 2021
———, *Shadow Lines: Searching for the Book Beyond the Shelf*, Salt, 2024
Ruby, Ryan, 'The Pundit', *NLR Sidecar*, 21 September 2022: https://newleftreview.org/sidecar/posts/the-pundit [accessed 16 June 2025]
Ruskin, John, *Sesame and Lilies*, George Allen, 1904
Russell, James, 'Souvenir from a Dream', in The *Griffin Brain and Other Stories*, Grand Iota, 2023
Sage, Lorna, *Moments of Truth*, Fourth Estate, 2001
Salwak, Dale, (ed.), *A Passion for Books*, Macmillan, 1999
Scarry, Elaine, *Dreaming by the Book*, Farrar, Straus and Giroux, 1999
Schulman, Sarah, *Conflict is not Abuse*, Arsenal Pulp Press, 2016
Schulte, Rainer, and John Biguenet (eds), *Theories of Translation: An Anthology of Essays from Dryden to Derrida*, University of Chicago Press, 1992
Schwartz, Lynne Sharon, *Ruined by Reading. A Life in Books*, Beacon Press, 1996
Scott, Clive, *Literary Translation and the Rediscovery of Reading*, Cambridge University Press, 2012
———, *The Work of Literary Translation*, Cambridge University Press, 2018
Sebald, W.G., *Austerlitz*, trans. Anthea Bell, Hamish Hamilton, 2001
Self, Will, *Why Read*, Grove Press UK, 2022
Seymour, Richard, 'Caedmon's Dream: On the Politics of Style', *Salvage Zone*, 5 July 2019: https://salvage.zone/

caedmons-dream-on-the-politics-of-style/ [accessed 16 June 2025]
Sillitoe, Alan, 'Mountains and Caverns', in ed. Dale Salwak, *A Passion for Books*, Macmillan, 1999
Sinclair, Iain (ed.), *Conductors of Chaos: A Poetry Anthology*, Picador, 1996
Smith, Ali, *Public Library*, Hamish Hamilton, 2015
Smith, Emma, *Portable Magic: A History of Books and their Readers*, Allen Lane, 2022
Smith, Logan Pearsall, *All Trivia*, Penguin, 1986
Smyth, Adam, *The Book Makers*, Bodley Head, 2024
Spufford, Francis, *The Child that Books Built*, Faber, 2002
Taylor, Helen, *Why Women Read Fiction*, Oxford University Press, 2019
Terry, Philip, *Inferno*, Carcanet, 2014
———, 'Three Cantos from Dante's Purgatorio', *Translation and Literature* 31.1, 2022
Tóibín, Colm, 'Dissecting the Body', *London Review of Books*, Vol. 28, No. 8, 26 April 2007: https://www.lrb.co.uk/the-paper/v29/n08/colm-toibin/dissecting-the-body [accessed 16 June 2025]
Watt, Adam, *Reading in Proust's A la recherche: 'le délire de la lecture'*, Clarendon Press, 2009
White, Edmund, *The Unpunished Vice: A Life of Reading*, Bloomsbury, 2018
White, Heather Cass, *Books Promiscuously Read: Reading as a Way of Life*, Farrar, Strauss and Giroux, 2021
Wittgenstein, Ludwig, *Tractatus Logico-Philosophicus*, Kegan Paul, 1922
Wood, James, *The Nearest Thing to Life*, Brandeis University Press, 2015

———, *The Fun Stuff and Other Essays*, Vintage, 2013
Wood, Michael, *Marcel Proust*, Oxford University Press, 2023
Woolf, Virginia, *The Letters of Virginia Woolf*, N. Nicolson and J. Trautmann (eds), Hogarth Press, 1975–80
Wordsworth, William, 'Preface' to *Lyrical Ballads* [1800], R.L.Brett & A.R. Jones (eds), Methuen, 1963
Zalewski, Daniel, 'The Background Hum', *The New Yorker*, 15 February 2009: https://www.newyorker.com/magazine/2009/02/23/the-background-hum [accessed 16 June 2025]

Acknowledgements

I don't remember when I learnt to read, but since it was before I went to school, I think I must begin by thanking my late mother and father for fostering what has become a lasting love of books. My father was extremely good at reading books aloud, and until he was supplanted by BBC Radio's *Children's Hour* and by my capacity to read for myself, his nightly performances were eagerly anticipated and greatly enjoyed. I revisited many of the same books when I, in turn, was reading to my children. Thank you, Jacob, Johnny and Jamie.

The matters covered in this book reflect conversations over the years with too many friends, colleagues, teachers, poets, activists and booksellers for me to list them all, but a few from the last sixty years need to be mentioned and thanked here, with my apologies to all those who have not been named:

Ian Alister, Lisa Appignanesi, Laura Ashe, Deborah Bowman, Peter Brooker, Sue Collinson, Martin Crowley, the late Andrew Crozier, Philip Crozier, David Dernie, Peter De Bolla, Brian Dillon, the late Jenny Diski, Maud Ellmann, John Field, the late John Forrester, Louise Foxcroft, Heather Glen, Martin Golding, Mike Harrison, Richard Hewlings, the late Monty Johnstone, Lauren

Kassell, Richard Kuper, Emily LaBarge, Denise Laing, Leo Mellor, Rod Mengham, Lara Pawson, Christopher Prendergast, Mark Rawlinson, the late Tom Raworth, Denise Riley, Peter Riley, Jim Russell, Ali Smith, Lyndsey Stonebridge, Keston Sutherland, the late Tony Tanner, Deborah Thom (who endured twenty-five years with me), Martin Thom, Nick Totton, Trevor Turner, Ben Watson, John Wilkinson, Clair Wills, Sarah Wood, Patrick Wright.

Mary Kay Wilmers at *The London Review of Books* commissioned an article about losing my books that provoked the thinking that resulted in this book: I owe her many thanks on many fronts. Some of the material in Chapters 3 and 7 also started life as essays in the *LRB*: I am grateful to the editors for permission to give it a new form.

Almost every year from about 2000 until it was interrupted by the pandemic, either Rod Mengham, Leo Mellor or I convened a small symposium in Cambridge, the Centenary Symposium, devoted to a writer who would have been a hundred that year, and whose work in our view had not received sufficient critical notice, among them Rex Warner, Nigel Balchin, Rumer Godden and Maeve Brennan. I'm very grateful to all those who were involved, and from whom I learnt such a lot.

In the beginning, David Dernie's brilliant eyes helped me to see the real potential of the coach house to become a library. Henry Freeland's wonderful designs and careful supervision turned the idea into a plan. Roger Gladwell and his amazing workforce – Noel, Jamie and all the others – turned the plans into the library. My thanks to everybody involved.

I was very fortunate in the friendships I made and the

intellectual stimulus I found in my four years as a research fellow at King's College, Cambridge, and then as a fellow of Queens' College for almost twenty years after that. I'm particularly grateful to the then-president of Queens', John Eatwell, and his wife Suzi Digby for all their friendship and care over the years. At Queens' I was also the Fellow Librarian, and learnt a huge amount about libraries, both the student library and the rare books library, from the staff there, especially from Dr Tim Eggington.

I have taught hundreds of students over the years: there is nothing like reading a poem with a group of interested and opinionated students for revealing aspects of it that you hadn't seen before, so I shall always be grateful for the opportunity to read such a variety of poems with such acute readers. I'd also like to mention for particular thanks the graduate students of the course I taught for some years on 'Reading Difficult Poems'. My ten years as a bookseller were greatly enhanced by all I learnt about books and the book trade from generous friends and colleagues in the PBFA, particularly from the late Stephen Francis Clarke, and Veronica Watts.

Thanks, too, to my agent, David Godwin, and finally a huge thank you to everybody at Weidenfeld & Nicolson, especially my editor, Jenny Lord, and all the people who so brilliantly changed my words from a manuscript into a book, all those who designed, copy-edited, proofread, managed the publicity and did all else needful for it.

About the Author

Ian Patterson is a widely published poet and translator, and a former academic. The translator of *Finding Time Again*, the final volume of the Penguin Proust, he is also the author of *Guernica and Total War* and *Nemo's Almanac*. He won the Forward Prize for Best Poem in 2017, with an elegy for his late wife, Jenny Diski. He worked in further education between 1970 and 1984, had a second-hand bookselling business for ten years after that, and from 1995 until 2018 was an academic, teaching English Literature at the University of Cambridge. Many of his students have gone on to shape the world of publishing and writing, both in the UK and the US, including Zadie Smith, Helen Macdonald and Emily Witt.

Index